Unit 6

spreadsheets

databases

Unit 7

Anne Kelsall

Graham Manson

Ruksana Patel

Steve Cushing

Consultant: Keith Parry

OCR level
Nationals
ict

www.payne-gallway.co.uk

✓ Free online support
✓ Useful weblinks
✓ 24 hour online ordering

01865 888070

PAYNE-GALLWAY

Payne-Gallway is an imprint of Pearson Education Limited, a company incorporated in England and Wales, having its registered office at Edinburgh Gate, Harlow, Essex, CM20 2JE. Registered company number: 872828

www.payne-gallway.co.uk

Text © Anne Kelsall 2007

First published 2007

12 11 10 09 08
10 9 8 7 6 5 4 3 2

British Library Cataloguing in Publication Data is available from the British Library on request.

ISBN 978 1 905292 12 7

Edited by Melanie Birdsall
Designed by Kamae Design
Produced and Typeset by Sparks, Oxford – www.sparks.co.uk
Printed in China (GCC/02)
Cover photo/illustration © Steve Shott

Acknowledgements
Microsoft product screenshots reprinted with permission from Microsoft Corporation.

Every effort has been made to contact copyright holders of material reproduced in this book. Any omissions will be rectified in subsequent printings if notice is given to the publishers.

Websites
The websites used in this book were correct and up-to-date at the time of publication. It is essential for tutors to preview each website before using it in class so as to ensure that the URL is still accurate, relevant and appropriate. We suggest that tutors bookmark useful websites and consider enabling students to access them through the school/college intranet.

Ordering Information
Payne-Gallway, FREEPOST (OF1771),
PO Box 381, Oxford OX2 8BR
Tel: 01865 888070
Fax: 01865 314029
Email: orders@payne-gallway.co.uk

Contents

Series Introduction   iv

Unit 6:   Spreadsheets – Design and Use   1

Chapter 1   Spreadsheets – Skills   2

Chapter 2   Design a Spreadsheet to Meet the Needs of an Organisation   35

Chapter 3   Creating and Formatting Your Spreadsheet   49

Chapter 4   Sort Data and Use Simple Filters   55

Chapter 5   Carrying out Modelling Activities Using a Spreadsheet   61

Chapter 6   Analyse Data Using Graphs and Charts   66

Chapter 7   Macros   77

Unit 7:   Databases – Design and Use   95

Chapter 8   Databases – Skills   96

Chapter 9   Design a Relational Database to Meet the Needs of an
Organisation   131

Chapter 10 Construct the Database According to the Design   162

Chapter 11 Interrogate the Database   179

Chapter 12 Create Reports   187

Chapter 13 Create a User Interface   198

Chapter 14 Test the Database   209

Index   217

Series Introduction

Introduction

This book is one of a series of books that has been designed to guide you in your work for the OCR Level 2 Nationals in ICT. Each book covers two or three units and explains the skills and concepts that are needed for each. It also sets out in detail how to create a portfolio to achieve a **Pass**, **Merit** or **Distinction** for each Assessment Objective.

Spreadsheets – Design and Use and *Databases – Design and Use* cover the Assessment Objectives for Units 6 and 7 of the specification. In addition, an introductory chapter for each unit gives you the opportunity to learn and practise the skills you need to work through the Assessment Objectives.

If you would like to learn and practise other skills not in the introductory chapters, go to Unit 6 or 7 under Student Resources on the www.payne-gallway.co.uk website.

How to use this book

The book is divided into two sections which guide you through each Assessment Objective (AO) as set out by OCR for Units 6 and 7. Every chapter helps you to understand how you would build evidence for your portfolio through clearly identified Scenarios, helpful Tips and structured Activities using step-by-step instructions. At every stage clear guidance is given as to the level of evidence required for a **Pass**, **Merit** or **Distinction** so that you are able to plan your own progress effectively.

Each student book in the series is further supported by data files for use with some of the activities. These are available for download at the Payne-Gallway website www.payne-gallway.co.uk.

UNIT 6

Spreadsheets – Design and Use

In this unit you will cover the following...

AO1 Design a spreadsheet to meet the needs of an organisation

AO2 Create the spreadsheet according to the design and format it to make it user friendly

AO3 Sort data and use simple filters

AO4 Carry out modelling activities using a spreadsheet

AO5 Analyse data using appropriate graphs and charts

AO6 Create macros to automate procedures in a spreadsheet

CHAPTER ①
Spreadsheets — Skills

Overview:

In this chapter you will learn about some basic spreadsheet formulas and functions. You will also use simple formatting techniques. Although this chapter will help you remember some basic spreadsheet features it is assumed that you have already completed Unit 1 and so have some experience in using simple formulas and formatting cells, for example currency.

This chapter was written for Microsoft Excel 2003. It can be used with other versions of Excel although some screenshots and methods may not exactly match these versions.

As you work your way through the different sections and activities in this chapter you will learn about some of the formulas that you can use later on when you come to design your own spreadsheet for your portfolio. You will use the various types of formula in specific examples but don't forget that they can all be used in a variety of situations.

In order to complete the activities in this chapter you will need access to a number of additional files. These files are contained in the Chapter 1 Resources zip file which can be downloaded from the OCR Nationals in ICT (Units 6 & 7) Student Resources page on the Payne-Gallway website: www.payne-gallway.co.uk.

The Chapter 1 Resources folder also contains some extra activities and explanations to help you complete this unit. These are contained in a folder called Additional Activities and are as listed below:

Pass level activities:
a   Simple formulas
b   Random numbers and rounding

Merit/Distinction level activities:
c   More lookup tables
d   More complex IF statements
e   More advanced logical functions

f	Lookups using the MATCH function
g	Reference functions
h	Text functions
i	Advanced trigonometric functions
j	The Goal Seek command

Key terms

Formula

This is an instruction you enter, such as **=A1+B1**, which tells the spreadsheet to make a calculation. You might see the plural as either **formulas** or **formulae**. Both are now equally acceptable.

All formulas must start with an **=** sign. This is what tells Excel that it is a formula.

Function

This is a special type of formula, using a keyword, which has been set up to represent a formula that would otherwise be very long and complicated, or which is used a lot. For example **=SUM( )** which calculates the total of a block of cells.

Formatting

This term is used to describe anything you do to change the way cells appear on a spreadsheet. For example, you can change the font, size and colour of text; the shading and border of a cell; the height and width of rows and columns. You can also format the numbers in the cells so that they show the appropriate number of decimal places, £ signs, % signs, etc.

Arithmetic and statistical functions

We often need to add together a long list of numbers. Although this can be done using a long formula with lots of **+** signs, the function **=SUM()** allows us to do this much more easily. All we need to do is put the first and last cells inside the brackets and the spreadsheet will automatically add up all the numbers in the list. So **=SUM(A1:E1)** is an equivalent, but much neater, formula to **=A1+B1+C1+D1+E1**.

Useful functions for summarising data include:

- **=AVERAGE()** – calculates the mean average of a group of numbers, so **=AVERAGE(A1:E1)** is a much neater alternative to **=(A1+B1+C1+D1+E1)/5**.
- **=MAX(range)** – finds the largest number from the cells in the range.
- **=MIN(range)** – finds the smallest number from the cells in the range.
- **=MEDIAN(range)** – finds the median of the cells in the range. This is the middle number, if the numbers are written in order.

- **=MODE(range)** – finds the mode of the cells in the range. This is the most commonly occurring number. However, if there is more than one mode, this formula will only give the first one that it finds. So if cells A1 to A13 contain 1,1,2,2,2,3,4,4,5,5,5,6,6 **=MODE(A1:A13)** will give 2, even though 5 is also the mode.
- **=COUNT(range)** – tells you the number of cells from the range that contain a number or a date.
- **=COUNTA(range)** – tells you the number of cells from the range that are not empty.
- **=COUNTIF(range,target)** – this very useful function tells you how many cells from the range contain the target given. So **COUNTIF(A1:A13,4)** will count the number of cells from A1 to A13 that contain 4. If cells A1 to A13 contain 1,1,2,2,2,3,4,4,5,5,5,6,6 then **COUNTIF(A1:A13,4)** will be 2.

Activity 1 gives an example of how these formulas can be used to summarise data.

Activity 1: Arithmetic and statistical functions…

In this activity you will:

- use **SUM** to add a range of numbers
- use **MAX** and **MIN** to find the largest and smallest number in a range
- use **AVERAGE**, **MEDIAN** and **MODE** to find the three types of average
- use **COUNT** and **COUNTA** to count the number of cells that contain different types of entry
- use **COUNTIF** with numeric, text and cell references as targets.

A group of children have entered a competition to guess the number of sweets in a jar. Some have had more than one guess. You are going to use statistical functions to find information about their guesses.

▶ Load the file **Activity 1.xls** or enter the data shown in Figure 1.1 into a blank workbook.

You are going to add formulas to summarise this data.

▶ Add the headings shown in Figure 1.2 to column D.

Now enter the following formulas:

▶ In E1 a formula to add up all the guesses in column B. This will be **=SUM(B2:B21)**

▶ In E2 a formula to find the highest guess. This will be **=MAX(B2:B21)**

▶ In E3 a formula to find the lowest guess. This will be **=MIN(B2:B21)**

	A	B
1	Name	Guess
2	Adam	144
3	Adrian	370
4	Aled	172
5	Alex	171
6	Amir	244
7	Andrew	237
8	Angela	365
9	Anil	137
10	Anju	306
11	Anjum	229
12	Ann	109
13	Arun	119
14	Asaf	244
15	Attiq	184
16	Angela	222
17	Angela	101
18	Anju	265
19	Ann	327
20	Attiq	296
21	Attiq	176

Figure 1.1: *Children's guesses for the number of sweets in a jar.*

D
Sum
Maximum
Minimum
Average
Median
Mode
No of guesses
guesses of 100
Ann's guesses
guesses above 200
No of formulas

Figure 1.2: *Headings to enter in column D.*

⊙TIP

Although you can type in all your formulas in the normal way, if you click on the Σ button on the toolbar, Excel will enter the SUM formula and guess at the cells you want to include. You must always check that these are actually the cells you want to add. It is good practice, however, to highlight the cells you wish to include before clicking on the Σ button to prevent Excel guessing.

If you click on the down arrow Σ ▾ you can quickly access some other common formulas too.

▶ In E4 a formula to find the mean average guess. This will be **=AVERAGE(B2:B21)**

▶ In E5 a formula to find the median guess. This will be **=MEDIAN(B2:B21)**

▶ In E6 a formula to find the most common guess. This will be **=MODE(B2:B21)**

▶ In E8 a formula to count the number of guesses that have been made. Since these are all numbers you can use **COUNT**. The formula you need will be **=COUNT(B2:B21)**

▶ In E9 you need a formula to count the number of guesses of 100. This will be a **COUNTIF** formula because you only want to count the guesses if they are =100. The formula needed will be **=COUNTIF(B2:B21,100)**.

▶ In E10 you need a formula to count the number of guesses Ann has made. This will be a **COUNTIF** formula that looks in column A for the word "Ann". Whenever we look for something other than a straightforward number we need to put it into inverted commas, so you need: **=COUNTIF(A2:A21,"Ann")**

▶ In E11 you need a formula that will count the number of guesses that are over 200. Spreadsheets use the mathematical sign **>** to mean 'more than', so you are looking for guesses **>200**. As this is more than just a simple number, this needs to go into inverted commas too, so you need: **=COUNTIF(B2:B21,">200")**

⊙TIP

> means 'more than'
< means 'less than'
>= means 'more than or equal to'
<= means 'less than or equal to'
<> means 'not equal to'

▶ In E15 you need a formula that will show the number of different formulas you have used in rows 2 to 11 to summarise the data. Using **COUNTA** on column D will count the number of formulas you have now used, so enter **=COUNTA(D1:D11)**. You could get the same result by using **COUNT** on column E.

⊙TIP

COUNT counts the number of cells that contain a number (including dates). COUNTA counts ALL cells, apart from completely blank ones. There is also a formula COUNTBLANK, which counts just the blank cells.

One very useful feature of **COUNTIF** is that you can put a cell reference as the target.

▶ Enter the headings shown in Figure 1.3 at the top of columns G and H.

We want to be able to type any name into G2 and be told the number of guesses that person has made. The formula to do this is **=COUNTIF(A2:A21,G2)**.

G	H
Name	No of guesses

Figure 1.3: *Headings to enter at the top of columns G and H.*

▶ Type this formula into cell H2.

▶ Try out this new formula by typing some names into cell G2.

Formatting a sheet to make it easier to use

The spreadsheet you produced in Activity 1 is an efficient way of summarising the data. However, there is a lot that can be done to make it easier to read and to use.

- Most spreadsheets benefit from having a main heading that shows what the sheet is about. This is usually larger than the rest of the text and may be spread across a number of cells.
- Titles should stand out on the sheet so they are usually bold and centred.
- If you have a column of numbers that need to be added up, it is a good idea to have them aligned to the right of the cells, so that the units, tens, hundreds, etc. are underneath each other. But if you are just looking at the numbers, they are sometimes easier to read if they are centred like the headings.
- Sometimes a spreadsheet is split into clear sections – for example in Activity 1, columns A and B show the children's guesses, columns D and E show the summary data and columns G and H allow you to enter a child's name and find out how many guesses he or she had. If a sheet is split in this way then shading each section in a different colour can make it clearer.
- Simple instructions can be added so that a user knows exactly what to do. For example, an instruction could tell a user of your spreadsheet to enter a child's name into cell G12.

In Activity 2 below you will add some formatting to make the spreadsheet from Activity 1 easier to use. You should remember these ideas whenever you create a spreadsheet, especially if it is to be used by someone else.

Activity 2: Adding formatting to make a spreadsheet easier to use...

In this activity you will:

- change the font and size of cells
- adjust row heights and column widths
- make cells bold
- centre data in cells
- merge cells
- add shading and borders
- add instructions for a user.

Make sure you have open your spreadsheet from Activity 1.

First you will add a title:

▶ Highlight row 1 and insert a row (right click and choose **Insert**).

To allow the title to stand out, this row needs to be bigger than the others.

▶ Leaving the row still highlighted click the right-hand mouse button (this is called **right clicking**) and choose **Row Height**. The row will show as currently 12.75 units high. Make this much higher by changing the height to **30**.

You are going to put a title across the top of columns A to H.

▶ Start by highlighting cells A1 to H1, then right click and choose **Format Cells**.

▶ Click on the **Alignment** tab at the top then change both **Horizontal** and **Vertical** alignment to **Center** and click in the box to **Merge cells**. Then click on **OK**.

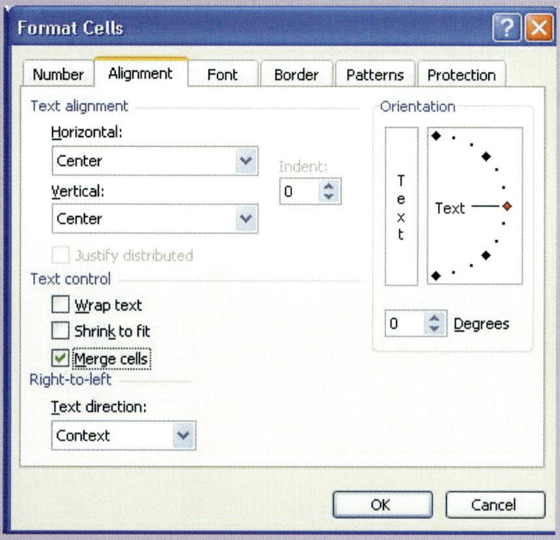

Figure 1.4: *Merging the cells.*

▶ Now enter the title **Number of sweets in the jar – guesses** into the new large cell you have created.

▶ Use the toolbar to choose a more suitable font size and style. In Figure 1.5 the title has just been made larger and bold. You can choose your own options.

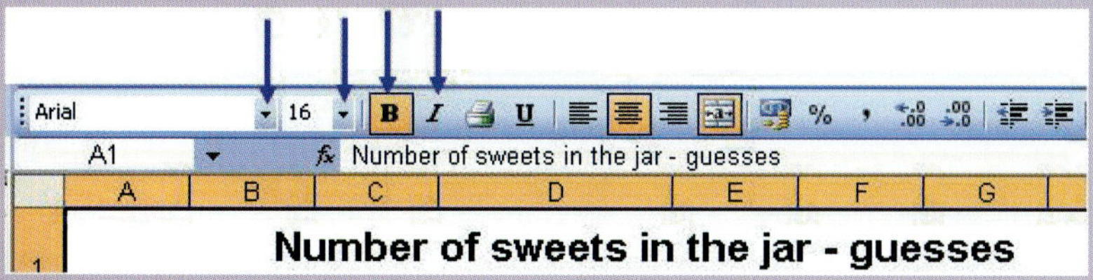

Figure 1.5: *Changing the font size and style.*

▶ Now highlight the column headings and make them bold and centred.

▶ Make the headings in column D bold too.

> You might have to make some columns a little wider to make sure the text all fits. Do this by double clicking on the boundary line in the column headings row.

Figure 1.6: Widening column H.

(!)TIP

There are three ways to change column widths and row heights.

- **Use the menu and type in a number as you did for row 1.**
- **Double click the boundary line as you did here.**
- **Drag the boundary line to where you want it to be.**

> Highlight the cells from B3 to B22 and centre them.

> Centre cell H3.

> Highlight cells E2 to E16 and centre these. Have a look and decide whether you think this column looks best centred, or right-aligned as it was. If you want to go back to the original right-aligned, then press the Undo button.

Now you need to separate the different sections.

> Highlight cells A2 to B22 and choose a shading colour from the toolbar. If you choose a dark colour you may need to change the font colour too.

Now you have shaded in the cells, you can't see the gridlines, so you need to add borders to the cells:

> Keep cells A2 to B22 highlighted and use the Borders tool next to the shading tool to choose the **All Borders** option.

> Now add some shading and borders to cells D2 to E16, then to G2 to H3.

> You might also like to add some colour and a border to the title.

The last thing that is needed is an instruction.

(!)TIP

Don't forget that the Undo and Redo buttons are very useful buttons if you make a mistake or change your mind.

(!)TIP

There are a few more colours available if you right click and choose Format Cells, then choose the Patterns or Font tab.

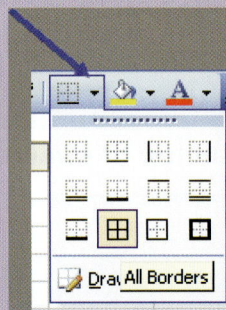

*Figure 1.7: Choosing **All Borders** from the Borders tool.*

▶ First highlight cells G2 to H3, then right click and choose **Cut**. Now move to cell G11 and right click then choose **Paste**. This will move the block down to make room for instructions.

▶ Highlight cells G6 to H10.

▶ Right click and choose **Format Cells** then **Alignment**.

▶ Choose **Center** for both **Horizontal** and **Vertical** alignment and click in the box to **Merge cells**, as you did for the title. However, this time you will be typing too much to fit on one line, so click on the **Wrap text** box too.

▶ Click on **OK**.

▶ Shade this box in the same colour as cells G11 to H12, to show that they belong together.

▶ Type an instruction into the new box. This could be something like **Type a name into the blank box below to find out how many guesses that person has had.**

One final thing that will show that this instruction belongs to the boxes below is to put a wider border around the section.

▶ Highlight cells G6 to H12, then go to the border tool on the toolbar and choose the **Thick Box Border**.

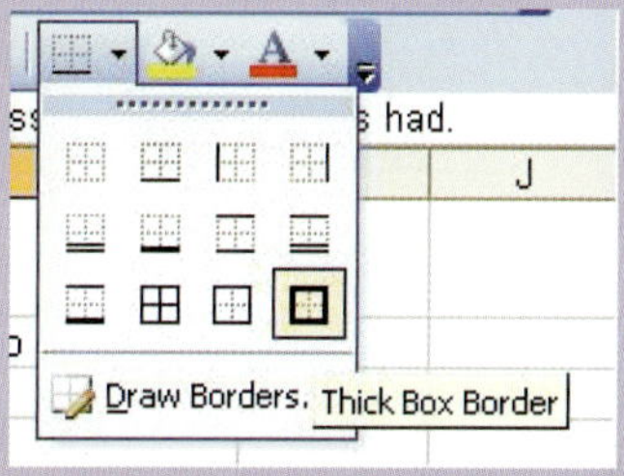

Figure 1.8: Adding a thick box border.

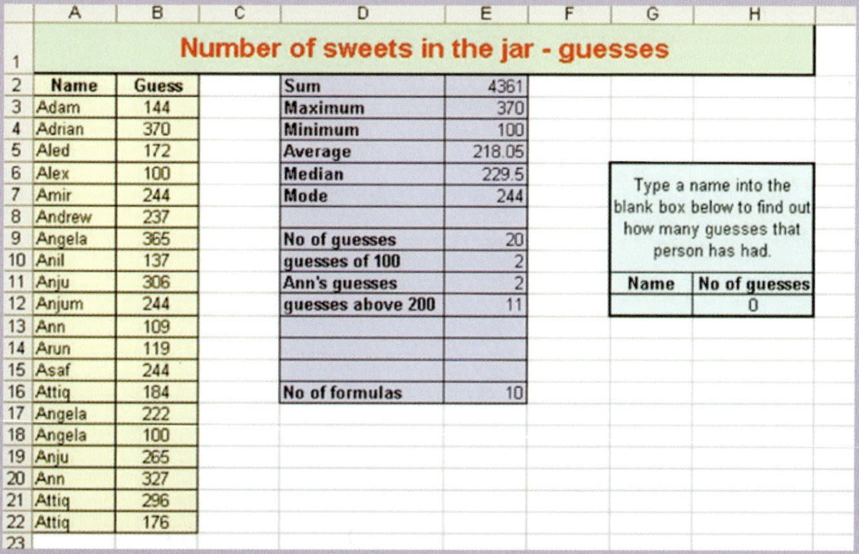

Compare your sheet to the one shown in Figure 1.9.

You might also be able to compare the sheets produced by other students in your group.

Discuss which you think are the most effectively formatted sheets.

	A	B	C	D	E	F	G	H
1	**Number of sweets in the jar - guesses**							
2	**Name**	**Guess**		**Sum**	4361			
3	Adam	144		**Maximum**	370			
4	Adrian	370		**Minimum**	100			
5	Aled	172		**Average**	218.05			
6	Alex	100		**Median**	229.5			Type a name into the
7	Amir	244		**Mode**	244			blank box below to find out
8	Andrew	237						how many guesses that
9	Angela	365		**No of guesses**	20			person has had.
10	Anil	137		**guesses of 100**	2			
11	Anju	306		**Ann's guesses**	2		**Name**	**No of guesses**
12	Anjum	244		**guesses above 200**	11			0
13	Ann	109						
14	Arun	119						
15	Asaf	244						
16	Attiq	184		**No of formulas**	10			
17	Angela	222						
18	Angela	100						
19	Anju	265						
20	Ann	327						
21	Attiq	296						
22	Attiq	176						
23								

Figure 1.9: An example of what the formatted spreadsheet might look like.

Formatting numbers

You should already be familiar with some of the ways you can format numbers, for example by specifying the number of decimal places, as currency with £ signs, as percentages with % signs.

You should never type symbols, such as £, %, into a spreadsheet cell, as this stops the entry being a number and so prevents the software being able to carry out any calculations with the data. Instead, you should always use the formatting option to add these symbols.

In Activity 3 we will look at an example of a simple spreadsheet and use formatting to display the numbers in the most effective way.

Activity 3: Formatting numbers — a reminder...

In this activity you will:

- insert rows
- format numbers, currency and percentages in a simple spreadsheet
- add simple formulas.

Jesi runs a business selling catalogue items to people in her local area. She wants to use a spreadsheet to calculate and print bills.

▶ Load the file **Activity 3.xls**, which shows the spreadsheet Jesi has started to create for one of her customers.

The maximum number of items any customer has ever ordered at once is 10. Jesi needs more rows to insert order lines, so that there is room for 10 items if necessary.

▶ Highlight rows 5 to 11 and then right click and choose **Insert**. You highlight the number of rows that you want to insert. In this case you are inserting 7 rows, giving a total of 10 rows for orders.

The numbers in cells B2 to B11 are amounts of money, so they need formatting as currency.

▶ Highlight cells B2 to B11, right click and choose **Format Cells**. Select the **Number** tab if it is not already selected, then choose **Currency**. Make sure that **Decimal places** is set to **2** and the **Symbol** is **£**, then click **OK**.

The VAT rate of 0.175 in cell B13 is a percentage – 0.175 is the same as 17.5%.

▶ Right click in cell B13 and choose **Format Cells**. Choose **Percentage** and set **Decimal places** to **1**.

Column D needs formulas to multiply the price per item by the number required.

▶ Enter a suitable formula into cell D2 and copy it down to cell D11.

▶ Format these cells as currency.

▶ Cell D12 needs a formula to add cells D2 to D11. Enter this.

▶ Cell D13 needs to show the amount of VAT. This is the amount in D12 multiplied by the percentage in B13. The formula you need here is **=D12*B13**.

▶ You should now be able to add a formula to cell D14, to add the VAT to the total price of the goods.

If you have entered all the correct formulas you should have a total in D14 of £41.51.

You can check your formulas against Figure 1.10 on the next page.

	A	B	C	D
1	**Item code**	**Price/1**	**No reqd**	**Cost**
2	A32/657	6.5	2	=B2*C2
3	A33/428	12.49	1	=B3*C3
4	C65/284	3.28	3	=B4*C4
5				=B5*C5
6				=B6*C6
7				=B7*C7
8				=B8*C8
9				=B9*C9
10				=B10*C10
11				=B11*C11
12	Total			=SUM(D2:D11)
13	VAT	0.175		=D12*B13
14	**Total to pay**			=D12+D13
15				
16				

Figure 1.10: *Here are the correct formulas for Activity 3.*

Date and time functions

The function **=TODAY()** will automatically insert today's date, which will be updated every time a document is opened. If you need the time as well as the date you can use **=NOW()**

Your computer stores the date as a number (it is actually the number of days since 1st January 1900), so it is important always to use the **Format Cells** option to show the date correctly in the cell. Take care when choosing a format, as Americans write their dates in a different order to us. If you want to write the date in numbers, for example 30/09/2006, you need to make sure that it is showing the day first, then the month and not the other way around. We call this format **dd/mm/yyyy**, which means 'two digits for the day, followed by a '/', then two digits for the month, followed by a '/', then the year in full.

> **⊘TIP**
>
> It is very important that your computer's regional settings are set to the UK and not to the United States. If they are wrongly set, then you may not have the right options for date formats, or they may not show correctly on your computer.

There are also functions that split up the various parts of a date:

- **=YEAR**(cell**)** will give the year of a date in the cell
- **=MONTH**(cell**)** will give the month, as a number from 1 to 12
- **=DAY**(cell**)** will give the day of the month
- **=WEEKDAY**(cell**)** will give the day of the week, as a number, so Sunday = 1, Monday = 2 through to Saturday = 7.

So if cell A1 contains the date 30/09/2006, then **=YEAR(A1)** will give 2006, **=MONTH(A1)** will give 9 and **=DAY(A1)** will give 30. As 30th September 2006 was a Saturday, **=WEEKDAY(A1)** will give 7.

=YEAR(TODAY()),=MONTH(TODAY()),=DAY(TODAY()) and **=WEEKDAY(TODAY())** will give the year, month and day of today's date.

YEAR, **MONTH** and **DAY** need formatting as numbers, not as dates. **WEEKDAY()** can be formatted as a number but it can also be formatted to show the day as a word, by using the **Custom** format option and typing **ddd** or **dddd** into the **Type** box.

Activity 4 allows you to experiment with the use of the **=TODAY()** and **=NOW()** functions with different format options.

Activity 4: Inserting the date and time...

In this activity you will:

- use **=TODAY()** to insert today's date and **=NOW()** to insert the date and time
- experiment with different date formats.

▶ Start a new spreadsheet workbook and enter the formula **=TODAY()** into cell A1

▶ Enter the formula **=NOW()** into cell B1

▶ Highlight these two cells and copy the formulas down as far as row 7.

There are many different ways that dates can be displayed. You are now going to investigate these:

▶ Right click in cell A2 and choose **Format Cells**. Select the **Number** tab if it is not already selected.

▶ Choose **Date** and make sure that the location is set to **English (United Kingdom)**

There are a number of different formats you can choose from. As a general rule you should not use the ones with an asterisk (*), as these could cause problems if you use your file on a machine that is not set up with the correct regional settings.

▶ Choose the first option without an asterisk.

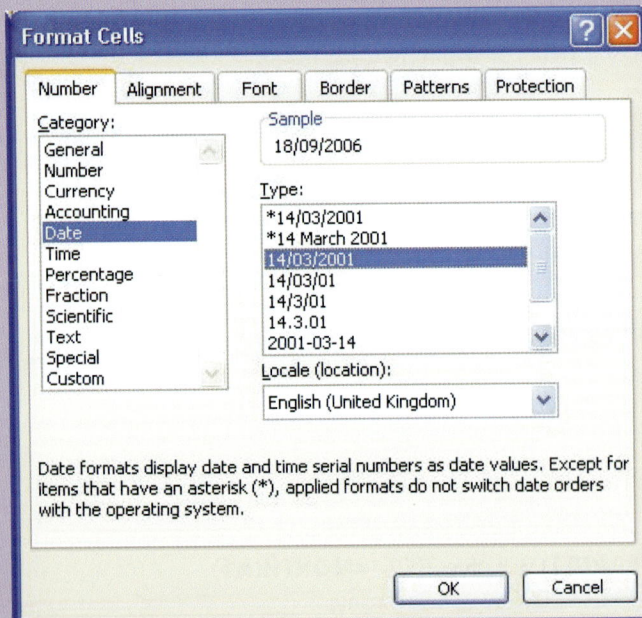

Figure 1.11: *Choosing a format for a date.*

▶ Now format the dates in cells A3 to A7, choosing a different date format for each one.

▶ Right click into cell B2 and choose **Format Cells**. This time choose **Time** and choose the first format without an asterisk.

▶ Format the next three times in the same way, using the different options available.

You can select your own format too.

▶ Format cell B6 and choose the **Custom** option in the **Format Cells** box. Type in the format **h.m, dddd** as shown in Figure 1.12 (**h** is for hour, **m** for minutes, **d** for day).

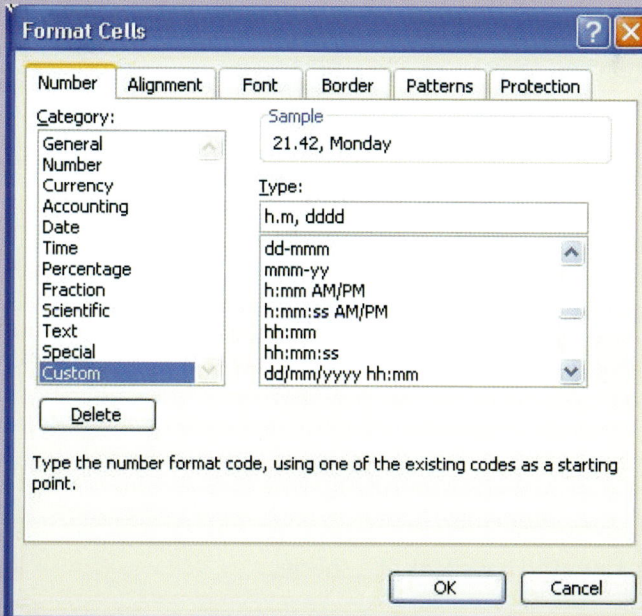

Figure 1.12: Entering your own custom format.

You will notice that Excel shows you what your format will look like in the **Sample** box before you click on **OK**.

▶ Format cell B7 in a different way using a custom format of your own.

You will see the times updating every time you make a change to the sheet. If you want to update the times without making a change, press the **F9** key.

▶ Now click into cell A9 and enter the formula **=YEAR(A1)**. At first this may seem to give the wrong result, but if you format the cell as a number, to 0 decimal places you should see the correct year.

▶ Now enter the formula **=MONTH(A1)** into cell A10 and format it as a number to 0 decimal places.

▶ Add the formulas **=DAY(A1)** to cell A11 and **=WEEKDAY(A1)** to cell A12. Format these both as numbers to 0 decimal places.

▶ Now click into cell A13 and add the formula **=WEEKDAY(A1)** but this time when you format it choose the **custom** option and enter **dddd**.

You might like to print off this sheet and keep it to remind you of the different formats you can use for dates and times.

Making decisions with the logical function IF

This is a particularly important section if you wish to gain a **Merit** or **Distinction**. Although the requirements are quite flexible about the functions you can use in your final spread-sheet, it is essential that you use at least one **IF** statement, as introduced here, if you are to gain more than a **Pass**.

Often we want the computer to make a decision. Some common examples of situations where this is necessary include:

- a teacher's mark book showing test results. The teacher might want a formula that gives 'Pass' for all pupils with a mark above a certain level, and 'Fail' for the rest
- a spreadsheet for calculating pay in a business where staff earn a bonus if they have made a certain amount of sales in a month but no bonus if they do not achieve that amount of sales
- a spreadsheet for calculating prices for customers, where 10% needs to be taken off the order cost if a customer has a discount voucher

In general, any time when there are two options, and you want the computer to carry out a different calculation for each option, you will need to use an **IF** statement.

An **IF** statement looks like this:

=IF(decision,if_true,if_false**)**
where **decision** is a statement that can be true or false, **if_true** is the value required if the statement is true and **if_false** is the value required if the statement is false.

This might seem a bit complicated and is easier to understand if we look at a specific example.

You might be creating an invoice for a mail order company where the total cost of the order is in cell D10. There is a postage and packing charge of £1.50 for orders under £30 but no charge for orders of £30 and over. This is an example of a situation with two options (an order under £30 or an order of £30 and over) where you want something different for each option.

In this example the computer needs to decide whether the value in D10 is less than £30 or not, so the **decision** is **D10<30**. If this statement is true the value needed is £1.50, so **if_true** will be **1.5**. If the decision statement is false, i.e. D10 is not less than 30, the value needed is 0, so **if_false** will be **0**.

This gives us a formula of **=IF(D10<30,1.5,0)**. This formula can be read as 'if the value in D10 is less than 30 then enter 1.5, otherwise enter 0'.

IF (D10<30 , 1.5 , 0)

If the value in D10 is less than 30 then enter 1.5, otherwise enter 0

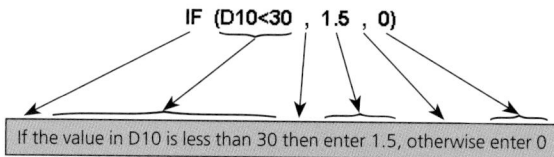

*Figure 1.13: The parts of an **IF** statement, showing what they mean.*

Activity 5 allows you to work through an example situation showing how **IF** can be useful.

Activity 5: Logical functions...

In this activity you will:

● use an **IF** statement to make a decision in a spreadsheet.

⊙ Load the ***Activity 5.xls*** spreadsheet.

This is an invoice for an office stationery order. It needs some formulas adding.

⊙ The cost for each item in column D is calculated by multiplying the price for the item by the number required. You should be able to enter an appropriate formula into cell D2 that multiplies the price in cell B2 by the number required in cell C2.

⊙ Copy your formula down as far as row 9.

⊙ You now need to enter a formula into D10 to find the total cost of all these items. If you have entered all the correct formulas so far this should give a total cost of £55.20.

⊙ In D11 you need a formula to calculate the amount of VAT. This will be the total cost from D10 multiplied by the VAT percentage in B11.

⊙ You now need a formula in D12 to add the VAT in D11 to the total cost in D10. If you have entered all the correct formulas this should give a total including VAT of £64.86.

You can check your formulas so far by looking at Figure 1.15 over the page.

There is a postage and packing charge of £3.50 for orders under £50 but no charge for orders of £50 and over. This needs an **IF** formula. If the total is less than 50 then we need 3.50, otherwise we need 0. The formula will therefore be **=IF(D12<50,3.5,0)**.

⊙ Enter this formula in cell D13.

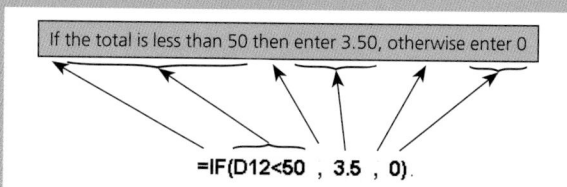

If the total is less than 50 then enter 3.50, otherwise enter 0

=IF(D12<50 , 3.5 , 0).

*Figure 1.14: The **IF** formula needed to add postage and packing to the invoice.*

▶ You will then need to format cell D13 to currency to match the rest of the column.

▶ Now insert a formula in cell D14 to add the postage and packing charge in cell D13 to the total including VAT in cell D12 to give the final total.

▶ Change the amounts in the **No Reqd** column to order just two of each item. This should give a total including VAT of £4.32 and you will see this time that your **IF** formula produces a postage and packing charge, giving a final total of £7.82.

	A	B	C	D
1	Item	Price/1	No Reqd	Cost
2	Pencils	0.1	50	=B2*C2
3	Red pens	0.12	20	=B3*C3
4	Black pens	0.12	50	=B4*C4
5	Ring binders	0.45	60	=B5*C5
6	Rulers	0.08	30	=B6*C6
7	Erasers	0.15	10	=B7*C7
8	scissors	0.55	10	=B8*C8
9	glue sticks	0.27	20	=B9*C9
10	Total cost			=SUM(D2:D9)
11	VAT	0.175		=D10*B11
12	Total inc VAT			=D10+D11
13	Postage and packing			
14	Final total			
15				

Figure 1.15: *The formulas needed for the invoice spreadsheet in Activity 5.*

Lookup tables

In the last section you saw how **IF** can be used to make a decision between two alternatives. Although a very useful function, it is rather limited because it only makes a decision between **two** alternatives. Often there are more than two options, for example:

- a teacher's mark book showing test results where students can gain a 'Distinction', a 'Merit', a 'Pass' or a 'Fail'
- a spreadsheet for calculating pay in a business where staff can earn three different levels of bonus according to the amount of sales they make in a month
- a spreadsheet calculating prices for customers, where there are four different types of voucher, each of which offers a different percentage discount.

When you want a spreadsheet to make a choice between more than two options you will usually need to enter the options into the spreadsheet. This is called a **Lookup table**. There are then special **LOOKUP** functions that will use the table to find the correct values.

The main **LOOKUP** formula you need to know about is:

VLOOKUP(target,range,column,TF**)**
Here:

- **V** stands for **vertical**. This means that the formula needs a lookup table where the different options are in a vertical column
- **target** is the item you are looking for

- **range** is the range of cells where the lookup table (such as the table of charges in our example) is held
- **column** is the column in the range where the answer can be found
- **TF** is either **TRUE** or **FALSE**. If you are looking for an exact match, which you usually are, this should always be **FALSE**.

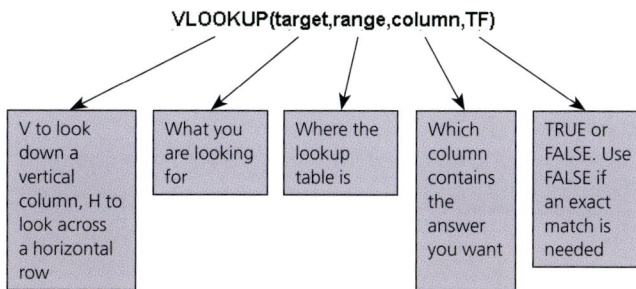

VLOOKUP(target,range,column,TF)

V to look down a vertical column, H to look across a horizontal row	What you are looking for	Where the lookup table is	Which column contains the answer you want	TRUE or FALSE. Use FALSE if an exact match is needed

Figure 1.16: *The structure of a VLOOKUP statement.*

Like **IF**, although **LOOKUP** functions can be used in any situation where a choice is needed, it is easiest to see how this works by looking at a specific situation.

Treetops House and Park has three admission prices for coach parties booked in advance:

- entry to the house and gardens – full adult price £8, concessions (children, students and pensioners) £5
- entry to the gardens only – full adult price £3, concessions (children, students and pensioners) £1.50
- entry to the house and gardens, with lunch in the restaurant – full adult price £15, concessions (children, students and pensioners) £10.

Spreadsheet software can be used to produce estimates and invoices for coach parties. One way of doing this would be to have a printed sheet of charges and look up the relevant cost each time to enter into the spreadsheet. However, your computer is just as capable as you are of looking items up on a list. It does this using **LOOKUP** formulas.

First you need to enter a table of charges into the spreadsheet – this is the **lookup table**. Then you use **LOOKUP** formulas to find the prices from this table. All the user will need to enter each time is the customer's choice and the number of adults and concessions.

Let's look at how the **LOOKUP** function works for this example. The table in Figure 1.17 shows how the information about charges can be arranged in a lookup table. The choices have been coded – HG for house and garden, G for garden only and HGL for house, garden and lunch. This will mean the user has less to type in.

Suppose we typed a choice into cell F2. We could then use the formula **=VLOOKUP(F2,A2:C4,2,FALSE)** to find the full price of the chosen option.

	A	B	C
1	Choice	Full	Concns
2	HG	£8.00	£5.00
3	G	£3.00	£1.50
4	HGL	£15.00	£10.00
5			
6			
7			

Figure 1.17: Lookup table for Treetops House and Garden.

- **VLOOKUP** says that you want to look up values in a **vertical** table (i.e. you read vertically down the first column).
- **F2** shows the value you are looking for – in this case the option you have typed in.
- **A2:C4** shows where the information table is
- **2** tells the computer to find the value from the second column.
- **FALSE** says that you are looking for an exact match for the choice typed into F2. If you type an invalid option you will get an error message, although it doesn't matter if you use capital letters or not.

So if you typed in **G** the computer would look for an exact match for G in the first column of the table in A2:C4 and would then look across to column 2 and find **3**.

Similarly **=VLOOKUP(F2,A2:C4,3,FALSE)** would find the price for a concession by looking across to column 3.

The lookup table could also be written the other way around, as shown in Figure 1.18.

	A	B	C	D
1	Choice	HG	G	HGL
2	Full	£8.00	£3.00	15
3	Concns	£5.00	£1.50	10
4				

Figure 1.18: Horizontal lookup table for Treetops.

In this case, you would need a slightly different formula **=HLOOKUP** which works in just the same way as **VLOOKUP** except that it looks up values by reading **horizontally** across the first row. The equivalent formulas would be:

- **=HLOOKUP(F2,B1:D3,2,FALSE)** to find the full adult price
- **=HLOOKUP(F2,B1:D3,3,FALSE)** to find the price for a concession.

Again, this might seem quite complicated. It will be much clearer if you try it out in a real spreadsheet.

Activity 6: Lookup functions...

In this activity you will:

- use **VLOOKUP** to look up values in a table
- use **IF** to prevent error messages when cells are blank
- use more than one sheet in a spreadsheet workbook
- rename, delete and hide sheets.

▶ Open the file **Activity 6.xls**, which contains the lookup table and headings shown in Figure 1.19.

	A	B	C	D	E	F	G	H	I
1	Choice	Full	Concns			Choice:			
2	HG	£8.00	£5.00				No	Price each	Total
3	G	£3.00	£1.50			Adults			
4	HGL	£15.00	£10.00			Concns			
5									
6						Final total			
7									

Figure 1.19 *Treetops House and Park ticket price calculator.*

You need to allow a user to enter the choice (HG, G or HGL) into cell G1 and the number of adults and concessions in the party into cells G3 and G4. The spreadsheet needs to insert the correct ticket prices in cells H3 and H4, then calculate the total costs of each type of ticket in I3 and I4, and the final total in I6.

▶ Enter the formula **=VLOOKUP(G1,A2:C4,2,FALSE)** for the adult price into cell H3. Don't worry that you will get an error message **#N/A** at first – that is because there is nothing in G1 to look up yet.

▶ Test that your formula works by entering each of the options (HG, G and HGL) into cell G1, one at a time.

▶ You should now be able to enter the correct formula into cell H4. This will be the same as the last formula, except that the computer needs to find the result from column 3 of the lookup table rather than column 2.

▶ When you are happy that both formulas work, add the required formulas into cells I3, I4 and I6. If necessary, check with the hint on the next page.

Your sheet now works, but could look better. It is not good to have the error messages **#N/A** whenever there is nothing entered into the choices cell.

You can prevent this happening by using **IF** to tell the computer to look in cell G1 first. If there is nothing there then you want nothing in the cell, but if there is something there you want to look it up in the lookup table using the formulas you have just entered.

▶ To tell the computer to look to see if there is nothing in G1 you need **=IF(G1= ""** (The "" is two sets of speech marks with nothing in between – that means 'nothing' or 'empty'.)

▶ Then you need to say what to do if it is empty, which is leave the cell empty. The formula is now **=IF(G1="","""**

▶ If G1 is not empty then you want the lookup formula you had last time, so the complete formula you need in cell H3 is: **=IF(G1="","", VLOOKUP(G1,A2:C4,2,FALSE))**

▶ You should now be able to edit the formulas in H4, I3, I4 and I6 so that they will remain blank until an option is given.

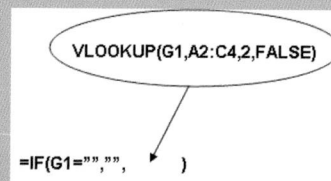

VLOOKUP(G1,A2:C4,FALSE)

=IF(G1="","",   )

Figure 1.20: *The formula for cell H3.*

!HINT

H4 =VLOOKUP(G1,A2:C4,3,FALSE)

I3 =G3*H3

I4 =G4*H4

I6 =SUM(I3:I4) (or I3 + I4 would be just as good)

Revised H4 =IF(G1="","",VLOOKUP(G1,A2:C4,3,FALSE))

Revised I3 =IF(G1="","",G3*H3)

Revised I4 =IF(G1="","",G4*H4)

Revised I6 =IF(G1="","",SUM(I3:I4))

▶ Test your spreadsheet to make sure that it carries out the correct calculations for each option.

The actual lookup table, in cells A1 to C4, is for the computer to use rather than for the user to see. It can be useful to move this to another sheet, where the computer can access it but it doesn't get in the way of the information the user wants to see.

▶ Highlight cells A1 to C4, right click and choose **Cut**. Then move onto **Sheet2** of your workbook by clicking on the **Sheet2** tab at the bottom of the screen.

▶ Click into cell A1 of this new sheet and choose **Paste**.

▶ Move back to **Sheet1** and look at your formulas. You should see that these have now changed to refer to the new sheet. You *can* type in formulas using these sheet references but the easiest way to create formulas like this is to click in the cells you want rather than to type them in, or to create them on the same sheet and then move them, as you have done here.

!TIP

If you want formulas to update when you move cells you must use cut and paste rather than copy and paste. If you use copy the formulas will still refer to the original cells.

▶ Now cut and paste your calculator table from F1:I6 to the beginning of the sheet, starting in A1.

▶ Add some suitable formatting to this sheet, to make it clearer and easier for someone else to use. There is no need to format Sheet2 as this is only for the computer to use.

You can label each sheet so that you can see more easily what it contains.

▶ Double click on the **Sheet1** tab at the bottom of the screen to highlight the name.

▶ You should now be able to rename **Sheet1** as **Main**.

▶ Now rename **Sheet2** as **Prices**. Move back to the **Main** sheet and look at your formulas – they will be automatically updated to account for the changed name of the lookup sheet.

For a neater solution you can now get rid of the unused **Sheet3**.

▶ Move to **Sheet3** by clicking on it. Make sure you are on the correct sheet, which should be empty, then go to **Edit** and choose **Delete Sheet**.

It is useful to be able to hide sheets when you are creating a spreadsheet for someone else to use. This will prevent them from seeing or altering certain information, such as the lookup table in this case.

▶ Move onto the **Prices** sheet and go to **Format** and choose **Sheet** and **Hide**.

You can always get a sheet back by going to **Format** and choosing **Sheet** and **Unhide**.

User-friendly spreadsheets

Formatting and preventing errors

Look back at your spreadsheet from Activity 6. When you formatted it, did you just make it *look* better, or did you add features to help the user?

● Did you use colours to help the user find the different parts of the sheet, such as the cells where input is needed?
● Did you remember to add a title?
● Did you remember to include some instructions?

Compare your sheet with Figure 1.21. Although this is not the only good way of formatting the sheet, you should be able to see how colour and instructions have been used to try to make the sheet easier for a new user to follow.

	A	B	C	D
1	**Treetops Ticket Calculator**			
2	Enter your choice (HG, G or HGL) in the green cell below, then enter the number of adults and concessions required in the yellow cells. Your final total price is shown in the blue box at the bottom.			
3	Choice:			
4		No	Price each	Total
5	Adults			
6	Concns			
7				
8	Final total			
9				

Figure 1.21: The Treetops spreadsheet, formatted to make it more user friendly.

However, it would be easy for a user to forget to use the correct codes here. This is a situation where further help would be appropriate.

You could add an instruction to your spreadsheet as you did in Activity 2. In addition to this method there is a range of techniques you can use to make a sheet simpler to use. Most spreadsheets should contain some form of help. One method isn't any better than the others, it will be up to you to choose the method you think is most appropriate for any sheet you create for your portfolio. In this section you will try out the following methods.

Type of help	What it does	How to add it
Comment	Appears in a text box whenever a user hovers over the cell.	Right click in the cell and choose **Insert**.
Input message	Appears whenever a user clicks into the cell and will stay on the screen until the user clicks into a different cell	Click in a cell, then choose **Data** from the menu bar and then **Validation**. Click on the **Input Message** tab and enter your message.
Validation	This sets limits to the data that can be entered into a cell.	Click in a cell and then choose **Data** from the menu bar and then **Validation**. Enter the allowable data using the **Settings** tab.

Validation settings include:

- **Whole number**: you can set these to between certain values – either values you type in or values from the spreadsheet
- **Decimal**: allows any number, including whole numbers – you can also set a range of acceptable values as for the **Whole number** setting
- **Date**: allows only dates – again you can set a range of acceptable dates
- **Time**: allows only times – again you can set a range of acceptable times
- **Text length**: allows any type of entry, but you can set the maximum number of characters that can be entered, or a range of acceptable lengths
- **List**: perhaps the most useful validation option. You can restrict entries to a list that is typed in somewhere on the sheet. This option also allows the user to enter data using a drop-down list rather than having to type.

When you have set validation settings then you can also add an **Error Alert** to be shown if a user enters something that does not fit into the limits set. You can choose whether to completely stop this being added, or to provide a warning, with an option of continuing or correcting the entry, or just to provide an information box. Usually you would choose to stop the entry, but some situations need one of the other options – for example, an order form where you might want a user to double check an especially large order in case it is a keying-in error, but you wouldn't want to prevent it!

Activity 7 gives you a chance to try out these techniques by making your Treetops spreadsheet from Activity 6 easier for an inexperienced person to use.

Activity 7: Comments and validation...

In this activity you will:

- add a comment to give information about a cell
- investigate the range of options available from the **validation** feature
- set data for entry from a drop-down box
- hide a column in a spreadsheet.

▶ Load the spreadsheet you created in Activity 6. Alternatively you can load the file *Activity 7.xls*.

▶ Click into cell B5 then right click and choose **Insert Comment**.

▶ Delete any text that might be in the box and add the instruction **Enter here the number of adults in your party**. Finish by clicking into any other cell.

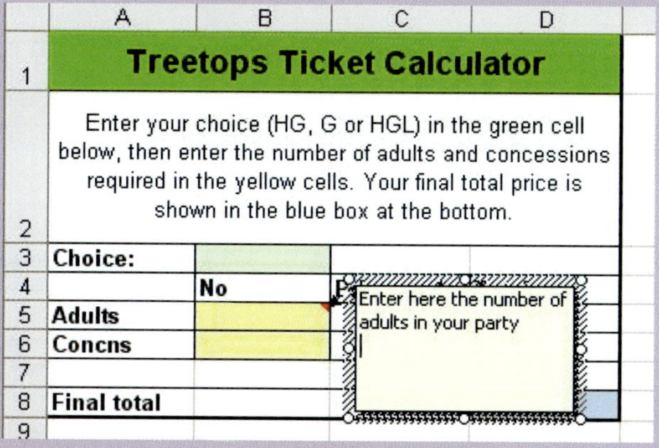

Figure 1.22: Entering a comment into cell B5.

You should see a little red triangle in the corner of the cell, indicating that there is a comment here.

▶ Hover your mouse over cell B5 and check that your comment shows correctly.

▶ If you need to change your comment, right click in the cell and choose **Edit Comment**. You will also find an option to **Delete Comment** if necessary.

▶ Click into cell B6 and add a comment with an appropriate instruction.

You are now going to add validation to cell B3 so that the user will only be able to enter one of the three acceptable codes: HG, G or HGL. To do this you need a list of acceptable codes somewhere on the sheet. The validation option does not allow you to use lists from other sheets.

You could simply type the codes into some blank cells, but as they are already typed into Sheet2 it would be better to use formulas pointing to these, so that if in the future the codes are changed you would only need to change them once.

▶ Go to the **Format** menu on the menu bar and choose **Sheet** then **Unhide**. You will then be shown the name of your hidden sheet – **Prices**. As this is already selected, you just need to click on **OK**.

▶ Click back onto your **Main** sheet.

It doesn't really matter where you put the list, so long as it is on the same sheet as the cell(s) to be validated and on a blank row or column. You are going to put it in column F.

▶ Click into cell F3. Press **=** to start a formula, then click onto your **Prices** sheet and click into cell A2 and press **Enter**. This will put a copy of cell A2 from your **Prices** sheet into cell F3 of your **Main** sheet.

▶ Copy this formula down from F3 into F4 and F5. This should give you a copy of the three codes.

	A	B	C	D	E	F
1	**Treetops Ticket Calculator**					=Prices!A2
2	Enter your choice (HG, G or HGL) in the green cell below, then enter the number of adults and concessions required in the yellow cells. Your final total price is shown in the blue box at the bottom.					
3	Choice:					HG
4		No	Price each	Total		G
5	Adults					HGL
6	Concns					=Prices!A4

(=Prices!A3 indicated)

Figure 1.23: *Cells F3 to F5 on the main sheet (with the formulas indicated).*

▶ Once you have the list you can hide your **Prices** sheet again – click onto the **Prices** sheet, then choose **Format/Sheet/Hide**.

Now you have the list on the right sheet you can set the validation.

▶ Click into cell B3 and choose the **Data** menu from the menu bar. Now choose **Validation**.

▶ Make sure the **Settings** tab is selected and choose **List** from the drop-down box.

▶ You now need to show Excel where the list of acceptable values is. Click on the button shown in Figure 1.24.

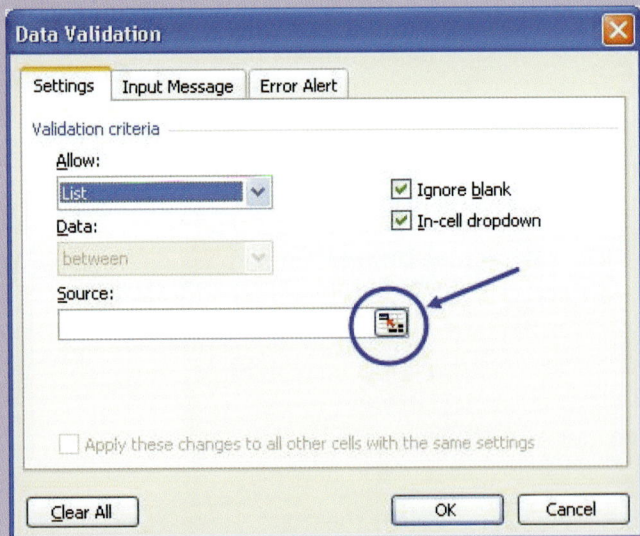

Figure 1.24: *Selecting the list.*

▶ Drag through cells F3 to F5 on your sheet to select them, then click on the button shown in Figure 1.25.

Figure 1.25: *Click here when you have selected the list.*

▶ Click on **OK** to set the validation you have chosen – only to allow values from the list in cells F3 to F5.

▶ Look at cell B3. The validation you have set has added a drop-down menu to this cell. Try it – you should find that it will allow you to enter just the three valid options.

Now that you have used the list in column F you don't want to see it any more – it is like the **Prices** sheet; it is just for the computer to use.

▶ Select the whole of column F by clicking on the **F** column heading.

▶ Right click and choose **Hide**.

Now that you have successfully created the drop-down box you can add further help by adding an input message and error alert.

▶ Click into cell B3 and choose **Data/Validation** again.

▶ Choose the **Input Message** tab and enter a suitably helpful message such as the one shown in Figure 1.26.

> **⊙TIP**
>
> You can easily hide rows and columns by selecting them, right clicking and choosing Hide. If you want to unhide these later, you must first select the rows/columns on either side before right clicking and choosing Unhide.

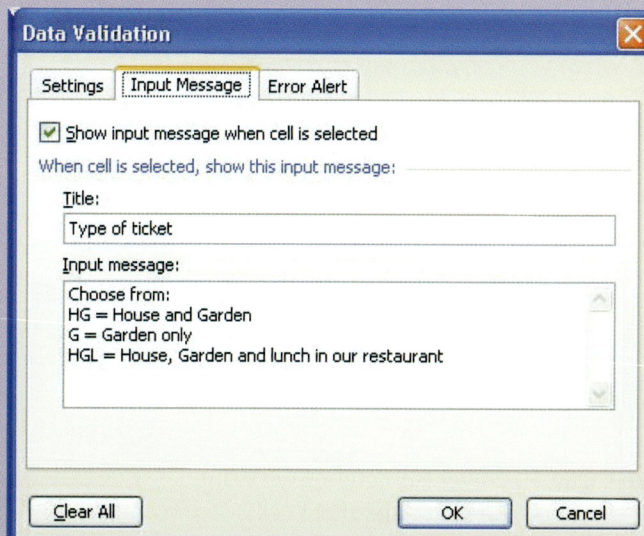

Figure 1.26: *Entering an input message into the* **Validation** *box.*

You have made it quite difficult to enter an incorrect code, but it is still possible to type into cell B3, so it is best to add a helpful error message.

▶ Select the **Error Alert** tab in the **Validation** box and enter a suitable error message such as the one shown in Figure 1.27.

Data Validation

| Settings | Input Message | Error Alert |

☑ Show error alert after invalid data is entered

When user enters invalid data, show this error alert:

Style:
Stop

Title:
Wrong code entered

Error message:
You must only enter one of the following:
HG, G or HGL

Clear All   OK   Cancel

*Figure 1.27: Entering an error message into the **Validation** box.*

▶ Click on **OK** to set your messages.

▶ You should now see your input message in cell B3. Try typing an invalid code to see your error message.

▶ Test your sheet by entering some different choices and values.

Absolute and relative cell referencing

You will have noticed that when you copy a formula down a column, then any references to other cells in that formula are automatically updated to refer to the correct row. The same thing happens if you copy a formula across a row.

For example: if cell C1 contains the formula **=A1*B1**, when you copy it down to row 2 it becomes **=A2*B2** and in row 3 it becomes **A3*B3**. These references are called **relative cell references** because they are not fixed – they are changed so that they are always in the correct place **relative** to the cell containing the formula, in this case the two cells multiplied together are always the two on the left of the formula.

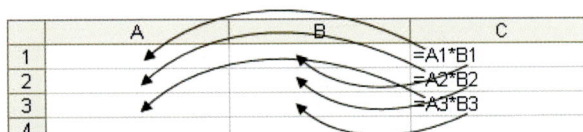

	A	B	C
1			=A1*B1
2			=A2*B2
3			=A3*B3
4			

Figure 1.28: Relative cell references copied down a column

Most of the time we want the cells to be relative in this way. However, sometimes we want to refer to a particular cell in a formula and we want this to be the same **absolute** cell no matter where the formula is. One example of this would be if you had a spreadsheet calculating the amount of VAT charged on a range of goods. If the VAT percentage was in a cell, say A1, then *all* the formulas calculating VAT need to refer to cell A1, no matter where the formula is. This sort of reference is called an **absolute cell reference.**

Absolute cell references are created by adding $ signs in front of each part, so the formula **=$A$1*B1** means A1 multiplied by B1 – A1 is an absolute cell reference, so will not be changed if the formula is copied.

	A	B	C
1			=$A$1*B1
2			=$A$1*B2
3			=$A$1*B3

Figure 1.29: Cell A2 as an absolute reference.

Although you can type in the $ signs, the quickest way to make a cell reference absolute is to press the **F4** key.

Each $ sign makes the row number or column letter after it fixed. So:

- $A$1 will not change the row number or column letter if it is copied down or across
- $A1 will not change the column letter if it is copied across but it will change the row number if it is copied down
- A$1 will change the column letter if it is copied across but will not change the row number if it is copied down.

Activity 8: Investigating relative and absolute cell references...

In this activity you will:

- try out different types of cell reference
- investigate the effects when formulas are copied across and down.

▶ Open the spreadsheet file *Activity 8.xls*. This contains the numbers 1 to 100 arranged in ten rows and 10 columns.

▶ Click into cell A15 and enter the formula **=A1.**

▶ Copy this formula across from A15 as far as J15. You should be able to anticipate the result.

▶ Click into some of the cells from B15 to J15 to check that the formula is what you expected.

▶ Highlight cells A15 to J15 and copy these formulas down as far as row 24. Again you should be able to anticipate the result.

▶ Click into some of the cells from A16 to J24 to check that the formulas are what you expected.

▶ Click back into cell A15 and click into the formula bar at the top of the screen.

▶ Press the **F4** key. You will see that this changes the **relative** cell reference **A1** to the **absolute** reference **$A$1**.

▶ Copy this formula across to J15 and then down to J24 as before. Look carefully at what has happened and click inside some cells to see what difference the $ signs have made.

▶ Click into cell A15 and click into the formula bar at the top of the screen again.

▶ Press the **F4** key as before. You should see that this changes the reference to **A$1**. This means that the column **A** is relative and the row **1** is absolute.

▶ What do you think will happen if you copy this formula across and down as before?

▶ Now copy the formula and see if you were right. Don't just look at the numbers displayed – have a look at some of the formulas too.

▶ Click into cell A15 once more and click into the formula bar at the top of the screen as before.

▶ Press the **F4** key – this will change the reference to **$A1**. Now it is the column **A** that is absolute and the row **1** is relative.

▶ What do you think will happen if you copy this formula across and down as before?

▶ Copy the formula and see if you were right.

	A	B	C
1	1	2	3
2	11	12	13
3	21	22	23
4	31	32	33
5	41	42	43
6	51	52	53
7	61	62	63
8	71	72	73
9	81	82	83
10	91	92	93
11			
12			
13			
14			
15	=A1	2	3
16	11	12	13
17	21	22	23

Figure 1.30: *Clicking into the formula bar to edit the formula.*

Now that you have seen the difference between absolute and relative cell referencing, Activity 9 allows you to work through an example of when absolute cell referencing is useful.

Activity 9: Using absolute cell references...

In this activity you will:

• use absolute cell references to keep a cell reference constant when the formula is copied down a column.

▶ Load the file **Activity 9.xls**.

This is a spreadsheet for calculating grades. You enter the percentage mark in cell A2 and the grade appears in cell B2. The sheet uses a lookup table on a hidden sheet called **Grades** (look back at Activity 6 if you need a reminder about hidden sheets).

▶ Use **Format/Sheet/Unhide** to show the **Grades** sheet.

The main formula in the spreadsheet is **=VLOOKUP(A2,Grades!A2:B10,2,TRUE)**. The **TRUE** at the end of the **LOOKUP** formula tells the computer to find the highest mark in the lookup table that is either matched or exceeded by the value in A2. For example, If you entered a mark of 50 into cell D2 the formula would look down the lookup table for the highest number that is either matched or exceeded by 50. This is 45. The formula would then look across to column B and give a result of **D**.

▶ Try this out by entering a range of different marks, both on and between grade boundaries shown on the **Grades** sheet.

You are going to change this into a sheet that a teacher could use to enter a whole group's marks.

▶ Highlight column A and **Insert** a new column. Label this column **Name**

▶ Rename columns B and C as **Mark** and **Grade**.

▶ Click into cell C2 so that you can see the formula. Click in between the **A** and the **2** of the reference to cell **A2** in the formula bar, as shown in Figure 1.31.

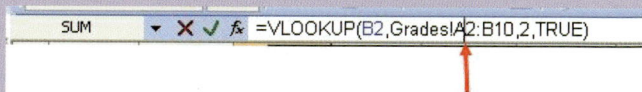

| SUM | ▼ X ✓ ƒx | =VLOOKUP(B2,Grades!A2:B10,2,TRUE) |

Figure 1.31: *Click in between the **A** and the **2**.*

▶ Now press the **F4** key to make this into an absolute cell reference.

▶ Now make **B10** in this formula into an absolute cell reference in the same way, so that the formula is now **=VLOOKUP(B2,Grades!$A$2:$B$10,2,TRUE)**

▶ Copy this formula down as far as row 30.

▶ Click into some of the cells in column C and look at the way the formula has copied this time.

▶ Check these formulas by entering some names and marks in different rows.

▶ Add some shading to the sheet to show clearly where names and marks need to be entered and where results can be found.

It would be better if no grade were shown unless a mark is entered. This can be done using an **IF** statement as you did in Activity 6.

▶ Change the formula in cell C2 by adding **IF(B2="","",** to the front and an extra **)** at the end. This should give a formula of **=IF(B2="","",VLOOKUP(B2,Grades!$A$2:$B$10,2,TRUE))**

▶ Copy this formula down the rest of the column as far as row 30.

Conditional formatting

You have learned many ways of formatting a spreadsheet to improve the way it looks and to make it easier to use. You have considered especially how different formatting can help a user distinguish important information.

Conditional formatting allows you to highlight particular cells if they meet particular criteria, so they can be easily seen. Here are some examples.

- In a financial spreadsheet you might want to highlight expenditures that are over a certain amount of money, or balances that are below a certain amount. If you had a spreadsheet calculating profit you might want to show different levels of profit in different colours to show very good, satisfactory and poor trading.
- The tracking spreadsheets used with this course use conditional formatting to show **Pass**, **Merit** and **Distinction** statements in three different colours.
- A teacher's mark book might use conditional formatting to highlight the students who are achieving different levels.

In Activity 10 you will use conditional formatting to highlight particular grades from the spreadsheet you created in the last activity.

Activity 10: Conditional formatting...

In this activity you will:

- add conditional formatting according to the value in the cell to be formatted
- add conditional formatting according to the value in another cell.

▶ Open up the mark book spreadsheet you saved at the end of Activity 9. Alternatively you can load the file ***Activity 10.xls***.

▶ Enter some data as shown in Figure 1.32.

The teacher would like to see at a glance which students gained an A* and which students gained a U. You are going to use conditional formatting to show the A* students in dark green and the U students in red.

▶ Highlight cells C2 to C30 and click on the **Format** menu on the menu bar and choose **Conditional Formatting**.

▶ Use the second drop-down box to choose **equal to** and type **A*** in the right-hand box, as shown in Figure 1.33.

	A	B	G
1	**Name**	**Mark**	
2	Adam	87	
3	Adrian	32	
4	Aled	30	
5	Alex	18	
6	Amir	66	
7	Andrew	48	
8	Angela	45	
9	Anil	20	
10	Anju	83	
11	Anjum	40	
12	Ann	47	
13	Arun	93	
14	Asaf	21	
15	Attiq	50	
16			
17			
18			
19			

Figure 1.32: *Student names and marks.*

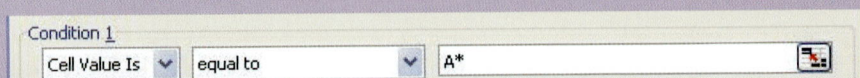

Condition 1			
Cell Value Is	equal to	A*	

Figure 1.33: *Setting the first condition.*

▶ Now click on the **Format** button to choose the format.

▶ Choose the **Patterns** tab to select a dark green background.

▶ Black text won't show well against this, so choose the **Font** tab and select white text in the **Color** option.

▶ Click on **OK**.

▶ Now click on the **Add** button to add another condition.

▶ Change the second condition to **Cell Value Is equal to U** and click the **Format** button.

▶ Choose a red background by clicking the **Patterns** tab and blue text from the **Font** tab.

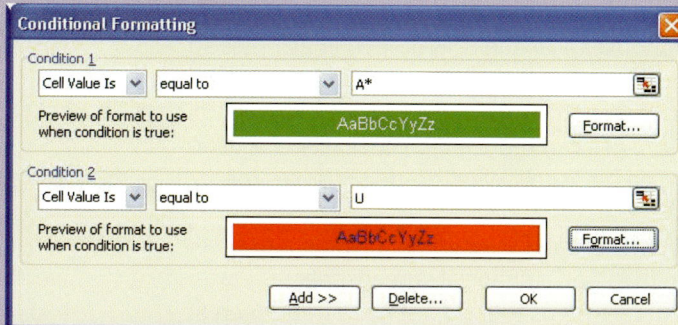

Figure 1.34: *Conditional formatting selected.*

▶ Click on **OK**.

▶ You should now see the formatting at work. Change some students' marks to see the true effect.

You can also format the students' names in this way, using the values in column C. To do this you use the first drop-down box to choose **Formula is** and enter a formula, starting with an **=** sign. When dealing with a group of cells, you enter the formula that would be needed in the first of these cells.

▶ Highlight cells A2 to A30 and choose **Format/Conditional formatting**.

▶ Create the conditions and formatting options shown in Figure 1.35.

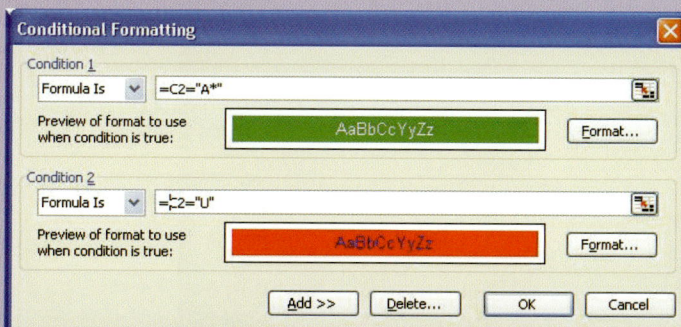

Figure 1.35: *Conditional formatting using a formula.*

▶ Now highlight cells B2 to B30 and create the same conditional formatting in the same way.

▶ Test your sheet with a few different marks. Try adding some new students at the bottom of the list.

Worksheet protection

Making a spreadsheet suitable for an inexperienced user

You have already met a number of methods that can be used to make a spreadsheet easier to use.

- Coloured text and shading can be used to make different parts of a sheet stand out from one another. For example, using one colour for cells the user needs to change and another colour for cells that are calculated by the spreadsheet.
- Borders can be used to show cells more clearly, using a thicker border to separate different sections of a sheet.
- Information and instructions can be added to the sheet, either by adding text to cells or by inserting cell comments. These have different uses – text in cells is seen at all times so is useful for general instructions, while comments are seen only when the user hovers over the cell, so are useful for instructions about what to enter in particular cells.
- Validation with input text and helpful error messages can reduce the possibility of a user entering the wrong data in a cell. Validation against a list allows drop-down boxes for easy data entry.
- Conditional formatting allows certain results to stand out, for example, helping a user see at a glance whether a profit or a loss has been made on a financial spreadsheet.
- Multiple sheets in a workbook allow you to separate items that do not need to be seen at the same time, so leaving sheets less cluttered.
- Hiding rows, columns and sheets prevents the user becoming confused by looking at information that is needed by the computer but that they do not need to see.

One other useful feature you need to know about is worksheet protection.

- Worksheet protection allows you to protect cells on the worksheet that must not be changed by a user. This is mostly used for protecting cells containing titles and formulas because, if an inexperienced user types a number into a cell where you have put a formula, the sheet will no longer work.

If you are ever creating a spreadsheet for someone else to use you should consider protecting it, so that the formulas cannot be changed or deleted. Activity 11 gives you an opportunity to see how worksheet protection is set and how it works.

Activity 11: Worksheet protection...

In this activity you will:

- look at another example of where multiple sheets can be used to make a spreadsheet workbook easier to use
- work with multiple sheets
- set worksheet protection to avoid a user altering the formulas in a workbook.

▶ Open the file *Activity 11.xls*.

This is a file for keeping monthly records for a school tuck shop. There is a sheet for each month where the organiser will enter the total amount taken against the date and the cost of any orders made against the date of the order. The total income and expenditure are then calculated as well as the total profit or loss. There is also a summary sheet for the year.

▶ Click on the sheet tabs and look at the layout of the sheets and the formulas used, so that you can understand what they do and how they work.

▶ Enter some data for a few months to see the calculations that are carried out, then look on the **Summary** sheet to see how the monthly total is transferred.

You are now going to lock the cells that contain formulas, so that the only cells a user can alter are the yellow **Sales** and **Orders** cells in each monthly sheet.

▶ Click into the **Summary** sheet. You should have noticed that all of the figures here are entered by formulas, taking values from the monthly sheets. A user will never need to alter any of these, so the whole sheet needs protecting.

▶ Click on **Tools** on the menu bar and choose **Protection**. Now choose **Protect Sheet**. There are many options available to you here, which you might want to investigate on your own, but for now just click on **OK**.

Figure 1.36: *Protecting a sheet.*

⊘TIP

When protecting a sheet you can enter a password. In general, if you are protecting a sheet against *accidental* changes there is no need to enter a password. If you enter a password and then forget it you won't be able to change anything on the sheet again!

▶ Try to type into some cells on this sheet. You should find that you are now prevented from doing this.

You now need to protect the remaining sheets. However, this time you don't want to protect every cell – you want to leave the yellow cells open for changes.

▶ Click on the **January** sheet tab, then scroll to the end, hold down **Shift** and click on the **December** sheet tab. This should select all 12 sheets so you can edit them together.

⊗TIP

You can select multiple sheets at once by holding down the Shift or Ctrl keys.

Shift selects all the sheets in between the two clicked on.

Ctrl selects just the sheets clicked on.

When more than one sheet is selected, any change made will be applied to all selected sheets.

▶ Highlight the first column of yellow cells – B5 to B35. Right click and choose **Format Cells**.

▶ Choose the **Protection** tab and uncheck the **Locked** option.

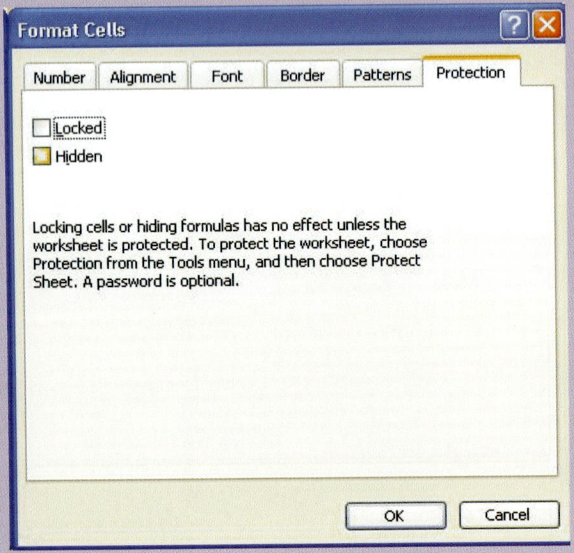

Format Cells	? ✕

Number	Alignment	Font	Border	Patterns	Protection

☐ Locked
☐ Hidden

Locking cells or hiding formulas has no effect unless the worksheet is protected. To protect the worksheet, choose Protection from the Tools menu, and then choose Protect Sheet. A password is optional.

[OK] [Cancel]

Figure 1.37: Unlocking cells B5 to B35.

▶ With all 12 sheets still selected, highlight cells E5 to E35 and unlock them in the same way.

Now that you have chosen the cells you want to remain unlocked you can protect the sheets as you did for the summary sheet. Unfortunately you cannot do this for multiple sheets so you will have to protect each sheet in turn.

▶ Click on the **Summary** sheet tab to deselect the sheets, then select the **January** worksheet. Protect this sheet using **Tools/Protection/Protect Sheet** as before.

▶ Test that your sheet is protected as you wanted – you should be able to enter data into any of the yellow cells but nowhere else.

▶ When you are happy that the **January** sheet is working as it should, protect all the sheets for the other months in the same way.

CHAPTER 2

→ Assessment Objective 1

Design a Spreadsheet to Meet the Needs of an Organisation

· ·

Overview:

Chapters 2 to 7 will take you through the assessment requirements of Unit 6. You will have the opportunity to use some of the formulas and formatting skills you have learned to create and use a spreadsheet of your own.

When you need to create a spreadsheet to solve a new problem, it is tempting to open up the software and start straight away. However, it is always best to do some planning first. Asking the following questions is a good way of going about this:

- What exactly does the spreadsheet need to do?
- What information needs to be entered?
- What results need to be calculated by the spreadsheet?
- What sort of formulas will be needed?
- What cell formats will be needed?
- Should there be more than one sheet in the workbook?
- What is the best way to lay out each sheet?

There are usually a number of possible ways of solving a problem and it is best to sit down and think about these before actually starting to create the spreadsheet.

Assessment Objective 1 requires you to create a plan for a spreadsheet showing the formulas and formatting that you will use. You can draw your plan by hand or you can use a word processor. For this assessment objective, you must not simply create the sheet using spreadsheet software, as this will not be considered to be a plan.

In order to complete the activities in this chapter you will need access to an additional file. This file is contained in the Chapter 2 Resources zip file which can be downloaded from the OCR Nationals in ICT (Units 6 & 7) Student Resources page on the Payne-Gallway website: www.payne-gallway.co.uk.

How this assessment objective will be assessed...

- A written description of the user requirements, including the purpose and intended user of the spreadsheet
- Sketches/designs of the sheet(s) you plan, showing layout, cell formats and formulas
- Higher grades are obtained by designing a more complex multi-sheet spreadsheet using a greater variety of formatting and functions, including IF and both relative and absolute cell referencing
- Higher grades also require more detail in the plans

Skills to use...

- Formulas using the arithmetic operators +, -, *, / and brackets
- Functions from some of the following categories:
  - Arithmetic and statistical functions such as SUM, AVERAGE, MAX, MIN, MEDIAN, MODE, COUNT, COUNTIF
  - Mathematical and trigonometric functions such as POWER, RAND, SIN, COS, TAN, RADIANS, DEGREES, ASIN, ACOS, ATAN
  - Rounding functions such as INT, ROUND, ROUNDUP, ROUNDDOWN
  - Logical functions such as IF, AND, OR and NOT
  - Lookup functions, such as VLOOKUP, HLOOKUP, MATCH
  - Reference functions such as ROW and COLUMN
  - Text functions such as LEFT, MID, RIGHT, LEN, VALUE, TEXT, CONCATENATE, FIND
  - Date and time functions, such as TODAY, NOW, YEAR, MONTH, DAY, WEEKDAY
- Relative and absolute cell referencing
- Formatting, including cell types, colours, borders and cell protection

Do not be worried by this long list. You do not need to use all of these in your portfolio, even to get a **Distinction**!

How to achieve...

Pass requirements

P1 You will produce a basic design for a spreadsheet in line with identified user requirements. The design will include basic details of spreadsheet layout, cell formats and formulas. Some of the choices may not be the most appropriate.

P2 You will use at least two of +, -, * and /.

P3 You will use functions from at least two of the eight categories listed in the 'Skills to use' section above.

Merit requirements

M1 The design will include more details of spreadsheet layout, cell formats and formulas. Most of the choices will be appropriate.

M2 You will use all of +, -, * and /.

M3 You will use functions from at least three of the eight categories listed in the 'Skills to use' section above. This must include an IF statement.

Distinction requirements

D1 The design will give comprehensive details of spreadsheet layout, cell formats and formulas. All choices will be appropriate.

D2 You will use all of +, -, *, / and brackets.

D3 You will use functions from at least four of the eight categories listed in the 'Skills to use' section above. This must include an IF statement.

D4 You will use both absolute and relative cell referencing.

You will probably have already completed Unit 1, in which you created a very simple spreadsheet. Even for a **Pass**, the spreadsheet you create for this unit needs to be more complex, using a wider variety of functions. You will also need to plan it more carefully and include designs in your portfolio.

Scenario

The scenario below sets the scene for an example task you are going to complete as you work through the rest of this unit.

For your own portfolio you will need to design a solution for a different task, which you will need to agree with your teacher. You must not use the example given here – your portfolio must show all your own, independent work.

You should be able to complete this task using skills learned in Chapter 1. If you are aiming only for a **Pass** in this unit, then you need to move to page 43.

Sam is the conference co-ordinator for a hotel. There are four conference suites available:

- the Elm Suite, which can accommodate 20 people, costing £200 per day
- the Birch Suite, which can accommodate 65 people, costing £300 per day
- the Maple PC Suite, which can accommodate 20 people, costing £350 per day
- the Oak Suite, which can accommodate 120 people, costing £800 per day.

A choice of three lunches can be provided:

- a sandwich buffet for £6 per person
- a salad buffet for £7 per person
- a hot meal for £10.50 per person.

There is a 10% discount on all bookings on Sundays.

Sam would like a system that will enable her to quickly enter details about bookings and which will then calculate final costs for customers. She would like to keep all the bookings for a month on the same sheet. She would then like to be able to use these monthly sheets to produce summary charts and figures so that she can see how many times the various suites have been used in the month and how popular each different type of lunch is. Our task is to produce a system using spreadsheet software. It needs to be easy to use as Sam has not used spreadsheet software before.

Initial design ideas

When tackling a complex problem, the first thing to do is to try to split it into smaller, more manageable parts, then consider each one in turn, starting with the more straightforward parts.

Firstly we need to consider how we will create the main sheet for Sam to enter booking details. This will need to calculate prices.

Later we can consider how summary charts and figures can be produced.

Here there are three main things that affect the price:

- the choice of suite – this part has the added complication that there is a maximum number of people for each suite
- the choice of lunch
- whether it is a Sunday or not.

There are four choices of suite and three choices of lunch. It would be best to set these up as lookup tables.

The choice of whether it is a Sunday or not is a choice between two things, so **IF** will probably be best here.

Figure 2.1 shows some initial thoughts on how to organise the choice of suite and lunch into lookup tables.

Sam also needs to be able to enter the number of people. This will be needed to check that the suite chosen can accommodate that number and also to calculate the cost of the meals, which are priced per person.

To show whether or not it is a Sunday we will need Sam to enter the date and then use the **WEEKDAY** formula to decide whether it is a Sunday or not.

It can be useful to jot down ideas about formulas at this early stage – not necessarily writing the formulas in full, but showing them in diagram form as shown in Figure 2.2. This helps decide what other information is needed. Here it becomes clear that we need a cell showing the date of the booking and also a cell showing the amount of Sunday discount, so that it could be changed later if necessary.

Suite	Max	Price
Elm	20	200
Birch	65	300
Maple	20	350
Oak	120	800

Lunch	Price
Sandwich	6.00
Salad	7.00
Hot	10.50

Figure 2.1: *The lookup tables needed for the conference bookings spreadsheet.*

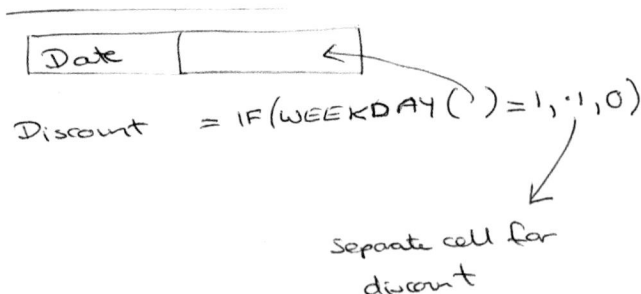

Figure 2.2: *Planning a formula to work out the Sunday discount.*

The next stage might be to draft out a plan of the screen Sam will need to **input** the customers' choices and produce the costing needed. We already know that we will need:

- the choice of suite
- the choice of lunch
- the number of people
- the date the booking is required.

We also need to think about the **output** Sam will need. Sometimes this is specified very clearly. Here we just know that we need to calculate costs. Where calculations are made up of many parts, as here, it is usually best to show each part separately. If we consider the stages we would need to calculate the cost of a booking, this will help us see the parts that the spreadsheet will need to calculate:

- the cost of the suite
- the cost of lunch per person
- the total cost of lunches
- the total cost of the suite and the lunches
- any discount
- the final bill.

We do not want to see the lookup tables themselves, so these will be best as another sheet.

If Sam is to enter all the bookings for a month, the most suitable design would be a table with one column for each item of input or output as given above. Sam could then start a new file each month.

An initial idea for the monthly sheet might look like the design in Figure 2.3. This doesn't show what the final sheet will look like — there isn't enough room on the plan to fit all of the column headings on the same line, so a second line has been started. However, writing down these ideas helps to consider:

- the data that needs to be input
- places where drop-down lists or other validation checks can be made
- some ideas about the formulas needed, though not a lot of specific detail.

This plan now tells us about other data we will need:

- the choices for the drop-down lists will need to be on the main sheet, although they can be copied by formulas from the lookup tables — these lists will then need to be hidden
- the maximum number for the chosen suite will also need to be found from the lookup table so that it can be used to check that the suite chosen can accommodate the number of people.

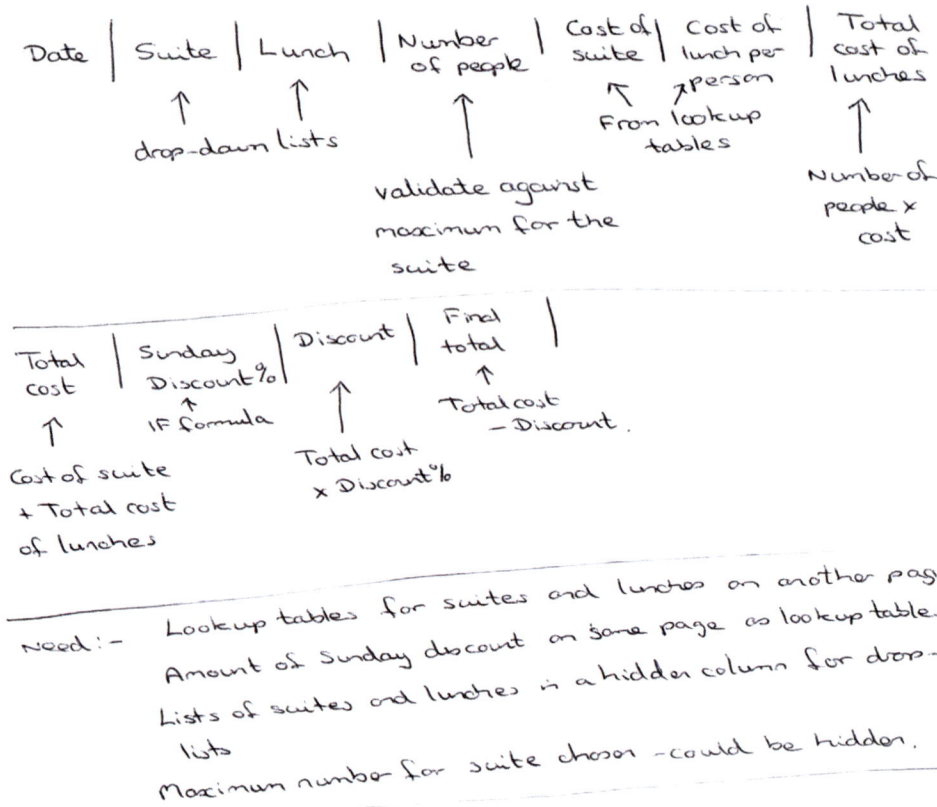

Figure 2.3: *Initial ideas for the main sheet (**Merit**/**Distinction** candidates).*

One more thing to consider is how many rows will be needed. This will tell you how far to extend formulas and formatting. In this case there are four suites and a maximum of 31 days in a month. Therefore the maximum number of bookings that could possibly be taken is 124. Although it is unlikely Sam will ever need all of these, we need to make sure that they are all available. Therefore we will need to have 124 rows for her to use.

When you have thought a little about the problem and had some initial ideas, then you can write up the **user requirements** for your portfolio. Here you identify clearly what it is that you need to do. Much of what you write might be repeating the task you have been given, but you can also be specific about the data the user will need to input and the information you will need your sheet to produce. Waiting until you have had some initial thoughts also gives you time to go back and find out more about the problem if necessary from the person who set you the task.

When you write about the user requirements it is important that you clearly identify the **audience** and **purpose** of the spreadsheet you are designing. In other words, **who** is going to use it and **what** they need it to do.

In this case a suitable description might be as follows:

User requirements

I am going to design a spreadsheet for use by Sam, who is the conference co-ordinator for a hotel. She makes bookings for conferences, where customers can choose between four suites for different group sizes. There is also a choice of three different types of lunch at three different prices.

Sam has asked me to create a spreadsheet system that will allow her to enter details of all bookings for a month. The system needs to calculate the cost of each booking and then allow Sam to produce summary charts and figures so that she can see how many times the various suites have been used in the month and how popular each type of lunch has been.

Sam has not used spreadsheet software before, so the system needs to be easy to use and have helpful instructions where necessary.

The prices Sam uses to calculate the costs of bookings are:

Suites:

- the Elm Suite, for up to 20 people, costs £200 per day
- the Birch Suite, for up to 65 people, costs £300 per day
- the Maple PC Suite, for up to 20 people, costs £350 per day
- the Oak Suite, for up to 120 people, costs £800 per day.

Lunches:

- a sandwich buffet costs £6 per person
- a salad buffet costs £7 per person
- a hot meal costs £10.50 per person.

There is a 10% discount on all bookings on Sundays.

Sam will need to input for each booking:

- the choice of suite
- the choice of lunch
- the number of people
- the date the booking is required.

The system will need to calculate for each booking:

- the cost of the suite
- the cost of lunch per person
- the total cost of lunches
- the total cost of the suite and the lunches
- any discount
- the final bill.

The system will need to be clear and easy to use and will also need summaries of the month's bookings, probably on a separate sheet.

Starting the design

Now we have some ideas about what is needed we can start to plan out the sheet in more detail, considering the cells to be used and the actual formulas. You can use the planning sheet provided with the resources for this chapter: ***Planning Sheet.doc***.

You might prefer to fill in your planning sheets using a pencil, so you can keep trying different ideas. You can use a word processor if you prefer but it is often very difficult to write long formulas into a cell-shaped space on a plan. If a formula is to be copied down a range of cells it is fine to write down the formula for the first cell in the column and show with an arrow that it will be copied down. Long formulas can be written sideways across the whole column, so long as you explain somewhere that this is what you have done. This is easily and quickly done by hand. Don't worry if your final design is not as neat and tidy as you would like – it is a working design, not a finished document.

For this scenario you will need to plan three sheets:

- the main sheet, where Sam can enter data about bookings and that will calculate prices
- the sheet containing the lookup tables
- a sheet that gives summary information about the month's bookings.

Your plan must show the column headings, cell formats and formulas that you will use. For **Merit** and **Distinction** your designs need to show full details of these. If there is not enough room to include details of formulas *and* formats on the same sheet, then you could use two planning sheets – one to show formulas and one to show cell formats.

Because the main sheet needs formulas that will look data up from the lookup tables, you will need to design the sheet containing these tables first.

You might like to draft out some ideas of your own before looking at the ideas on the next few pages. There are always several different ways of solving a problem and the designs in this book are not the only, or even necessarily the best, methods. The ideas given here are there to help you, but don't be afraid to experiment.

> **⚠TIP**
>
> It can be difficult writing exact formulas down on a plan. However, that is what is needed for a **Distinction**. You can always use a computer to test your idea for a specific formula before adding it to your plan.

Before or after?

The purpose of a design is to plan out what you are going to do *before* you start to get involved in the detail of actually creating it. Good planning can help you avoid wasting a lot of time creating something that eventually either does not work or does not meet the user's requirements.

To gain a **Distinction** your plan must contain comprehensive details of layout, format and formulas. If there are some formulas you are not sure about at first, there is nothing to stop you doing some investigations then filling in the extra detail on your plan at a later stage.

In Chapter 3, when you will actually create the sheet, you may find that you want to improve some of the formulas and add more formatting. This is quite acceptable providing you show it is an improvement to your original design. It is not necessary to go back and pretend you designed the final version all in one go!

Example designs

The JPEG files provided in the MeritDistinction folder inside the online Chapter 2 Resources folder show you what a design might look like for the task given in this chapter. You will see that the column headings and some short formulas have been entered into the planning sheets using a word processor, as this is easy to do, but details of long formulas and formatting that needs to go across many cells have been entered by hand, as have other comments.

The first sheet planned is the one containing the lookup tables with the price list. The plan is shown in ***Plan1_PriceList.jpg***. You need to give the sheet a name, so it has been called **PriceList**. It is not possible to include spaces in names of sheets, but two words can easily be used by using capital letters in this way. You will see that the data to be entered has been typed in, and details of format have been added by hand.

The main sheet needs too many columns to fit onto a single sheet of paper, so a second sheet has been used to show columns H to N. These designs are shown in ***Plan2_Main-Sheet1.jpg*** and ***Plan3_MainSheet2.jpg***. You will see that some thought has been given to the content and formatting of every cell and column.

Although you are designing a solution to a problem, you are also trying to demonstrate your skills in the use of spreadsheet software, so it is a good idea to find opportunities to use a range of techniques. Some of the techniques planned here are merging cells, rotating text, wrapping text, conditional formatting, cell comments, etc.

The summary sheet plans to summarise the number of bookings for the different rooms and the different lunch options. The plan for this is shown in ***Plan4_SummarySheet.jpg***. Where there is insufficient room to write down details of formulas, these have been clearly cross-referenced and written elsewhere where space was available.

A scenario for those working to Pass level

This section gives a scenario for those who are aiming for a **Pass** in this unit. If you are working on the main scenario described above, then you need now to move to the 'Portfolio builder' section on page 48.

Sam is the conference co-ordinator for a hotel. There are four conference suites available:

- the Elm Suite, costing £200 per day
- the Birch Suite, costing £300 per day
- the Maple PC Suite, costing £350 per day
- the Oak Suite, costing £800 per day.

A choice of three lunches can be provided:

- a sandwich buffet for £6 per person
- a salad buffet for £7 per person
- a hot meal for £10.50 per person.

There is a 10% discount on all bookings on Sundays.

Sam would like a system that will enable her to enter details about bookings and prices and which will then calculate final costs for customers. She will also need to enter the discount for Sunday bookings, so she would like the system to show her the day of the week when she enters a date.

She would like to keep all the bookings for a month on the same sheet. She would then like to be able to use the data to produce summary charts and figures so that she can see how many times the various suites have been used in the month. Our task is to produce a system using spreadsheet software. It needs to be easy to use as Sam has not used spreadsheet software before.

Initial design ideas

When tackling a complex problem the first thing to do is to try to split it into smaller, more manageable parts, then consider each one in turn, starting with the more straightforward parts.

Firstly we need to consider how we will create the main part of the sheet for Sam to enter booking details and costs. This will need to calculate prices.

Later we can consider how summary charts and figures can be produced.

We already know that the main sheet needs to allow Sam to enter details about bookings and prices. Now we need to think more carefully about exactly what details she needs to enter before costs are calculated:

- the choice of suite
- the price of the chosen suite
- the choice of lunch
- the price of the chosen lunch
- the number of people
- any discount for a Sunday booking.

Sam will also need to enter:

- the date the booking is required.

We also need to think about the **output** Sam will need. Sometimes this is specified very clearly. Here we just know that we need to calculate costs. Where calculations are made up of many parts, as here, it is usually best to show each part separately. If we consider the stages we would need to calculate the cost of a booking, this will help us see the parts that the spreadsheet will need to calculate:

- the total cost of lunches
- the total cost of the suite and the lunches
- the amount of any discount
- the final cost, with any discount taken off.

We have also been asked to calculate:

- the day of the week the booking is for, so that Sam can easily spot a Sunday booking.

If Sam is to enter all the bookings for a month, the most suitable design would be a table with one column for each item of input or output as given above. Sam could then start a new file each month.

An initial idea for the monthly sheet might look like the design shown in Figure 2.4. This doesn't show what the final sheet will look like – there isn't enough room on the plan to fit all of the column headings on the same line, so a second line has been started. However, writing down these ideas helps to consider:

* the data that needs to be input
* how data will be input – e.g. using short codes to save time when entering choices of suites or lunches
* some ideas about the formulas needed, though not a lot of specific detail
* places where extra instructions/information might be needed by the user – e.g. how to fill in the **Discount %** column.

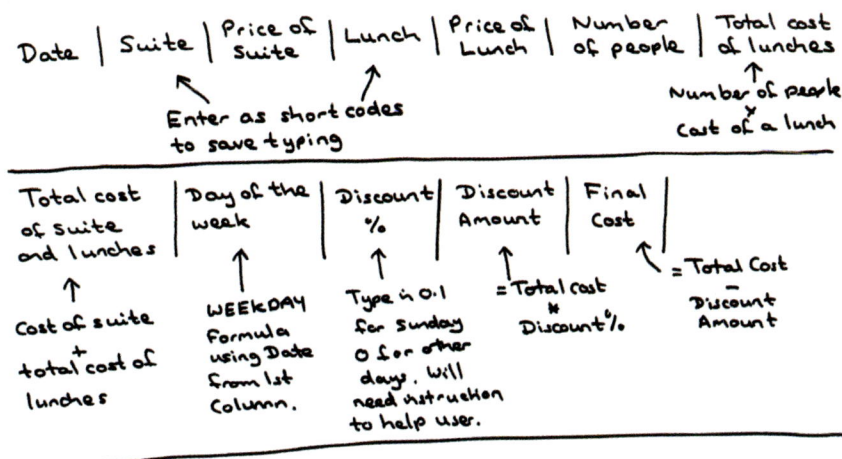

Figure 2.4: *Initial ideas for the main sheet (*Pass* candidates).*

One more thing that needs to be considered is how many rows will be needed. This will tell you how far to extend formulas and formatting. In this case there are four suites and a maximum of 31 days in a month. Therefore the maximum number of bookings that could possibly be taken is 124. Although it is unlikely Sam will ever need all of these, we need to make sure that they are all available. Therefore we will need to have 124 rows for her to use.

When you have thought a little about the problem and had some initial ideas, then you can write up the **user requirements** for your portfolio. Here you identify clearly what it is that you need to do. Much of what you write might be repeating the task you have been given, but you can also be specific about the data the user will need to input and the information you will need your sheet to produce. Waiting until you have had some initial thoughts also gives you time to go back and find out more about the problem if necessary from the person who set you the task.

When you write about the user requirements it is important that you clearly identify the **audience** and **purpose** of the spreadsheet you are designing. In other words, **who** is going to use it and **what** they need it to do.

In this case a suitable description might be as follows:

User requirements

I am going to design a spreadsheet for use by Sam, who is the conference co-ordinator for a hotel. She makes bookings for conferences, where customers can choose between four suites for different group sizes. There is also a choice of three different types of lunch at three different prices.

Sam has asked me to create a spreadsheet system that will allow her to enter details of all bookings for a month. The system needs to calculate the total cost of each booking and tell her the day of the week the booking is for. She then wants to be able to produce summary charts and figures so that she can see how many times the various suites have been used in the month.

Sam has not used spreadsheet software before, so the system needs to be easy to use and have helpful instructions where necessary.

The prices Sam uses to calculate the costs of bookings are:

Suites:

- the Elm Suite costs £200 per day
- the Birch Suite costs £300 per day
- the Maple PC Suite costs £350 per day
- the Oak Suite costs £800 per day.

Lunches:

- a sandwich buffet costs £6 per person
- a salad buffet costs £7 per person
- a hot meal costs £10.50 per person.

There is a 10% discount for Sunday bookings.

For each booking, Sam will need to input:

- the choice and price of suite
- the choice and price of lunch
- the number of people
- the date the booking is required
- the % of the Sunday discount if it applies.

For each booking, the system will need to calculate:

- the total cost of lunches
- the total cost of the suite and the lunches
- the day of the week, from the date
- the amount of any discount
- the final cost, including the discount.

It will also need to produce summaries showing the total number of bookings for each suite and each type of lunch.

The system will need to be clear and easy to use as Sam has not used a spreadsheet before.

Starting the design

Now we have some ideas about what is needed we can start to plan out the sheet in more detail, considering the cells to be used and the actual formulas. You can use the planning sheet provided with the resources for this chapter: ***Planning Sheet.doc***.

You might prefer to fill in the planning sheets using a pencil, so you can keep trying different ideas. You can use a word processor if you prefer but it is often very difficult to write long formulas into a cell-shaped space on a plan. If a formula is to be copied down a range of cells it is fine to write down the formula for the first cell in the column and show with an arrow that it will be copied down. Long formulas can be written sideways across the whole column, so long as you explain somewhere that this is what you have done. This is easily and quickly done by hand. Don't worry if your final design is not as neat and tidy as you would like – it is a working design, not a finished document.

Your plan must show the column headings, cell formats and formulas that you will use. If there is not enough room to include details of formulas *and* formats on the same sheet, then you can use two planning sheets – one to show formulas and one to show cell formats.

You might like to draft out some ideas of your own before looking at the ideas on the next few pages. There are always several different ways of solving a problem and the designs in this book are not the only, or even necessarily the best, methods. The ideas given here are there to help you, but don't be afraid to experiment.

Before or after?

The purpose of a design is to plan out what you are going to do *before* you start to get involved in the detail of actually creating it. Good planning can help you avoid wasting a lot of time creating something that eventually either does not work or does not meet the user's requirements.

In Chapter 3, when you will actually create the sheet, you may find that you want to improve some of the formulas and add more formatting. This is quite acceptable providing you show it is an improvement to your original design. It is not necessary to go back and pretend you designed the final version all in one go!

Example design

The JPEG files provided in the Pass folder inside the online Chapter 2 Resources folder show you what a design might look like for the task given in this chapter. ***Plan1_ColumnsA–G.jpg*** and ***Plan2_ColumnsH–N.jpg*** contain the main data for this scenario. ***Plan3_SummaryFormulas.jpg*** is the plan for the summary formulas that will go at the bottom of the sheet.

You will see that the column headings and some short formulas have been entered into the planning sheets using a word processor, as this is easy to do, but details of long formulas and formatting that needs to go across many cells have been entered by hand, as have other comments.

Although you are designing a solution to a problem, you are also trying to demonstrate your skills in the use of spreadsheet software, so it is a good idea to find opportunities to use a range of techniques. Some of the techniques planned here are merging cells, rotating text, etc. Colours and shading can be easily shown by using coloured pencils.

Portfolio builder

When you are working for your own portfolio you will need to agree on a problem with your teacher. It is important that the problem will allow you to use all of the features detailed in the 'How to achieve' section at the beginning of this chapter.

You should then design your own solution on paper, developing your ideas in the same way as has been done in this chapter. Start with your initial ideas and work through to some detailed designs.

When you have a design it is a good idea to check it again against the 'How to achieve' section at the beginning of this chapter. Sometimes it may be necessary to adapt the problem slightly to allow you to demonstrate the range of features you need. Although you wouldn't do this with a real-life problem, it is sometimes necessary when working towards a qualification to make sure you give yourself the opportunity to show the range of skills you have.

You will need to make sure that your portfolio contains:

1 your own explanation of the task and the user requirements
2 designs that you have created to show the formulas and formatting that will need to be used in your spreadsheet – these must be designs and not printouts of a completed spreadsheet.

Your designs must show formulas to be entered and formatting to be used. For a **Distinction** this needs to be fully detailed.

CHAPTER ③

→ *Assessment Objective 2*
Creating and Formatting Your Spreadsheet

Overview:

In this chapter you will use the design you drew up in Chapter 2 to create a spreadsheet for managing conference suite bookings in a hotel. Then you will carry out any additional formatting that is needed to make it easy for someone else to use. You will need to use some of the skills covered in Chapter 1 and may find it useful to refer back to that chapter from time to time.

This chapter will guide you through the process of creating and formatting a spreadsheet, which you will need to carry out for your own design as part of your assessed work for your portfolio.

In order to complete the activities in this chapter you will need access to the sample designs provided in the online Chapter 2 resources folder. Additional example files have been provided for you to refer to and are contained in the Chapter 3 Resources zip file which can be downloaded from the OCR Nationals in ICT (Units 6 & 7) Student Resources page on the Payne-Gallway website: www.payne-gallway.co.uk.

How this assessment objective will be assessed...

You need to provide sufficient evidence to show the various software features you have used, for example:

- Printout(s) of your sheet(s) showing formulas
- Printout(s) of your sheet(s) with data entered, showing that it works
- Printout(s) of your sheet(s) showing the formatting you have applied
- Screenshots showing any features you have used that are not evident from your printouts – e.g. cell comments, validation, worksheet protection
- Brief annotations to show the features used

Skills to use...

- Entering formulas according to the design
- Applying formatting using skills learned in Chapter 1

How to achieve...

Pass requirements

P1 You will produce a spreadsheet that works. It may only contain one sheet.

P2 You will use text and background colour and cell borders.

P3 You will adjust row height or column width.

P4 You will merge cells.

P5 You will set some text to appear at an angle or sideways in the cell.

P6 You will add at least one example of help for a user, such as an instruction, a cell comment or validation.

Merit requirements

M1 You will produce a working spreadsheet with more than one sheet.

M2 You will use text and background colour and cell borders to distinguish between different types of cell (e.g. cells to input data, cells that automatically calculate).

M3 You will adjust row height or column width and hide and show rows or columns.

M4 You will merge cells.

M5 You will set some text to appear at an angle or sideways in the cell and will set some text to wrap in a cell.

M6 You will add help for a user, including at least one cell comment and at least one appropriate use of validation.

M7 You will use conditional formatting.

Distinction requirements

D1 You will produce a working spreadsheet with more than one sheet, linked by formulas.

D2 You will use text and background colour and cell borders to distinguish between different types of cell (e.g. cells to input data, cells that automatically calculate).

D3 You will adjust row height or column width and hide and show rows or columns.

D4 You will merge cells.

D5 You will set some text to appear at an angle or sideways in the cell and will set some text to wrap in a cell.

D6 You will add sufficient help to allow an inexperienced user to use the spreadsheet with ease. This will include suitable cell comments and validation with useful feedback to users.

D7 You will set some cells for input from a drop-down list.

D8 You will use conditional formatting to make the output clearer.

D9 You will use worksheet protection to prevent a user changing or deleting formulas.

Creating your spreadsheet

Now that you have a design for your spreadsheet (see the sample designs provided in the online Chapter 2 Resources folder – refer to the Pass or MeritDistinction folder as appropriate) you need to actually create it. You will be using the formulas, functions and formatting that you included in the plan to make a working and user-friendly spreadsheet that will allow Sam to manage the conference room bookings at the hotel where she works.

Activity 1: Creating a spreadsheet from your design...

In this activity you will:

● use the design from Chapter 2 to create a spreadsheet to meet Sam's needs.

▶ Load your spreadsheet software, then take the design sheets one by one and add all the required text, formulas and formatting that are outlined on the designs.

▶ Make sure you follow the plan exactly. First enter the text and formulas, then make sure you add all the formatting on the design sheet. At this stage, resist the temptation to make any improvements to formatting or formulas.

▶ If you are creating more than one sheet, make sure you name these as shown on the plans. Delete any additional unwanted sheets.

▶ If you are aiming for a **Merit** or **Distinction**, you can find a hint for the conditional formatting in column A in Figure 3.1.

> **⊘TIP**
>
> In this scenario, many formulas need copying down from row 4 to row 127. First enter the formulas and set the formatting for the whole of row 4. Test it with a range of entries to make sure it works, *then* copy the cells down.

Condition 1
Formula Is =WEEKDAY(A4)=1

Preview of format to use
when condition is true: AaBbCcYyZz

Figure 3.1: Conditional formatting for cell A4, to highlight all dates that are a Sunday.

▶ When you have saved your work, use **Tools/Options/View** to show the formulas.

▶ Alter column widths as necessary to show complete formulas.

▶ Use **File/Print Preview** to preview your sheet(s) to show what they will look like when they are printed.

▶ Use the **File/Page Setup** options to improve the way your sheet will look and the way it will fit on the paper, including altering the margins as necessary.

▶ Add some headers and footers to show clearly that this is your spreadsheet showing the formulas. It is a very good idea to have page numbers showing – you will often need to print on more than one page and it is easy to get the printouts mixed up.

▶ Where you have the same formulas over many rows, there is no need to print every page – it is sufficient to show all the columns by printing the first page(s) at the top of the sheet. You can then simply add a note to say how far these formulas have been copied down.

▶ Print out your sheet(s) showing the formulas you have used.

▶ Remove the show formulas option so that you can see your spreadsheet in the form in which it will be used. Sometimes it is quicker just to reload the saved version.

▶ Enter some typical bookings for different days in a month. Make sure you test every different option for rooms and lunches, as well as every different day of the week. However, it is not necessary to fill in all the rows!

▶ Preview your sheet(s) again before printing, adjusting margins, headers, etc. as necessary.

▶ Print out your sheet(s) showing the data you have entered and the results shown.

Adding extra formatting to improve your spreadsheet

Although there will be a lot of detail about formatting on your plan, there will probably still be room for improvements. You should look and see if there are any ways in which it could be formatted to:

● improve the appearance
● make it easier to use.

Look at the checklists in the 'How to achieve' section at the beginning of this chapter. You need to make sure you have evidence of using all of the features listed for a particular grade.

Questions that you might consider include:

● Are there any improvements you could make to cell borders, shading and text colours? Can all text be read easily?
● Are there any cells/rows/columns where text would be better at a different size?
● Are there any column widths or row heights that could be adjusted, either to make the contents fit better or to reduce a column width so that more can be seen on the screen at once?
● Are there any rows, columns or sheets that are needed only by the computer and that would be best hidden?
● If you have set validation, have you added a suitable **Error Alert** message?
● Are there any additional instructions that you could add to make the use of the spreadsheet clearer? These might be written in a cell, added as comments or as validation input messages.

Candidates aiming for a **Distinction** also need to set worksheet protection – you need to think about which cells need unlocking first so that the user will still be able to edit data in them.

Activity 2: Improving the formatting...

In this activity you will:

- add any additional formatting you think will improve the spreadsheet you have created
- create screenshots to demonstrate any features that will not be easily shown from printouts.

▶ Load the spreadsheet file you created in Activity 1.

▶ Add any additional formatting that you have thought of. If you have more than one sheet then you must consider each sheet in turn.

▶ Print out your changed spreadsheet(s) to show the improvements.

▶ Make sure that you label the printout(s) to show that this is your improved version. You can do this by writing by hand on the printout(s) or by setting a custom header or footer.

▶ Make a note of any improvements you have made. You could do this using either handwritten annotations on your printouts or a separate short word-processed explanation.

▶ Look again at the checklist of features in the 'How to achieve' section. For each skill you have used, look to see if someone else could see what you have done just by looking at your printout(s).

▶ If there are features, such as comments, validation and cell protection that are not obvious, then you need to produce some screenshots to show that these features exist.

Further improvements

Although you have worked from a plan to produce your spreadsheet solution, it is quite normal to want to make improvements after you have constructed it according to your plan.

For example you may find:

- some formulas that don't give the result expected
- some formulas that could be improved by using **IF** statements to get rid of error messages
- other areas where, now the spreadsheet has been built, you think you could make it more efficient by adding and/or improving formulas.

Activity 3: Making improvements to your spreadsheet...

In this activity you will:

- make any improvements you think would improve your spreadsheet.

How much you do at this stage is entirely up to you. You may be completely happy with the solution, in which case there is no need to make any adjustments at all.

However, if you are working towards a **Merit** or **Distinction** you should consider how your formulas can be improved to avoid any error messages you can see. For a **Distinction** you need to have the most efficient formulas throughout your solution.

If you are working towards a Pass you may know of some ways to get the software to do more calculations and reduce the amount of input the user needs to do.

If you do make any improvements, you will need to create two more sets of printouts – one showing the formulas and one showing the data. You will also need to show where you have made changes. Again this might best be done by highlighting and annotating your printouts, or it might be done by writing a brief explanation using a word processor.

Some people go back and alter their designs at this point, to make it look as though the final spreadsheet is exactly as they designed it at the beginning. As long as your original design is detailed, you do not need to do this. Instead you should provide evidence of the improvements you have made to explain why your final spreadsheet doesn't completely match your design.

At this stage you should check against the checklists in the 'How to achieve' section in this chapter and in Chapter 2, to make sure you have evidence of using all the features listed there.

Portfolio builder

When you are working on your own problem you will need to create your spreadsheet solution, add all necessary formatting and add printouts to your portfolio to show:

1 the formulas you have used
2 some entered data to show that the spreadsheet actually works
3 the final formatting you have used
4 any improvements you have made to your design.

You should add a small amount of annotation to your printouts, so that someone else can see what they are showing.

You will also need to add any screenshots that are necessary to show all the formatting skills you have used, where these cannot be seen clearly from your printouts.

As a final check for your portfolio you should go through the checklists in the 'How to achieve' section and make sure that there is some clear evidence in your portfolio for every skill you have used. It is often useful at this stage to ask someone else to check this for you.

➡ *Assessment Objective 3*
Sort Data and Use Simple Filters

Overview:

Normally if you have a lot of data that you want to sort and/or search, you would use database software. However, spreadsheet software does have limited facilities to sort and search, and these can be useful if you have a lot of data in a spreadsheet.

In this chapter you will look at how sorts and searches can be used in your spreadsheet work. We will continue with the example of the hotel conference suite bookings spreadsheet.

> In order to complete the activities in this chapter you may need access to an additional file. This file is contained in the Chapter 4 Resources zip file which can be downloaded from the OCR Nationals in ICT (Units 6 & 7) Student Resources page on the Payne-Gallway website: www.payne-gallway.co.uk.

How this assessment objective will be assessed...

- Printouts showing a list of data that has been sorted
- Printouts showing filtered data

Skills to use...

- Sorting data using **Data/Sort**
- Filtering data using the **AutoFilter** tool
- Custom filter options on the **AutoFilter** tool

How to achieve...

Pass requirements

P1 You will sort a list of data using one field.

P2 You will filter a list of data using one field.

Merit requirements

M1 You will sort data using at least two fields.

M2 You will filter data using at least two fields.

Distinction requirements

D1 You will sort data using at least two fields.

D2 You will filter data using at least two fields, customising at least one filter.

Key terms

Sort

Sorting involves putting a list of data in **order** of one of the items. For example, in a list of names and addresses you might **sort** the list in order of last name.

Filter

This is also referred to as **searching**. The software looks through a list of data and finds all the records where certain **criteria** are met. For example, in a list of names and addresses you might **filter** the list to find all the people with a last name of **Jones**.

Sorting data in Excel

To sort a list of data it needs to be typed in a table, like the data you have entered on the spreadsheet for Sam to record her hotel bookings. Each separate booking is in a different row and the different items of information for each booking are in separate columns. We refer to the rows as **records** and the columns as **fields**.

There must not be any blank rows or columns in the middle of the data. It does not matter whether there are column headings or not – Excel can sort with or without headings.

To sort the data, you need to click in any cell in the list of data. Then click on **Data** on the menu bar and choose **Sort**. You are then given a choice of up to three fields you can sort on, in ascending or descending order. You also have a choice of whether or not you have column headings on your data.

Activity 1: Sorting a list of data...

In this activity you will:

- sort a list of data using one field
- sort a list of data on more than one field.

▶ Open the spreadsheet file you created in Chapter 3. Alternatively, if you have not entered a lot of data into your own spreadsheet, you can load either *Activity 1 MD.xls* for the **Merit**/**Distinction** file or *Activity 1 P.xls* for the **Pass** file.

▶ If you are using the **Merit**/**Distinction** version you need to be on the **Main** sheet.

▶ The *Activity 1 MD.xls* file has all sheets protected. You cannot sort data on a protected spreadsheet, so if you have protected the sheet you first need to use **Tools**/**Protection** to unprotect the **Main** sheet.

▶ Click on one of the dates. It doesn't matter which one, nor does it really matter which column you click on – it just needs to be somewhere in the list of data.

▶ Click on **Data** on the menu bar and choose **Sort**.

TIP

Excel should automatically find the whole list of data when you click on Sort. If ever this is not done correctly, you can always highlight the complete set of records yourself before choosing Sort.

- Make sure that the computer has correctly guessed that your data has column headings, then choose to sort by **Suite**.

It might be very useful for Sam to have the bookings in this order, so that she can see all the bookings for a particular suite together, rather than just seeing them in the order in which they were typed. And it might be even more useful if each section is then sorted so that she can see the bookings for each suite in order of the date of booking. This can be achieved by sorting on a **second** field – **Date**.

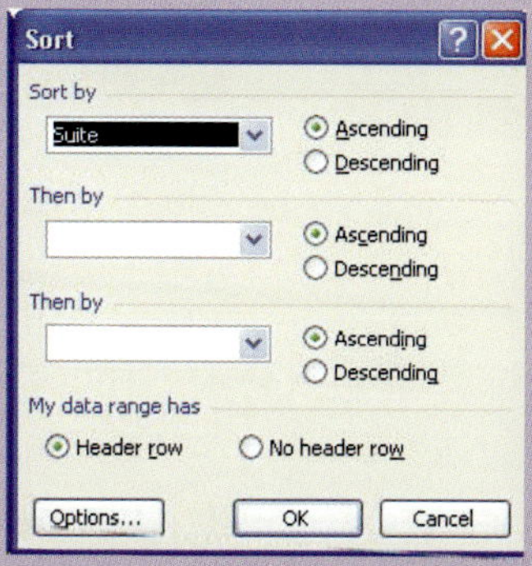

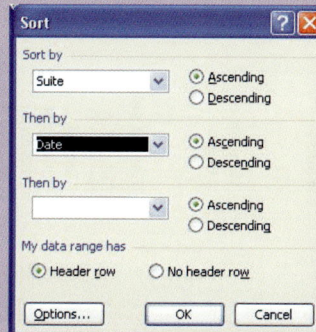

- Choose **Data/Sort** again, then choose to sort by **Suite**, then by **Date**.
- Click on **OK** then check to see what this has done.
- Experiment with a few more sorts. Try some in ascending order and some in descending order.
- Try sorting on three fields – perhaps sort by **Date** then **Lunch** then **Suite**.
- Do not save your file when you have finished – leave it in the original order. You've seen how easy it is to sort it into any order you want at any time.

***Figure 4.1:** Sorting the conference suite bookings data by **Suite**.*

***Figure 4.2:** Sorting by **Suite** and **Date**.*

Filtering data

Since computers are often used to store vast amounts of data, we cannot always easily find specific items of information just by looking through the data ourselves. Instead we use the computer to **filter** the data so that we can see only the records we are interested in.

For example, suppose Sam wanted a list of all the bookings for the **Elm** suite. She *could* sort according to suite, then just look at the section showing the bookings for the **Elm** suite, but it is also possible to get the computer to filter the data so that only the bookings she wants to see are visible. She can then see much more easily the information she needs and could even print out separate lists if she needed to.

The easiest way to filter data using Excel is to set an **AutoFilter**. This method is quite flexible and is the only method you need to know about.

To set the AutoFilter, choose **Data** from the menu bar, then select **Filter** and **AutoFilter**. This will give you a drop-down menu next to each column heading. You can use these to select the items you are looking for.

Sometimes you don't want to find a particular item of data, such as Elm, but you want to find a **range**, such as group sizes above a certain number, or dates between two particular days. This type of filter can be set by choosing the **Custom** filter option from the drop-down menu.

Activity 2: Filtering data...

In this activity you will:

- use **AutoFilter** to filter data on a single field
- reset a filtered list to show all the data again
- filter data using more than one field
- set a custom filter.

Filter data on a single field

▶ Open the spreadsheet file you used in Activity 1.

▶ If you are using the **Merit/Distinction** version you again need to be on the **Main** sheet.

▶ The **AutoFilter** tool is like **Sort** – it cannot be used on a protected spreadsheet, so you may need to remove the protection again to carry out this activity.

▶ Click on one of the dates and choose **Data/Filter/AutoFilter**. This will add a drop-down arrow next to each of your column headings:

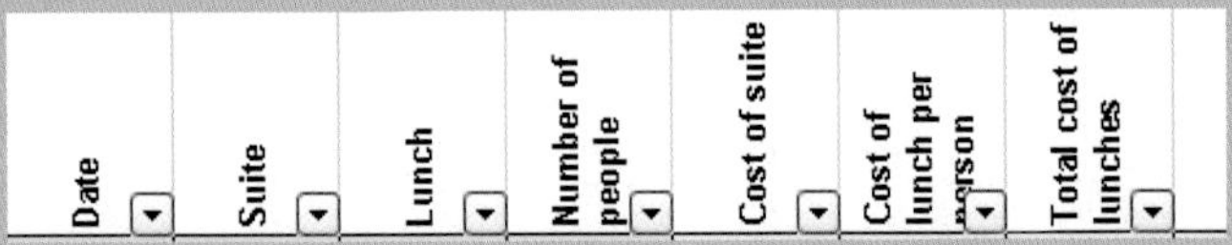

Figure 4.3: *The AutoFilter will add drop-down arrows next to each of the column headings.*

▶ Click on the arrow in the **Suite** column. You should be able to choose the option for the **Elm** suite, which will then show you just the bookings for this suite.

▶ To get the whole list back click on the drop-down arrow again, then choose **(All)**.

▶ Try a few different filters in this way, choosing an item from one of the drop-down lists, then choosing **(All)** to get the whole list back again.

Filter data on more than one field

Sam wants a list of all the bookings in the Elm suite which have ordered a hot lunch. This requires two filters – one for the suite and one for the lunch type. This is done in just the same way as before, but without retrieving all the records after the first filter:

▶ First make sure you have all the records showing, then choose the drop-down arrow for the **Suite** column and choose **Elm**.

▶ Now go straight to the drop-down arrow for the **Lunch** column and choose the **Hot** option.

▶ Check that you have got the results you expected.

To retrieve all the records again you can go back to each of the drop-down arrows in turn and select **(All)**. However, there is another way that is probably quicker when you have set more than one filter:

▶ Use the menu bar to choose **Data/Filter** then select **Show All**.

▶ Try a few more filters on more than one field – you can filter on as many fields as you like. Try out the two different methods of retrieving all the records afterwards, and decide which method you prefer.

Custom filter

Sam now wants a list of all bookings for 15 people or fewer.

▶ Click on the drop-down arrow next to **Number of people** and choose the **(Custom…)** option.

▶ Choose **is less than or equal to** in the first box, then type **15** in the second box.

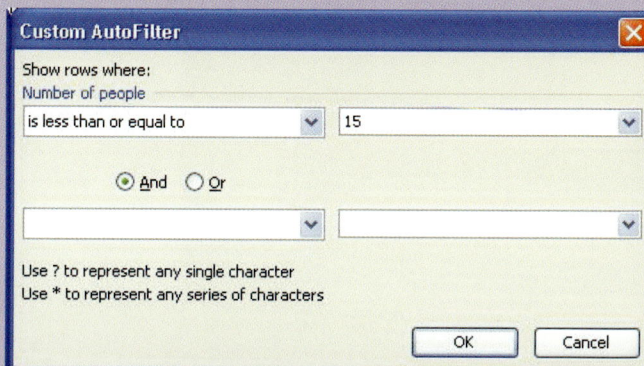

Custom AutoFilter	✕
Show rows where:	
Number of people	
is less than or equal to ⌄	15 ⌄
⦿ And ◯ Or	
⌄	⌄
Use ? to represent any single character	
Use * to represent any series of characters	
	OK Cancel

Figure 4.4: Setting a custom filter for bookings of 15 people or fewer.

▶ Click **OK** and then check that this filter has done what you expected.

You are going to find all the bookings between two specified dates. If you are using the *Activity 1 MD.xls* or *Activity 1 P.xls* files, you can look for bookings between 15th and 22nd February. If you are using your own file, you will need to choose some dates for which you know there are some bookings to be found.

▶ Choose a **(Custom…)** filter on the **Date** field.

▶ If you look down the options you will see that there is no '**between**' option. Instead you can use the two sets of boxes to choose dates that are after (i.e. **is greater than**) the 15th **And** before (i.e. **is less than**) the 22nd. This will give us the set of data that we want.

Custom AutoFilter	✕
Show rows where:	
Date	
is greater than ⌄	15/02/2007 ⌄
⦿ And ◯ Or	
is less than ⌄	22/02/07 ⌄
Use ? to represent any single character	
Use * to represent any series of characters	
	OK Cancel

Figure 4.5: Setting the custom filter to find dates between 15th and 22nd February.

▶ When you are happy you know what this filter has done, reset the list to show **all** the records.

Sam wants a list of all the bookings for both the Elm suite and the Birch suite. This can also be done with a custom filter, using the **Or** option as shown in Figure 4.6.

Custom AutoFilter

Show rows where:

Suite

| equals | Elm |

○ And ⦿ Or

| equals | Birch |

Use ? to represent any single character
Use * to represent any series of characters

OK   Cancel

Figure 4.6: Setting the custom filter to display all the bookings for the Elm and Birch suites.

▶ Experiment with some more filters, trying out the different options available in the custom filter.

Portfolio builder

For your portfolio you will have to show that you have carried out at least one sort and one filter on the spreadsheet file you create. For **Merit** and **Distinction** these will need to use more than one field and for a **Distinction** at least one of the fields must be filtered using a custom filter.

You will need to provide evidence of the filters and sorts you have set. This can be done by printing out screenshots such as those shown in Figures 4.1 to 4.6 and by printing out the resulting list each time.

You should remember this requirement when you are thinking of a suitable spreadsheet to create for your portfolio – it must contain at least one sheet where there will be a list of data that can be sorted and searched.

CHAPTER 5

→ Assessment Objective 4

Carrying out Modelling Activities Using a Spreadsheet

Overview:

Modelling is a term used to describe the use of computers to see **what** would happen **if** certain things change – we sometimes refer to these as **what-if** problems. You have already carried out many modelling activities in the activities in the previous chapters of this book – you have changed some data in the spreadsheet to see what effect this would have on the final result.

This chapter will clarify the sort of activity you need to carry out and the evidence you need to put into your portfolio for this assessment objective.

> In order to complete the activities in this chapter you will need access to the file you worked on in Chapter 4. This file is contained in the Chapter 4 Resources zip file which can be downloaded from the OCR Nationals in ICT (Units 6 & 7) Student Resources page on the Payne-Gallway website: www.payne-gallway.co.uk.

How this assessment objective will be assessed...

- Printouts of your spreadsheet before and after changes are made to the data
- Written comments making predictions about the results of these changes by looking at the spreadsheet results
- Written descriptions of investigations made, including predictions and decisions made as a result of what the spreadsheet shows

Skills to use...

- Changing data on a spreadsheet
- Interpreting the results provided by the spreadsheet

How to achieve...

Pass requirements

P1 You will change variables in your spreadsheet.

P2 You will make simple predictions.

Merit requirements

M1 You will change variables in your spreadsheet.

M2 You will make predictions or decisions.

M3 You will write about your investigations and the results you find.

Distinction requirements

D1 You will change variables in your spreadsheet.

D2 You will make suitable predictions *and* decisions.

D3 You will write about your investigations and the results you find.

Key terms

Modelling

Using a spreadsheet to find out **what** will happen **if** something changes. This is done by changing some data and seeing what effect this has on the results.

Predictions

When you change the data the formulas you have set up in your spreadsheet will calculate what will happen – this is a prediction.

Decisions

When you want a particular result, perhaps a final price that is less than a certain amount, you will need to make a decision about what to do to get that result.

Activity 1: A suitable modelling activity...

In this activity you will:

- use your hotel bookings spreadsheet to make predictions
- make decisions by experimenting with data on the spreadsheet
- create the type of evidence you will need in your portfolio for this objective
- print out selected parts of a spreadsheet

▶ Open up the spreadsheet you used in Chapter 4 (called *Activity 1 P.xls* or *Activity 1 MD.xls* if you are using the files provided on the Payne-Gallway website).

Make a prediction

Sam receives an enquiry from a customer who wishes to make a booking for 60 people, next Thursday, in the Birch Suite. However, he is not sure whether to book a hot lunch or a salad lunch. You can make a prediction for him by providing the prices for the two different lunches.

▶ Enter the details for this customer into the spreadsheet. Choose a hot lunch.

You should get a price of £930.

You now need to print out this booking. However, there is no need to print out the whole page of bookings:

▶ Highlight the row containing your new booking. Click on **File** on the menu bar and choose **Print Area** and **Set Print Area**.

▶ Choose **File** and **Print Preview** to make sure your work fits on the page before printing. If the row is too wide, click on the **Setup** button and choose the **Landscape** option from the **Page** tab.

Your printout would look better if you could see the column headings:

▶ Click on the **Close** button to take you out of print preview. Now choose **File** and **Page Setup**.

▶ Click on the **Sheet** tab.

▶ Click on the button that will allow you to choose **Rows to repeat at top** — see Figure 5.1.

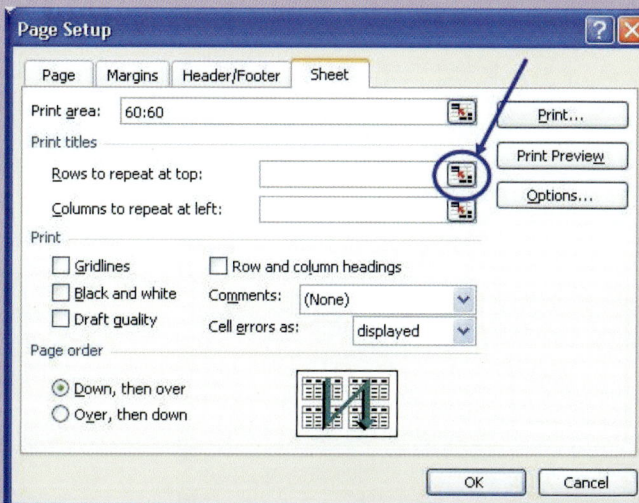

Figure 5.1: *Setting the column headings to print using **File/Page Setup**.*

▶ Click on a cell in the row containing your column headings, then click on the button on the right to take you back to the original dialogue box (see Figure 5.2).

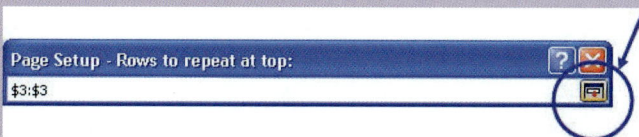

Figure 5.2: *Click here when you have chosen the row containing your column headings.*

▶ There is a **Print Preview** button on the dialogue box. Click it to see the effect.

▶ When you are happy that you have what you want and that it will print onto one page, choose **Print**.

▶ Write a comment on your printout, e.g. **New booking with a hot lunch. The total cost will be £930**.

> **!TIP**
>
> To print part of a spreadsheet, highlight the cells you want to print, then click on File on the menu bar and choose Print Area and Set Print Area. Then use Print Preview to make sure your work fits on the page before printing.
> Don't forget to clear the print area afterwards, using File/Print Area/Clear Print Area.

▶ Change the lunch option to a salad lunch and see what effect this has on the price.

You should find the new price is £720.

▶ Print out this changed booking. Write a comment on your printout, e.g. **New booking with a salad lunch. The total cost will be £720**.

You have now used your spreadsheet to make predictions. For a **Merit** or **Distinction** you will also need to write a short commentary explaining what the customer wanted, what you did and what results you found. This would be best done using a word processor.

Make a decision

A second customer contacts Sam to make an enquiry. She would like to book the Birch Suite next Saturday for 20 people, with a hot lunch.

▶ Enter these details as a new booking. You should find that the cost will be £510.

The customer decides this is too expensive – she has a maximum budget of £400.

There are a number of options you can now try for the customer: change the suite, change the lunch option or suggest a Sunday booking.

▶ Print out the original booking for £510. Add a sentence of explanation to your printout.

▶ Make changes to the booking to see what effect changing the suite, changing the lunch option and changing the date will have. You need to make the fewest possible changes to the customer's original options, yet still get the final cost to below £400.

▶ Print out the result each time, even if the cost is still too high and add a comment to each printout.

You should find that changing to the Elm Suite will reduce the cost to £410, changing to a salad lunch will give £440, a sandwich lunch will give £420, while changing the date to a Sunday will reduce the cost to £459. All of these are still over budget. However, the Elm Suite on a Sunday with a hot lunch will cost £369, the Elm Suite on the Saturday with a salad lunch will cost £340 and the Birch Suite on a Sunday with a salad lunch will cost £396. You could therefore offer the customer these three options.

For a **Merit** or **Distinction** you should make at least one decision to solve a problem such as this, and again you will need to write a short commentary explaining the problem, what you did, the results you obtained and the decision you made.

To find out how to use the **Goal Seek** command to make decisions using spreadsheets, try the activity in *j The Goal Seek command.doc*, available with the downloadable resources for this chapter.

Portfolio builder

When you have designed and created your own spreadsheet for your portfolio you will need to think of two or three different situations, such as the ones in the activities in this chapter. To gain a **Pass** you will need to:

- carry out at least two **what–if** investigations to **predict** what will happen **if** a particular thing is changed
- print out your sheet (or a relevant part of it) **before** and **after** you make the change – label each printout to show what the spreadsheet is predicting.

To gain a **Merit** or **Distinction** you also need to:

- write a separate, word-processed explanation of the problem you were investigating, explaining which cell(s) you changed and the final prediction(s).

To gain a **Distinction** you also need to:

- use the spreadsheet to help you make at least one decision. This means that you will have a fixed outcome and need to decide what can be changed to obtain the outcome you want. You can do this by experimenting, as in the second part of Activity 1
- print out your spreadsheet showing the options you investigated – this might be a number of printouts as in Activity 1
- a word-processed explanation of the problem you had to solve, explaining what you did and the final decision you made, with reasons.

Although you will need to solve these problems yourself – make your own predictions and decisions – you may ask your teacher to help suggest suitable problems to investigate if you cannot think of any yourself.

CHAPTER ⑥

→ *Assessment Objective 5*
Analyse Data Using Graphs and Charts

Overview:

You have already seen how statistical functions can be used to summarise lists of data in a spreadsheet. Spreadsheet software also allows us to easily create graphs and charts to show the data more visually.

In this chapter we will look at how bar charts, pie charts and line graphs are created, as well as the sort of data that is best suited to each. We will also consider the use of graphs to compare two sets of data.

In order to complete the activities in this chapter you will need access to a number of additional files. These files are contained in the Chapter 6 Resources zip file which can be downloaded from the OCR Nationals in ICT (Units 6 & 7) Student Resources page on the Payne-Gallway website: www.payne-gallway.co.uk.

How this assessment objective will be assessed...
- Printouts to show at least one bar chart, pie chart and line graph

Skills to use...
- Creating bar charts, pie charts and line graphs
- Choosing the most appropriate type of graph
- Adding titles and appropriate labels
- Creating charts with more than one set of data

How to achieve...

Pass requirements
P1 You will create at least two different types of graph/chart.

Merit requirements
M1 You will create at least one example of each type of graph from bar chart, pie chart and line graph.

M2 At least one graph will compare values from at least two sets of data.

M3 All graphs will have titles and appropriate axis labels.

Distinction requirements

D1 You will create at least one example of each type of graph from bar chart, pie chart and line graph.

D2 All graphs created will be appropriate.

D3 At least one graph will compare values from at least two sets of data.

D4 All graphs will have titles and appropriate axis labels.

Creating bar charts and pie charts

You are probably already quite familiar with the use of spreadsheet software to create graphs and charts. You do not need to know any more for a **Pass** in this assessment objective. Activity 1 allows you to practise your skills in this area and to find out what evidence you will need to produce for your portfolio.

One useful feature of Excel is that once you have created a chart it will constantly update as you change your data. So you can save a chart with a file – there is no need to keep on recreating the same chart just because you have changed the data.

Activity 1: Creating simple charts...

In this activity you will:

● create a bar chart
● create a pie chart
● add a title to a chart
● add suitable labels to a chart
● show and hide the legend on a chart

▶ Open the hotel suite bookings spreadsheet you have been using in Chapters 4 and 5 (called **Activity 1 P.xls** or **Activity 1 MD.xls** if you are using the files provided on the Payne-Gallway website).

▶ Find the summary table showing the number of bookings for each room and each type of lunch. This sort of table is the most useful form for data to be graphed. It is at the bottom of the **Pass** sheet and on a separate sheet in the **Merit/Distinction** version.

131	Suite	Number	Perce
132	E	14	24
133	B	15	26
134	M	14	24
135	O	14	24
136	Total	57	

*Figure 6.1: Highlighting the data on the **Pass** version of the spreadsheet.*

	Summary Sheet		
1			
2			
3	Suite	Number of bookings	Percentage
4	Elm	14	24.6%
5	Birch	14	24.6%
6	Maple	14	24.6%
7	Oak	15	26.3%
8	Total	57	

*Figure 6.2: Highlighting the data on the **Merit/Distinction** version of the spreadsheet.*

Bar chart

First you are going to create a bar chart to show the number of bookings for each room:

▶ Highlight the cells containing the titles, names of suite and number of bookings. Make sure you don't include the total or the percentage. Figures 6.1 and 6.2 show what you should have selected if you are using the files provided.

▶ Click on the **Chart Wizard** icon on the toolbar or, if you can't see this, you can choose **Chart** from the **Insert** menu on the menu bar.

There are a large number of options you can choose from here. Although some may look more exciting than others, it is important to remember that a chart's purpose is to make data clearer to understand. Some types of chart are for very particular purposes. A good rule is that if you don't know what the chart means, then don't use it!

Figure 6.3: *The Chart Wizard icon.*

You have probably met bar charts, pie charts and line graphs, so these are safe to use. Excel calls bar charts with vertical bars **Column** charts and those with horizontal bars **Bar** charts.

▶ With **Column** selected you can see further choices. If you only have one column of data, as we have here, you only need look at the first choice in each row. Click on each one, then hold down the **Press and Hold to View Sample** button to see what it will look like with your data.

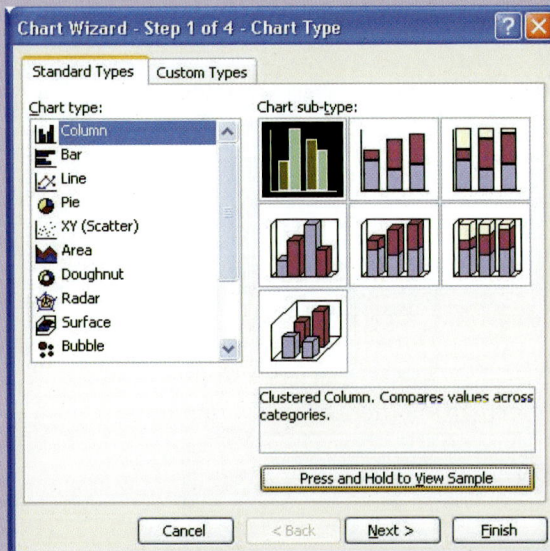

Figure 6.4: *Choices of column chart styles.*

▶ You should find that either of the first options in the top two rows shows the data most clearly. Choose one of these and click on **Next**.

▶ You will now be shown a preview of your chart. If it looks correct, which it usually will, then click on **Next**.

▶ The next dialogue box allows you to choose a title and axis labels for your chart. Enter some appropriate text, such as that shown in Figure 6.5, then click on **Next**.

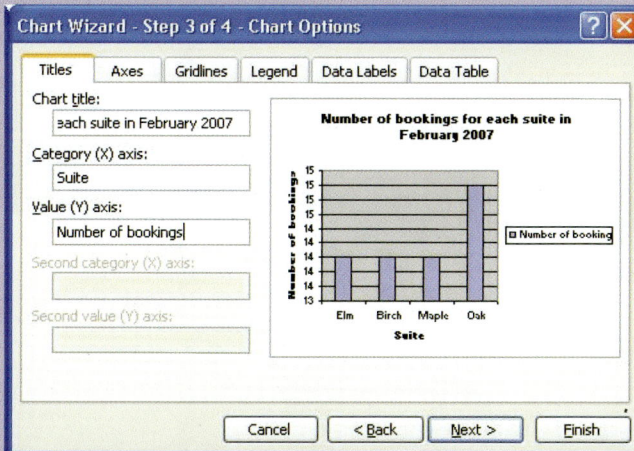

Figure 6.5 *Entering a title and appropriate axis labels.*

The last choice you need to make is whether to add the chart to your sheet of data or to create it on a new sheet. It is usually best to use a new sheet, as this will prevent your data sheet getting cluttered, and you can always copy and paste the graph wherever you want afterwards.

▶ Choose **As new sheet**, and type in a name for the sheet to show what the chart is about (see Figure 6.6).

▶ Then click on **Finish**.

Figure 6.6: *Choosing to create the chart on a new sheet.*

▶ You will now see your chart, with a toolbar that allows you to change any of the options you have set. You might like to investigate these options. However, don't choose the **By Row** option as this will get rid of all the labels on the bars and is not intended for use with the sort of data you have used.

▶ One thing that does need to be changed is the legend 'Number of bookings'. This is showing that the blue bars represent the number of bookings. Since there are only blue bars, this legend is unnecessary. Change this so that the legend is not showing, by clicking on the **Legend** button of the Chart toolbar.

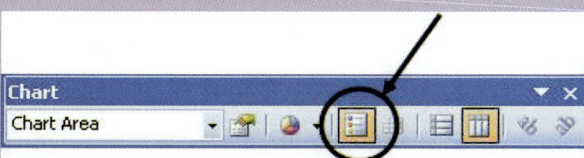

Figure 6.7: *Click this button to turn off the legend.*

> **!TIP**
>
> If you ever want to format a chart and find that the toolbar is missing, click on View on the menu bar, choose Toolbars and Chart.

If you are working to Pass level only you may be wondering where your own spreadsheet of details has gone.

▶ Look at the tabs at the bottom of the screen: click on **Sheet1** and you should see your original sheet.

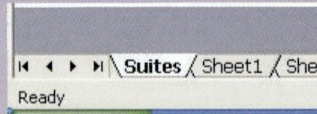

If you ever need to delete one of these extra sheets, click on the tab for the sheet you want to delete, then choose **Edit** from the menu bar and click on **Delete Sheet**.

▶ Try changing some of the bookings to different suites. Go back and see the effect these changes have on your chart.

Figure 6.8: *Use the sheet tabs to get back to your original sheet.*

Pie chart

Now you are ready to create a second chart.

▶ Go back to your summary tables and highlight the table showing the number of each type of lunch booked.

▶ Click on the **Chart Wizard** icon again and select a **Pie** chart. You can choose the type of pie chart you think is best, and enter your own title.

▶ This time you should agree that the legend is needed to show which type of lunch each sector of the pie represents.

You can add more details to your pie chart:

▶ Click inside the pie and then choose the **Format** button on the **Chart** toolbar: It should say **Format Data Series**. If it doesn't you can change this using the first drop-down menu on the toolbar.

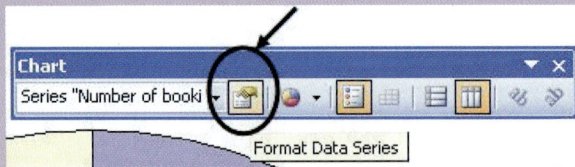

> **!TIP**
>
> It is a good idea to save your spreadsheet before deleting a sheet, so that if you delete the wrong sheet by mistake you can get it back again.

Lunches	Number of bookings	
Sandwich	17	2
Salad	24	4
Hot	16	2

Figure 6.9: *Selecting the data for the number of lunches booked.*

Figure 6.10: *Choosing the **Format** button.*

▶ There are a number of options you can now choose, but the most useful is the **Percentage** option on the **Data Labels** tab. Click this to label each sector of the pie chart with the appropriate percentage (to the nearest whole number).

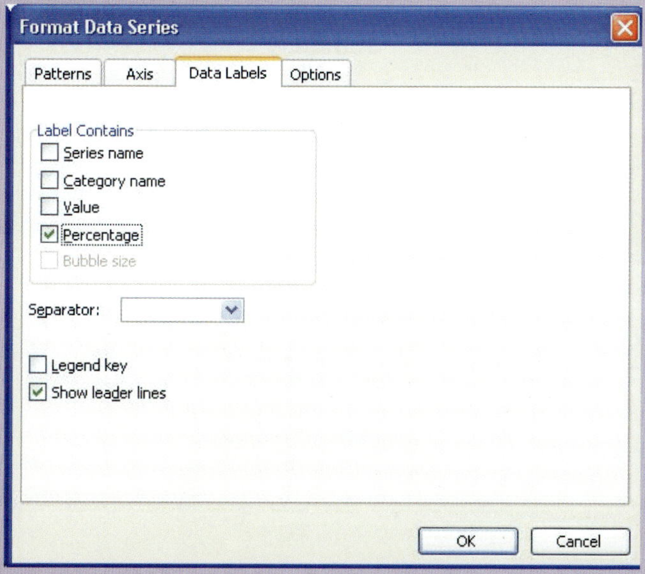

Figure 6.11: *Adding labels to show the percentages on the pie chart.*

The best way of finding out what all the options will do is to experiment. Spend a little time altering the format until you are happy with the resulting pie chart.

▶ Print each of the charts you have produced.

If you are working to Pass level only you do not need to do any more than this for your portfolio.

Comparative graphs

To gain a **Merit** you need to be able to create a graph to compare two different sets of data. This would be useful when you have the same type of data recorded for different periods of time. For example, Sam might want to compare the use of the different suites over two months.

Since Sam is keeping a separate sheet for each month, she will need to copy and paste summary values from two or more separate tables and put them together onto one sheet. Don't worry if you find in your own work that you don't have appropriate values to compare in your main spreadsheet. It is fine to create a new sheet to add extra data.

Activity 2: Comparative graphs...

In this activity you will:

- create a new sheet summarising data from three months
- create a bar chart comparing the three sets of data.

▶ Open up the spreadsheet file *Activity 1 MD.xls*. This contains bookings for February 2007 and can be found in the Chapter 4 resources folder.

▶ Now open the two files for this chapter: *Activity 2 March.xls* and *Activity 2 April.xls*. These contain bookings for March and April 2007.

▶ Start a new blank workbook where you will create a table to compare bookings for these three months.

▶ Highlight the first two columns of the summary tables on the **Summary** sheet of *Activity 1 MD.xls*, then right click and choose **Copy**.

▶ Move back to your new worksheet and click into cell A1.

▶ Right click and choose **Paste Special** then choose **Values** to paste the values from this table without pasting the formulas.

▶ Since the figures in column B are from February, replace the two column headings with the heading **February**, as shown in Figure 6.13.

▶ Go to the **Summary** sheet of the *Activity 2 March. xls* workbook and copy and paste the values from column B into column C of your new worksheet. Replace the two column headings with the heading **March**, as shown in Figure 6.14.

▶ Now copy column B from the **Summary** sheet of the *Activity 2 April.xls* file and paste the values into column D of your new worksheet. Alter the column headings to **April**, as shown in Figure 6.15.

	A	B	
1			Summary She
2			
3	Suite	Number of bookings	
4	Elm	14	25.
5	Birch	14	25.
6	Maple	14	25.
7	Oak	14	25.
8	Total	56	
9			
10	Lunches	Number of bookings	
11	Sandwich	16	28.
12	Salad	24	42.
13	Hot	16	28.
14			

Figure 6.12: *Highlight the first two columns of the summary tables.*

	A	B
1	Suite	February
2	Elm	14
3	Birch	14
4	Maple	14
5	Oak	14
6	Total	56
7		
8	Lunches	February
9	Sandwich	16
10	Salad	24
11	Hot	16
12		

Figure 6.13: *Column B headings changed to* **February**.

	A	B	C
1	Suite	February	March
2	Elm	14	16
3	Birch	14	14
4	Maple	14	16
5	Oak	14	15
6	Total	56	61
7			
8	Lunches	February	March
9	Sandwich	16	20
10	Salad	24	15
11	Hot	16	26
12			

Figure 6.14: *Column C values pasted from the* **March** *sheet.*

	A	B	C	D
1	Suite	February	March	April
2	Elm	14	16	17
3	Birch	14	14	13
4	Maple	14	16	17
5	Oak	14	15	14
6	Total	56	61	61
7				
8	Lunches	February	March	April
9	Sandwich	16	20	29
10	Salad	24	15	16
11	Hot	16	26	16
12				

Figure 6.15: *Column D values pasted from the* **April** *sheet.*

▶ Save your new summary sheet. Call it **Bookings Feb_Apr**.

▶ You should now be able to close down the other files.

▶ Now that the figures from all three months are in the same table you can create a chart to compare the three months.

▶ Highlight cells A1 to D5 and create a bar (column) chart with this data. Experiment with the different options available until you have a graph that clearly shows all the data.

(▶) You will see that the legend is useful for this chart. When you have more than one set, or **series**, of data you need to know which bar refers to which series. In this case we have three series — February, March and April. Each series has a different coloured bar and the legend makes it clear which bar is which.

(▶) Create a comparative bar chart to show the bookings for the different types of lunch over the three months. Choose some different formatting options for this chart. For example, if you have chosen two-dimensional bars for the first chart, try using three-dimensional bars for this new one.

Creating line graphs

Although you *could* have chosen a line graph for either of the charts in Activity 1 it would not have been appropriate. Line graphs are designed to show **continuous** data, whereas bar charts and pie charts show **discrete** data. The best way of telling the difference between two types is to ask 'Does it make sense to think of a halfway point between two points on the chart?'. For example, you created a bar chart to show the number of bookings for each of the different suites, so you had one bar for Elm and one bar for Birch. Does it make sense to ask how many there might be for halfway between the two? Of course it doesn't — there's no such thing as an 'Elm and a half' suite! **Discrete** means 'completely separate'. So as there are four completely separate suites, this is **discrete** data.

Similarly there are three completely separate choices for lunch. There is no option for booking something halfway between a sandwich lunch and a salad lunch. So the lunch data is also **discrete** data.

Line graphs should not be used for discrete data. The mid-point on a line graph should actually mean something. You can think of the line showing a **trend**.

For example, Sam wants to show the number of bookings for a particular suite over a number of months, so she might use a line graph to show whether there is a trend for an increase or decrease in the number of bookings. The mid-point between February and March would give an indication of the number of bookings that might be expected from the middle of February until the middle of March.

Activity 3: Line graphs...

In this activity you will:

- create a line graph to show a trend
- create a comparative line graph with more than one data series.

Creating a line graph

(▶) Open up the **Bookings Feb_Apr** file you saved in Activity 3. (Alternatively, open the file ***Activity 3.xls*** provided with the resources for this chapter.)

Sam wants to show how the total number of bookings has changed over these three months.

Row 6 shows the total number of bookings. You *could* just highlight this row and create a graph but it is always useful to include column headings as well as the data.

▶ Highlight cells A1 to D1. Now hold down the **Ctrl** key and highlight cells A6 to D6. This should enable you to keep the column headings highlighted while highlighting row 6 as well.

	A	B	C	D	
1	Suite	February	March	April	
2	Elm	14	16	17	
3	Birch	14	14	13	
4	Maple	14	16	17	
5	Oak	14	15	14	
6	Total	56	61	61	
7					
8	Lunches	February	March	April	
9	Sandwich	16	20	29	
10	Salad	24	15	16	
11	Hot	16	26	16	
12					

Figure 6.16: *Highlighting the column headings and the data in row 6.*

▶ Now click on the **Chart Wizard** and choose a **Line** graph.

▶ Choose the first option from either the first or second row. You should resist the temptation to use a 3-D line as it is very difficult to read accurate details from this and your aim should be to show the data as clearly as possible.

▶ You should then be able to follow through the stages, adding suitable labels, until you have your final graph.

▶ With only one set of data, again it is best to switch off the legend.

You can also produce a line graph to show how bookings for a particular suite have changed.

▶ Highlight cells A1 to D2 and produce a line graph to show how bookings for the Elm suite have changed over the three months. Choose a different option for the style of line graph this time, so you can compare the result with your first graph.

Creating a comparative line graph

You can put more than one line on a graph, so you could compare the trends for all three suites.

▶ Highlight cells A1 to D5 and choose **Chart Wizard**.

▶ Choose a **Line** graph and click **Next**.

Up to now you have not needed to change this next option. However, the chart shown in the preview is not what we want here – we want to see the trend over the three months for each suite, so we want the **months** along the bottom axis, just as you have had for the last two graphs.

▶ Click to show **Series in Rows**, which tells the computer to draw a separate line for each row of data.

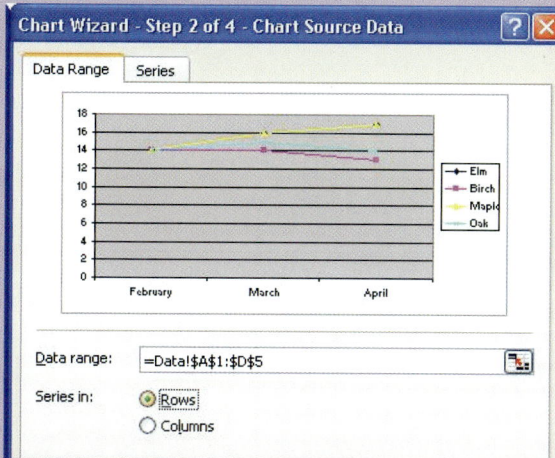

Figure 6.17: Changing to Series in Rows.

▶ Complete this graph by adding suitable labels and choosing to create it **As new sheet**.

▶ You should leave the legend showing, as it shows which suite each line shows. Look carefully to see the trend for each suite. At first you may not see the line for **Elm**. Because the values are the same for Elm and Birch the **Birch** line is covering up most of the **Elm** line. This is not an error, it is just what has to happen if the values are the same.

Although this graph has been created from the same data as the comparative bar chart you created in Activity 2, you will be able to see that the data is shown in a completely different way. The bar chart in Activity 2 shows clearly the number of bookings for each suite each month, whereas the graph you have just created allows you to compare more clearly the trends over the months between the three suites.

You can find examples of all the charts covered in this chapter in the file *Chapter 6 Final*.

Bar chart, line graph or pie chart?

To gain a **Distinction** in this assessment objective you need to show that you have used the most appropriate type of chart at all times.

Here you must resist the temptation to use some of the more obscure options just because they look good to you. You need always to think about how clearly the data is being shown.

The best type of graph/chart to use depends on what you want to show:

● **Bar charts:** A bar chart (called **Column** chart in Excel) is the best way to show the popularity of different options, showing clearly the actual numbers of each in a way that makes it easy to compare values. It is easy to see, for example, how much higher one bar is than another, showing us how much more popular one option is than another.
   Bar charts are also a good way of comparing more than one set of data on the same chart, by having different coloured bars for each set of data.

● **Pie charts:** Although pie charts can show the same data as a bar chart, they emphasise **proportions** rather than absolute **amounts**. For example, in the pie chart of lunch choices you created in Activity 1 it is easy to see what *proportion* of the bookings were for each type of lunch, but less easy to compare the *actual numbers* of each booking. That is why it is usual to add percentages rather than absolute values to pie charts. If you try to compare different sets of data using pie charts you get a different pie for each set of data. This usually makes it less easy to compare the two sets of data.

● **Line graphs:** A line graph is the best way to show **trends**, usually over time. Line graphs are also a good way of comparing the trends of more than one set of data, by having different coloured lines for each set of data.

If you are aiming for a **Distinction**, you should take time and care when choosing each chart you create, maybe trying out more than one option until you are sure you have displayed the data in the best possible way.

Portfolio builder

For a **Pass** in this objective you simply have to create and print out two different types of chart, for example a pie chart and a bar chart. You should be able to choose suitable data to create your charts from the spreadsheet you create. The bar chart and pie chart might show the same data, or different data.

For a **Merit** or **Distinction** you must create and print at least one bar chart, one pie chart and one line graph. If necessary you can use additional data, so long as it is connected to your main spreadsheet solution, just as we created the additional file **Bookings Feb_Apr** in this chapter. At least one of these should be a comparative graph showing more than one set of data. All graphs need to be given appropriate titles and axis labels.

It is not necessary to provide any evidence of *how* you create your graphs and charts, so long as you print out the final results.

For a **Distinction** your graphs all need to be appropriate, showing the data in the best possible way. When you have created each chart or graph you should always test it by asking yourself the following questions:

1 Does the chart show all the data I wanted it to?
2 Does the title explain what the chart shows?
3 Is there a label on each axis of a bar chart or line graph?
4 Is the legend necessary?
5 Can I see clearly what each bar/segment/point is showing?
6 Is the data continuous? (i.e. do halfway points have a meaning?) If so, a line graph is usually best.
7 Is the data discrete? (i.e. is the idea of halfway points meaningless?) If so, then a line graph should not be used.
8 Do I want to show actual **amounts** or **proportions**? Amounts are best shown by a bar chart, while proportions are best shown by a pie chart.

You might want to clarify your reason for each chart by adding a sentence of explanation to your printout.

CHAPTER 7

➔ Assessment Objective 6

Macros

Overview:

Sometimes when you are using a spreadsheet there are certain tasks you might want to do quite often. For example, you might often want to save and print your file, or sort a sheet in a particular order. You might often need to move from one sheet to another, or perhaps move from the top to the bottom of a long sheet.

Some commonly used tasks, such as printing, are already easy to do because there is an icon on the toolbar. Macros are ways of automating other tasks, so that they can be just as easily accessed.

In this last chapter of Unit 6 you will learn how to create macros to make working with your spreadsheet even easier for the user. You will record some common routines and look at the code created. You will create keyboard shortcuts, toolbar buttons and worksheet buttons to run your macros.

In order to complete the activities in this chapter you will need access to a number of additional files. These files are contained in the Chapter 7 Resources zip file which can be downloaded from the OCR Nationals in ICT (Units 6 & 7) Student Resources page on the Payne-Gallway website: www.payne-gallway.co.uk.

How this assessment objective will be assessed...

- Printouts of macro code
- Annotated screenshots showing buttons and keyboard shortcuts
- Written descriptions of what the macros do
- Annotated macro code showing the function of key lines

Skills to use...

- Recording macros
- Accessing macro code
- Creating buttons to run macros

How to achieve...

Pass requirements

P1 You will record a simple macro to automate at least one task.

P2 This macro will be set to run by either a keyboard shortcut or a button on the sheet or a toolbar.

P3 You will access the macro code and print it out.

Merit requirements

M1 You will record a macro to automate a sequence of at least two tasks.

M2 This macro will be set to run by both a keyboard shortcut and a button on the sheet or the toolbar.

M3 You will access the macro code and print it out.

M4 You will describe what the macro does and how it can be run.

Distinction requirements

D1 You will record two macros, each of which will automate a sequence of at least two tasks.

D2 Each macro will be set to run by both a keyboard shortcut and a button on the sheet or the toolbar.

D3 You will access the code for each macro and print it out.

D4 You will annotate the macro codes to show the function of at least three items of code.

D5 You will describe what each macro does and how it can be run.

Recording a macro

Any sequence of key strokes and menu choices can be recorded in a macro. It does not matter how simple or complex the routine is, the procedure is the same:

1 Click on **Tools** on the menu bar and choose **Macro**, then **Record New Macro**.

2 A dialogue box will appear, allowing you to name your macro, assign a keyboard short-cut, decide where to save the macro and write a brief description.

Figure 7.1: The **Record Macro** dialogue box.

3 When you have completed the dialogue box, click on **OK**.

4 A new toolbar will appear, containing two buttons. This is called the **Stop Recording** toolbar. Ignore this to start with.

5 Carry out the procedures you want to automate.

6 Click on the **Stop Recording** button that is on the left of the new toolbar.

Figure 7.2: *The **Stop Recording** toolbar.*

What sort of procedures do you record in a macro? Anything you can do using keystrokes and mouse clicks can be recorded. A range of examples are given in the activities in this chapter, but any time you find yourself doing the same few procedures frequently this can be recorded in a macro. Alternatively, if there is a feature on one of the menus that you want an inexperienced user to access easily, you can create a macro to access it. You will be able to create your own button on the worksheet, making it easier for the user, who no longer has to remember where to find the command.

Activity 1: Recording a simple macro...

In this activity you will:

- record a macro to move the cursor to a different point in a worksheet
- create a keyboard shortcut to run the macro.

▶ Open the file ***Activity 1.xls***. This is the Pass level version of Sam's booking spreadsheet. It contains all the bookings at the top of the sheet and the summary table at the bottom. If you have not used this file before, scroll down to see the summary table.

Sam might open this file just to see the summary table. It is not very convenient having this 'hidden' at the bottom of the sheet, as every time Sam opens the file to see the summary table she has to move down to row 131. The fact that she will frequently need to do the same thing – move down to row 131 – suggests that a macro could be useful.

▶ Click on **Tools** on the menu bar and choose **Macro**, then **Record New Macro**.

You will now be shown the **Record Macro** dialogue box to complete.

The macro name must not contain any spaces, so you can use capital letters to make the name as meaningful as possible (see Figure 7.3).

You can choose any letter key as a keyboard shortcut. It is best if this is chosen to make it easy to remember, so here we have chosen **Ctrl+s** for a macro that will move to the **s**ummary table. However, you should not use a keyboard shortcut that you use for anything else, so if you commonly use Ctrl+s to save a file you should choose another key instead.

Most macros are created for use in a specific workbook, so you need to choose **This Workbook**. Any macro that you want to be available every time you use Excel needs to be saved in your **Personal Macro Workbook**, but it is unlikely you will ever want to use this option.

It is tempting not to bother writing a description of the macro, but if you record a number of macros, you might later regret not taking the time to describe what each one does.

▶ Complete the dialogue box as shown in Figure 7.3, then click **OK**.

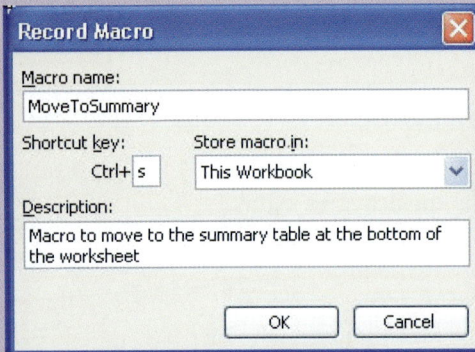

Figure 7.3: *Completing the **Record Macro** dialogue box.*

▶ Click in cell A131 of the worksheet. If you cannot see this straight away, use the arrow keys to take you there, as using the mouse and the scroll bars will give you a lot of unnecessary code in your macro.

▶ Click on the **Stop Recording** button on the **Stop Recording** toolbar.

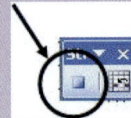

Figure 7.4: *Stop recording.*

You have now recorded a macro! Next you should test it to see if it works:

▶ Move to a different point on the worksheet – anywhere except cell A131.

▶ Hold down **Ctrl** and press **s** (or whichever letter you chose as your shortcut key). You should see that the cursor has moved to cell A131.

▶ If this doesn't happen, go to **Tools/Macro** and choose **Macros**. You should see the macro you have just recorded listed. Make sure this macro is selected, then choose **Delete**. Then try to record it again.

NB: You should not delete your macro if it works!

Figure 7.5: *Deleting a macro.*

▶ Now record a new macro. Call it **MoveToTop** and give it a suitable keyboard shortcut and description — to move back to cell A1.

▶ Test your new macro.

You should now have a quick way of moving to the summary sheet and then back to the top of the sheet again.

Sam needs to know about these macros in order to be able to use them. This is best done by adding an instruction.

▶ Double click at the end of the instruction in row 3.

▶ Press **Alt** and **Enter**. This allows you to start a new line in a cell with wrapped text. Enter a suitable instruction to tell a user how to get to the summary table and back to the top of the sheet again.

▶ You will probably need to increase the height of row 3. You might also like to make the text larger.

▶ Save your file — call it ***Activity 1 with macros***. Then close it down and open it again. You should find that the macros still work.

Macro code

You may have wondered how the computer stored the macros you recorded in Activity 1. Every macro is stored as a list of instructions. These instructions are written in codes using a language called **Visual Basic for Applications** or **VBA** for short.

For a **Pass** in this unit you need to be able to record a simple macro such as the one in Activity 1, then you need to access the code and print it out.

You can see any available macros by holding down **Alt** and pressing the **F11** key. This shows the **Visual Basic Editor** (**VBE**) window.

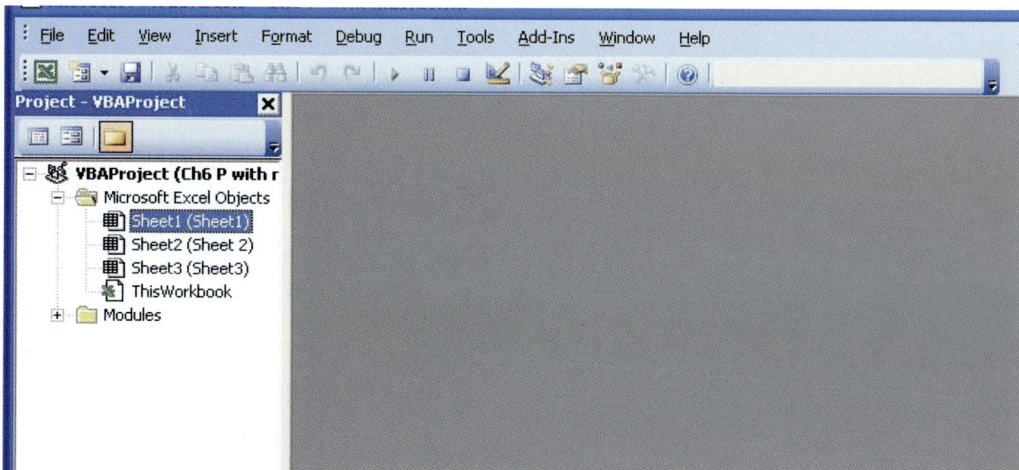

Figure 7.6: *The VBE window.*

In the top left of the screen you will see a reference to every workbook that is currently open. In Figure 7.6 you can see that only one workbook is open.

The macro code is inside the **Modules** folder. It can be seen by double clicking on **Modules**, then on any modules inside this folder. If you have recorded all your macros in the same session they will all be in a single module called **Module1**.

When you double click on a Module a window showing the code for any macros will open up. Figure 7.7 shows the code for the macros recorded in Activity 1:

```
Ch6 P with macros.xls - Module1 (Code)

(General)                                          MoveToSummary

Sub MoveToSummary()
'
' MoveToSummary Macro
' Macro to move to the summary table at the bottom of the worksheet
'
' Keyboard Shortcut: Ctrl+s
'
    Range("A131").Select
End Sub

Sub MoveToTop()
'
' MoveToTop Macro
' Macro to move to cell A1 at the top of the worksheet.
'
' Keyboard Shortcut: Ctrl+t
'
    Range("A1:L1").Select
End Sub
```

Figure 7.7: *The code for the macros recorded in Activity 1.*

Once the code window is open it can be printed using **File/Print**.

Activity 2: Printing macro code...

In this activity you will:

- access the code for recorded macros
- print the code.

▶ Open the file that you saved at the end of Activity 1. Alternatively open the file ***Activity 2.xls***.

▶ Press **Alt** and **F11** to access the VBE window.

▶ Double click on **Modules**.

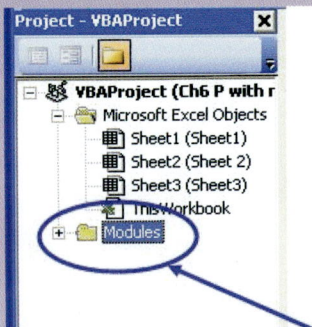

Figure 7.8: *Double clicking on **Modules** to access the code.*

▶ Double click on **Module1**.

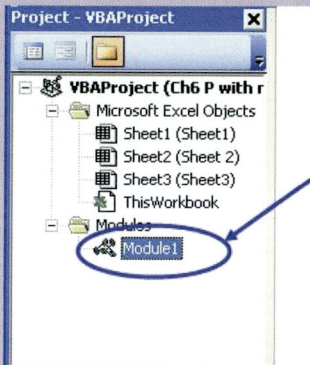

*Figure 7.9: Double clicking on **Module1** to open the code window.*

▶ Click on **File** on the menu bar and choose **Print** to print your code.

▶ Close down the code window to see the spreadsheet behind.

▶ Don't forget to save your spreadsheet before closing it down, so that the code will be saved with it.

> ⊘**TIP**
>
> You can close down the VBE window at any time. Your VBA code will be saved when you save your file.

The code window can easily get cluttered with attempts at macros that are no longer needed. That is why it is a good idea always to use **Tools/Macro/Macros** to delete any failed attempts. If you still have unwanted macros in the VBE window you can delete them just by deleting the text but you need to be careful to delete all of the macro from **Sub** to **End Sub** and not to delete part of any other macro by mistake.

You have now learned how to record a macro and print out the code. These are the skills you need to show with your own spreadsheet in order to gain a Pass for this objective.

Creating a button to run a macro on the worksheet

Keyboard shortcuts are quick ways to run macros that are used often, but they are not particularly user friendly – unless you add specific instructions, a user might not even know a macro exists. It is often much more helpful and appropriate to add a button to a worksheet.

Once you have created your macro, you then need to use the **Forms** toolbar to draw a button on your worksheet:

1 Click on **View** on the menu bar and choose **Toolbars**. Select the **Forms** toolbar.
2 Choose the **Button** icon on the **Forms** toolbar.
3 Drag out a box in a suitable empty space on the sheet. This will be the button.

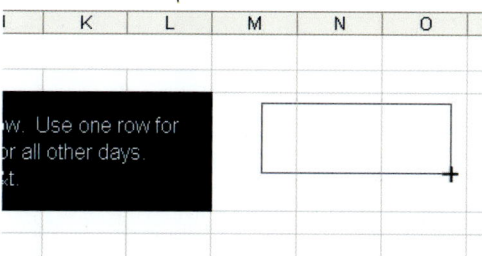

*Figure 7.10: Choosing the **Button** icon.*

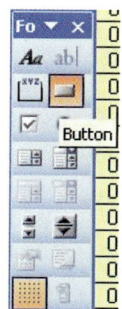

Figure 7.11: Dragging out a box to form the button.

4 You will then be asked to choose a macro to assign to this button. Choose the macro you want, then click **OK**. Figure 7.12 shows the first macro you created in Activity 1 being assigned to a button. Here you will see another good reason for making sure you give your macros appropriate names.

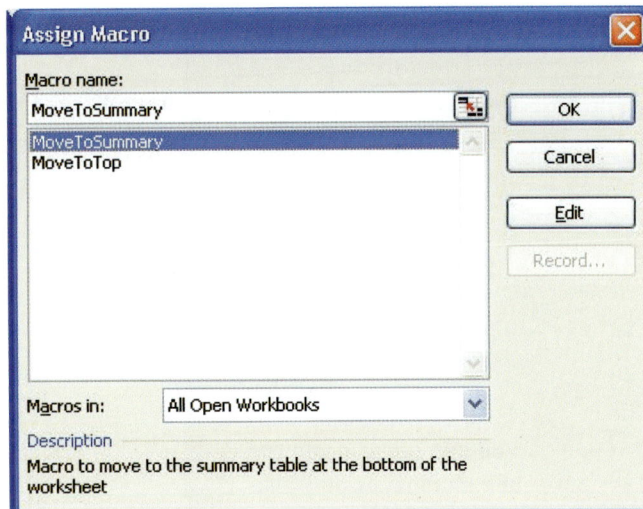

Figure 7.12: *Assigning a macro to a button.*

5 Click onto the text on the button and type in something more appropriate. For example, the button for the macro to take you to the summary table could just be labelled **Summary**.
NB: You can only do this straight after you have created the button. If you want to alter the label on a button at a later stage you need to right click on it and choose **Edit Text**.

6 Click in a cell away from the button.

7 Next time you hover over the button your cursor should turn into a pointing finger. If you click on the button now it will run your macro.

When you have added all the buttons you need you should remove the **Forms** toolbar by clicking on the cross at the top, just as you would close down any other window.

Activity 3: Creating buttons to run macros...

In this activity you will:

- create buttons on a worksheet to run macros.

▶ Open the file you saved at the end of Activity 2. Alternatively open the file **Activity 3.xls**.

▶ Use **View/Toolbars** to show the **Forms** toolbar.

▶ Use the **Button** tool to create a button to the right of the instructions, as shown in Figure 7.11.

▶ You will be asked to choose a macro to assign to this button. Choose **MoveToSummary** and click on **OK**.

▶ Click onto the text of the button that has been created and edit this so that the button now says **Summary**.

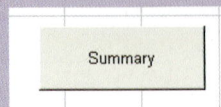

Figure 7.13: *The Summary button.*

▶ Click into any cell, away from the button.

▶ Now click on the button again. This time it will activate your macro and you should be taken to cell A131.

▶ Create another button, next to the summary table, to activate your **MoveToTop** macro.

▶ Close down the forms toolbar, then test your buttons a few times.

More macros

So far you have recorded two simple macros, each of which carried out a single task – moving to a different place on a worksheet. There are many more tasks that can be carried out using macros.

For a **Merit** in this objective the macro you create must carry out at least **two** tasks. For a **Distinction** you must create at least **two** macros, each of which must carry out at least **two** tasks.

When recording more complex macros it is a good idea to plan them out first – think carefully about *exactly* what you want your macro to do. You might make a note of all the tasks. Then carry out a 'dry run' – a practice of these tasks, to make sure you get it right, before you record the macro. This is just like a group of musicians recording a song – they would practise first to make sure they had got it absolutely right before recording.

Activity 4 gives you some more ideas for macros you can produce. When you create your own spreadsheet for your portfolio you should be able to think of plenty of macros that could be useful.

Activity 4: More macros...

In this activity you will:

● create macros that carry out more than one process
● create buttons to run the macros.

As Sam is using her spreadsheet regularly to enter bookings she will want to save and print her sheet regularly. She can do this by first choosing to save, then choosing to print. However, it may be convenient to create a macro that will do both of these things at once:

▶ Open the file you saved at the end of Activity 3. Alternatively open the file *Activity 4A.xls*.

To avoid wasting paper while testing this macro, it is suggested you should select just part of the sheet to print each time.

▶ Highlight the summary table in cells A131 to G136, then choose **File/Print Area/Set Print Area**

▶ Choose **Tools/Macro/Record New Macro**. Call this macro **SaveAndPrint**, choose a suitable keyboard shortcut and enter a brief description. Then click on **OK**.

▶ Now **save** your spreadsheet file in the usual way, then **print** it.

▶ Click on the **Stop Recording** button.

▶ Press **Alt** and **F11** to view your code. You will probably have to open **Module2** to see this new code, as a new module is started if you record a macro in a different session from other macros.

▶ The code for this macro is shown in Figure 7.14. You should be able to see that the first instruction line tells the computer to save the file, then the next one tells the computer to print the current worksheet.

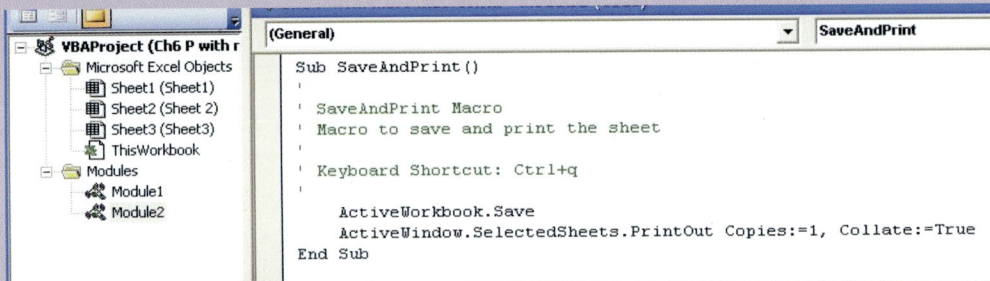

```
VBAProject (Ch6 P with r    (General)                              SaveAndPrint
  Microsoft Excel Objects   Sub SaveAndPrint()
    Sheet1 (Sheet1)         '
    Sheet2 (Sheet 2)        '  SaveAndPrint Macro
    Sheet3 (Sheet3)         '  Macro to save and print the sheet
    ThisWorkbook            '
  Modules                   '  Keyboard Shortcut: Ctrl+q
    Module1
    Module2                     ActiveWorkbook.Save
                                ActiveWindow.SelectedSheets.PrintOut Copies:=1, Collate:=True
                            End Sub
```

Figure 7.14: *Code for a macro to save and print a file.*

▶ Print off your code and add a suitable description of what the macro does and how it can be run.

▶ Create a suitable button at the top of this worksheet, to run this macro.

▶ Create a screenshot showing this button. Annotate your screenshot to say that this shows the button used to run your save and print macro.

A simple macro such as this is sufficient to gain a **Merit** in this unit. For a **Distinction** you will need to create at least two different macros, though neither has to be any more complex than this one.

▶ If you have been working on the **Merit** and **Distinction** version of the spreadsheet solution in chapters 4 to 6, then close down your current file and open the **Merit** and **Distinction** version that you have been using. Alternatively you can open the file **Activity 4B.xls**.

You should now be able to think of some useful macros for this spreadsheet. For example:

▶ On the main sheet, unprotect the sheet, sort in order of suite, then protect the sheet again.

▶ On the main sheet, unprotect the sheet, sort in order of date, then in order of suite, then protect the sheet again.

▶ On the main sheet, unprotect the sheet, sort in order of date, then in order of lunch choice, then protect the sheet again.

> **⊘ TIP**
> You cannot add buttons to a protected sheet so you will need to unprotect it before creating these. Remember to protect it again afterwards.

▶ On each sheet, add a separate macro and button to take you to cell A1 of the other sheet.

▶ Create a new worksheet, which will simply be a menu sheet. Add a suitable large heading and some large text to explain what the workbook does. Then add buttons to take you to the other sheets of the workbook. Don't forget you have already recorded these macros. This menu sheet can then be protected.

> ▶ Move to the main sheet and create a new macro that takes you back to the menu sheet and then saves the file. Create a new **Save** button on every sheet that activates this macro. That will make sure that so long as the file is saved using this button it will open up with the menu sheet showing.

Creating a button on a toolbar to run a macro

Buttons on the worksheet are probably the most obvious and so most helpful way of running a macro for an inexperienced user. However, there may not be space on the screen to create a button and too many worksheet buttons can make the screen very cluttered. The other option is to create a button on a toolbar.

One advantage of a toolbar button is that it does not take up space on the worksheet itself. Another advantage is that it is always visible, even if you scroll down a long worksheet, or if you move from one worksheet to another.

For your assessment in this objective you only need to create one type of button and the button on the worksheet you have already learned to create is probably the most useful and most straightforward to create. However, you may wish to know how to create different types of button.

Most macros are designed to be used for particular workbooks. You don't want the buttons to be shown all the time. In order to do this you first need to create a new toolbar for your button, so that you can have this toolbar showing only when the relevant workbook is in use.

The following steps will tell you how to create a new toolbar.

1 First you need to choose **View** from the menu bar, then **Toolbars** and choose **Customize** from the bottom of the list.
2 Choose the **Toolbars** tab and click on the **New...** button.

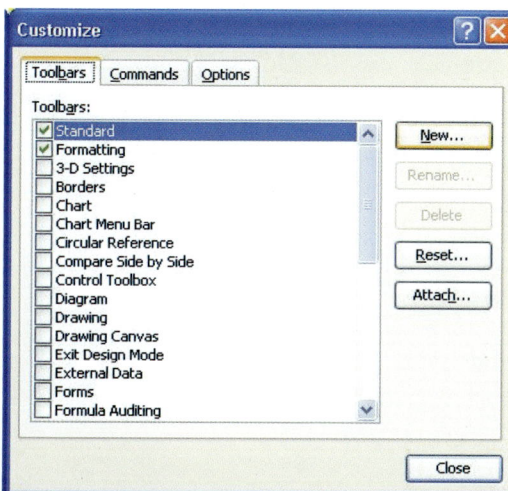

Figure 7.15: Creating a new toolbar.

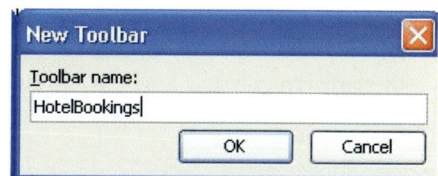

Figure 7.16: Naming the toolbar.

3 You will then be asked to name the toolbar. It is a good idea to choose a name that will remind you of the workbook it will be used with.

4 You will now be given a very short, empty toolbar, that you can move to wherever you like.

Now you are ready to add buttons to this toolbar.

1 Select the **Commands** tab on the **Customize** dialogue box and scroll down and choose **Macros**. Hold onto the **Custom Button** option and drag it onto your new toolbar.

*Figure 7.17: Drag the **Custom Button** onto your toolbar.*

2 You now need to assign your macro to the button. Right click on the button and choose **Assign Macro**. You will then be shown all available macros and you can select the macro to assign to the button and then click **OK**.

3 You now have a new button that will activate your macro. However, it would be easy for a new user not to notice this, especially if you put your toolbar at the top with all the usual tools. Also, the icon doesn't give any clue about what the button does. You can change this by right clicking on the button and choosing **Image and Text**.

4 At first the text is not helpful as it just says **Custom Button**, but if you right click again you can click on **Name**, which will allow you to enter a more helpful name for the button. For example, a button to move to a worksheet called **Summary** could just be labelled with the word **Summary**.

5 There is also an option on the right click menu to **Change Button Image**, although there is a limited number of choices.

6 When you have set all of these options you can close down the **Customize** window and if you then click on your new button it should run your macro.

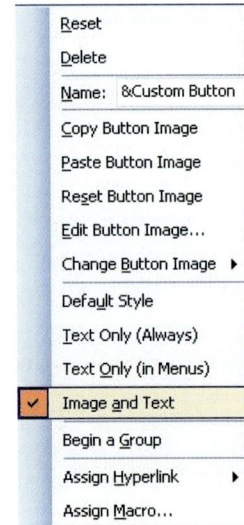

*Figure 7.18: Choosing **Image and Text**.*

Figure 7.19: Changing the button name.

⊘TIP

If you ever need to remove a button from a toolbar, choose View/Toolbars/
Customize and simply drag the button off the toolbar.

Activity 5: Creating a new toolbar with buttons...

In this activity you will:

● create a new toolbar for your hotel bookings sheet
● add buttons for all your macros to the new toolbar
● add a macro and button to the menu page to load the new toolbar.

▶ Open the version of the hotel bookings spreadsheet that you saved at the end of Activity 4. Alternatively you can load the file *Activity 5.xls*.

▶ Use **View/Toolbars/Customize** to open the **Customize** dialogue box, then choose **Toolbars** and click the **New** button. Call your toolbar **HotelBookings** and click **OK**.

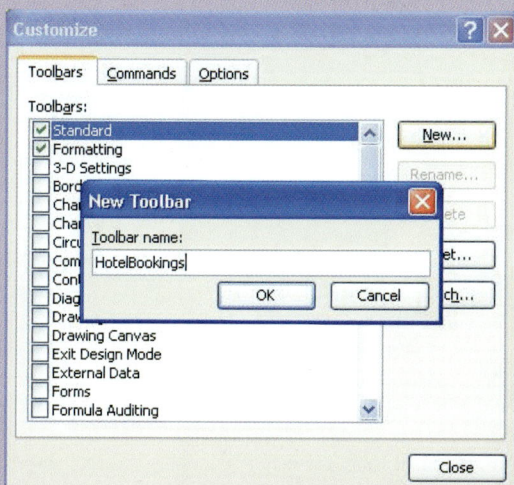

Figure 7.20: Creating a new toolbar for the hotel bookings spreadsheet.

▶ Click on the **Commands** tab and scroll down to choose **Macros**, then drag the **Custom Button** onto your new toolbar:

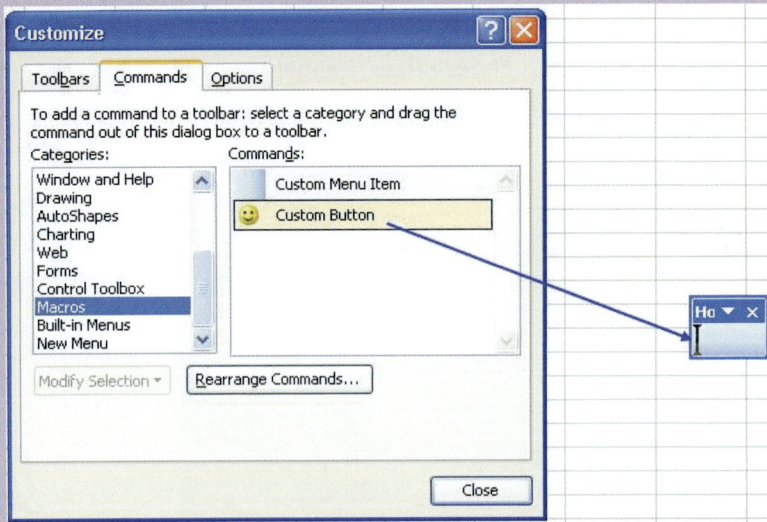

Figure 7.21: Dragging the custom button onto your toolbar.

▶ Right click on your new button and use **Assign Macro** to assign it to one of your macros. Adjust the button by adding appropriate text and/or changing the image as you see fit.

▶ Now add buttons for all of your other macros to this toolbar.

▶ Choose a different image for each button, or you might prefer just to use the 'text only' option for some or all of your items.

Figure 7.22: Toolbar for the macros created in Activity 4.

▶ Adjust the shape and position of the toolbar so that it does not obscure any of the sheets – you can treat it just like any other Windows window. Figure 7.22 shows one possible result. Leaving the toolbar 'floating' rather than locked into the toolbar space at the top of the screen makes it much easier to delete it if it is not required.

Now you have a toolbar to go with your workbook you need an easy way of showing this.

▶ Close down the new toolbar.

▶ Record a macro to select **View/Toolbars** and your **HotelBookings** toolbar. Create a button on your menu page to run this new macro.

▶ Save your file, then close down the new toolbar.

▶ Open up the file, use your new button to show the toolbar and test it.

▶ Now you have your new toolbar you don't really need all of the other buttons on the sheets – just the one that opens up your toolbar. If you want to delete any of the other buttons, make sure the sheet is unprotected, then right click on each button and choose **Cut**.

Activity 6: Creating macros to show and hide a toolbar as a workbook is opened and closed...

In this activity you will:

* create an **Auto_Open** macro to run automatically when a workbook is opened
* create an **Auto_Close** macro to run automatically when a workbook is closed.

▶ Open up the file you saved at the end of Activity 5. Alternatively you can use the file *Activity 6.xls*.

▶ Make sure your new toolbar is **NOT** showing.

▶ Record a new macro to show your new toolbar. There is no need to give it a keyboard shortcut but you **MUST** name it **Auto_Open**. This name must be typed exactly.

Figure 7.23: Recording an **Auto_Open** *macro.*

A macro that is called **Auto_Open** is recognised by Excel as one which should be automatically run when a workbook is opened.

▶ Save your file, then close it down and close down your toolbar.

▶ Load your file again. You should see the toolbar appear automatically.

Now all you need is to be able to close the toolbar automatically whenever you close the file. A macro to run automatically whenever a file is closed needs to be called **Auto_Close**.

▶ Record a new macro, called **Auto_Close**, which hides the new toolbar.

Figure 7.24: Recording an **Auto_Close** *macro.*

> ▶ Save your file, then open it and close it a few times to see these new macros working.
>
> ▶ You no longer need the button on the menu page to open the new toolbar, so you can delete it by right clicking and choosing **Cut**.

Looking at the macro code

For a **Merit** or a **Distinction** in this objective you need to write on the printout of your code to show what each macro does. This is made easier if you always enter a **Description** in the dialogue box before you record your macro.

Figure 7.25 shows the code for the first macro you created in Activity 1:

```
sub MoveToSummary()
'
' MoveToSummary Macro
' Macro to move to the summary table at the bottom of the worksheet
'
' Keyboard Shortcut: Ctrl+s
'
      Range("A131").Select
End Sub
```

Figure 7.25: *The code for the first macro you created, which moves to the summary table at the bottom of the worksheet.*

- Every macro begins with the code **Sub *name_of_macro* ()**. Here you can see that this macro is called **MoveToSummary**. You should see now the advantage of using a name that describes what the macro does.
- Any lines in green and starting with **'** are not macro commands, they are information for you. They show you the name of the macro, the description you typed in when you recorded it and also the keyboard shortcut if you chose one.
- Any lines below these lines of information are the coded instructions. Here there is only one instruction – **Range("A131").Select**. Although the **syntax** (that means the way the instruction is written) may look strange, you should be able to see what this piece of code is telling the computer to do – select the cell A131.
- Every macro ends with the code **End Sub**.

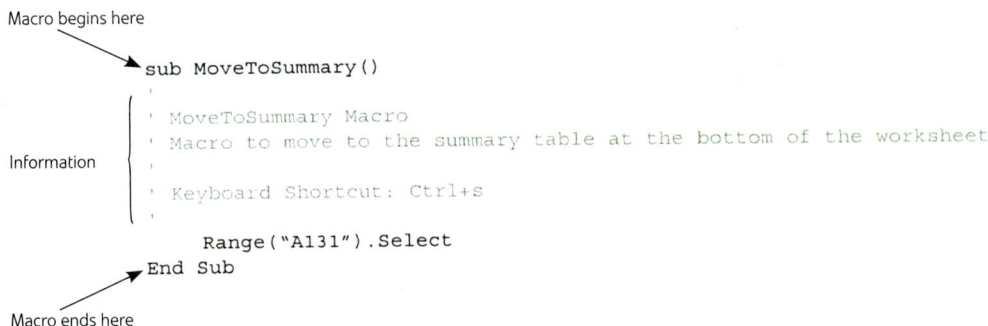

```
Macro begins here ──▶ sub MoveToSummary()
                      '
                      ' MoveToSummary Macro
                      ' Macro to move to the summary table at the bottom of the worksheet
Information           '
                      ' Keyboard Shortcut: Ctrl+s
                      '
                            Range("A131").Select
Macro ends here ──▶ End Sub
```

Figure 7.26: *The different parts of the macro code.*

Now we will look at the **SaveAndPrint** macro you created in Activity 4, with more than one command:

For a **Merit** you simply need to identify a macro and write down what it does and how it can be run, as shown in Figure 7.27.

```
sub SaveAndPrint()
'
' SaveAndPrint Macro
' Macro to save and print the sheet
'
' Keyboard Shortcut: Ctrl+q
'
    ActiveWorkbook.Save
    ActiveWindow.SelectedSheets.PrintOut Copies:=1, Collate:=True
End Sub
```

This macro saves the workbook and then prints it out. It can be run from the keyboard shortcut Ctrl and q or from the button I put on the sheet.

Figure 7.27: *Annotating the code with a description of what the macro does and how it can be run.*

For a **Distinction** you need to identify particular items of code and say what each one does. You will need two different macros and between these you will need to show at least **three** different lines of code.

Figure 7.28 shows the same macro, annotated to explain two lines of code. For a **Distinction** you would then need to explain at least one different line of code on another macro.

```
sub SaveAndPrint()
'
' SaveAndPrint Macro
' Macro to save and print the sheet
'
' Keyboard Shortcut: Ctrl+q
'
    ActiveWorkbook.Save
    ActiveWindow.SelectedSheets.PrintOut Copies:=1, Collate:=True
End Sub
```

This line saves the sheet

This line prints the sheet

This macro saves the workbook and then prints it out. It can be run from the keyboard shortcut Ctrl and q or from the button I put on the sheet.

Figure 7.28: *Annotating the code to show the function of two items of code.*

It is usually quite easy to work out what the lines of code do. If in doubt, record separate macros for each procedure you want to include, so you can see which line of code performs each procedure. You might also ask your teacher for advice if there is a particular piece of code you cannot work out.

Portfolio builder

In the other assessment objectives in this unit, you have created your own spreadsheet solution and carried out sorting, searching, modelling and graph/chart creation. For Assessment Objective 6, you need to think of a macro or macros that will make the use of your spreadsheet easier.

A simple 'save and print' macro is almost always useful, but it would be better if you could find something a little more individual to your own solution.

To gain a **Pass** in this objective you need to record a simple macro that can be run by a keyboard shortcut and print out the code.

To gain a **Merit** your macro must automate at least **two** tasks. You should also create a worksheet button to run your macro. You will need to print out a screenshot of your worksheet button as well as the code. You need to annotate the code giving a written description of what the macro does and the different ways it can be run.

To gain a **Distinction** you must create at least **two** macros, each of which must automate at least **two** tasks. You need to print out screenshots to show the buttons that will run your macros. You must then annotate your macro code not only to describe what each macro does and how it can be run, but you must also explain what at least **three** different items of macro code do. This must be lines of instruction code and not the name or lines of information at the top or the **End Sub** at the end.

UNIT ⑦

Databases – Design and Use

In this unit you will cover the following...

- **AO1** Design a relational database to meet the needs of an organisation
- **AO2** Construct a database according to the design
- **AO3** Interrogate a database using queries to sort and search
- **AO4** Create reports
- **AO5** Create a user interface
- **AO6** Test the database

CHAPTER 8
Databases – Skills

Overview:

It is assumed that you have already completed Unit 1 of the OCR National, so you have some experience of using a simple database to search and sort data. You are likely also to have used reports to output data.

This chapter reviews some of the basic database skills that you should already have used. It briefly looks at the creation of different types of query and report. You are recommended not to skip this section, as there may be some types of query introduced here that you have not met before.

Later in the chapter we will look at the use of more complex databases, containing more than one table of data, linked together. Such databases are called **relational databases**. You will learn about how these databases are structured and how the links can be used to enable queries and reports to combine data from more than one table.

In the later chapters of this unit you will be creating a relational database in order to fulfil the assessment requirements of this unit.

In order to complete the activities in this chapter you will need access to a number of additional files. These files are contained in the Chapter 8 Resources zip file which can be downloaded from the OCR Nationals in ICT (Units 6 & 7) Student Resources page on the Payne-Gallway website: www.payne-gallway.co.uk.

The Chapter 8 Resources folder also contains some extra activities and explanations to help you complete this unit. These are contained in a folder called Additional Activities and are as listed below:

Preliminary activities:

k Basic database terminology
l Forms

Key terms

Record

All the data about one item in the database. In a database about people, a record is all the data about one person. If the database is about books, then a record is all the data about one book. If the database is about cars, then a record is all the data about one car...

Field

One item of data in a record. In the pupil database, the fields include FirstName, LastName, Gender, etc. In a database about books, the fields might include title and author. In a database about cars, the fields might include make, model and registration number.

Key field

A unique field, used to identify a record. It is often necessary to have a special key field, such as a number, as two people might have the same name, two books might have the same title, etc. If there is already a field that is unique (for example, in a database about cars, the registration number will be different for every car), then that field can be used as the key field.

File

The complete collection of records, which you can think of as the complete table.

Flat-file database

A database where all the data is contained in a single table.

Queries

Often you will want to search the database and show only certain fields. For example, in a database of books you might want to see a list of titles of all the books by a certain author. In a database of houses for sale you might want to find all the houses in a certain price range and in a certain area, then just print out the addresses of these houses, in order of price.

Queries are a very flexible way of searching for particular records in a database. Once created they can be saved and used again and again, making them very useful when creating a database for inexperienced people to use.

Queries have three main features. They allow you to:

- choose the fields you want to see.
- choose any search criteria you want to set, so that you find only records that meet these criteria
- choose any fields you want to sort on, so you can have your final list in any order.

Queries are accessed by clicking on the **Queries** tab in the **Objects** panel of the main database window. When you first open the Queries window, there are no queries available, but you have the choice to create a new query in design view or by using the wizard.

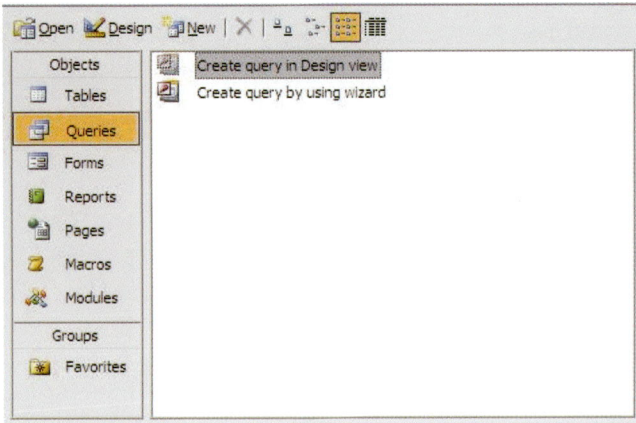

Figure 8.1: *Clicking on the **Queries** tab in the main database window.*

Although wizards are often very useful, the query wizard is very limited and it is just as easy to create your own query using **Design view**.

To see how to create a query, we will use an example from the database **School Data.mdb**, which is available in the online resources for this chapter. Suppose we wanted to print out a list showing the names and tutor groups of all the pupils in Maths group M8_1, but we want the list in alphabetical order of last name.

When you choose **Create query in Design view** you are asked where the data you want to use is stored. In a flat-file database such as **School Data** there is only one table of data, called **Pupils:tbl**, so you simply click on **Add** and then **Close** the window.

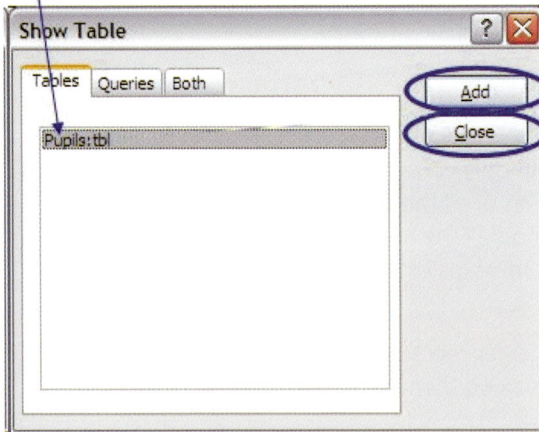

Figure 8.2: *Choosing the **Pupils:tbl** table and closing the window.*

You will now see the main **query design** window. This allows you to choose the fields you want to use in your query and to set any search and sort criteria.

We want to print out a list showing the names and tutor groups of all the pupils in Maths group M8_1. We therefore need to use the following fields:

- last name (LastName)
- first name (FirstName)
- tutor group (TutGp)
- maths group (MathsGp)

You choose the fields you want by double-clicking on them, one at a time, in the box showing the field names at the top of the design window:

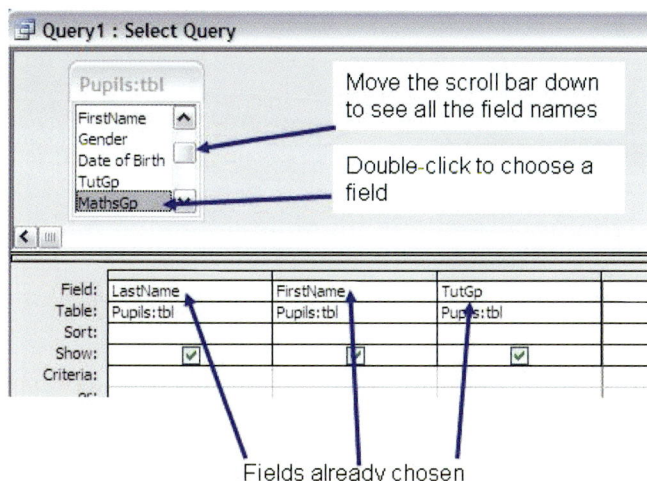

Figure 8.3: *Choosing the fields to include in a query.*

You can then type in any **search criteria** you want to use in order to find the records that you want. In this case we want those records where the maths group is **M8_1**. To find these you need to type **M8_1** into the **Criteria** box in the **MathsGp** column:

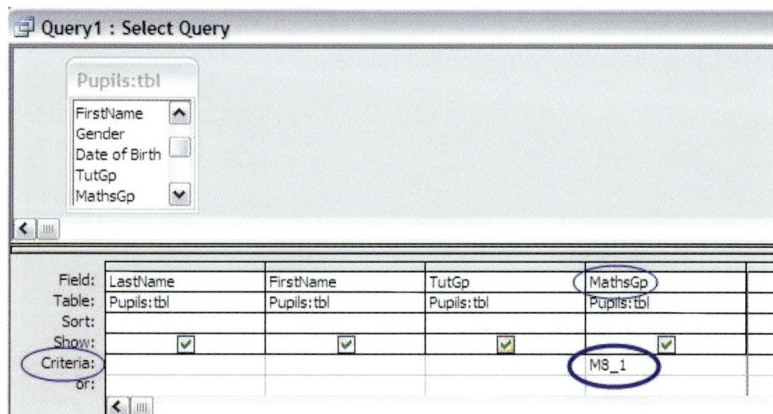

Figure 8.4: *Typing in the search criteria.*

When you have entered this, Access will add speech marks. That means you don't have to worry about these.

Next you think about whether or not you want to set any fields to **sort** on. In this example we want our list sorted in order of **LastName**. To do this you click in the **Sort** box in the **LastName** column and choose **Ascending** from the drop-down box.

Figure 8.5: *Setting a sort.*

Once the search and sort criteria have been set you can test the query by clicking the **Run** button on the toolbar.

Figure 8.6: *The **Run** button on the query toolbar.*

You can then check to make sure that you have got the output you expected. You should see the pupils from Maths group M8_1 listed in alphabetical order of last name.

LastName	FirstName	TutGp	MathsGp
Bibi	Shamir	8AA	M8_1
Collins	Steven	8AA	M8_1
Davies	Lee	8AA	M8_1
Coates	Gary	8DT	M8_1
Kaur	Narinder	8DT	M8_1
Whitehouse	Thomas	8DT	M8_1
Jacques	Steven	8EW	M8_1
Whitehouse	Adam	8EW	M8_1
Windsor	Emma	8EW	M8_1
Ali	Nazim	8GM	M8_1
OReilly	Matthew	8GM	M8_1
Vincent	Joanne	8GM	M8_1
Corden	Daniel	8JW	M8_1
Howells	David	8JW	M8_1
Lloyd	Adam	8JW	M8_1
Mackay	Gary	8LJ	M8_1
Parker	Sarah	8LJ	M8_1
Carter	Tanya	8RS	M8_1
Thompson	Abigail	8RS	M8_1
Rahman	Rahma	8SB	M8_1
Bennett	Adam	8SG	M8_1
Downing	Caroline	8SG	M8_1
Girn	Manjinder	8SG	M8_1
Post	Kelly	8SG	M8_1

Figure 8.7: *The completed query for pupils in Maths group M8_1.*

Look carefully at Figure 8.7. Although this is useful output to make sure the query works, if we had been asked to produce a list of pupils in this Maths group there would be no need to actually print the **MathsGp** column, as this is the same for all pupils. We can now change the design of the query to prevent this field being shown.

To go back to the query design screen you click on the **View** button on the left of the toolbar. This button shows a pencil, ruler and set square, which is the icon for **Design view**. If you ever need to provide evidence of a query you have created you should always produce a screenshot of the design view as well as the output created.

You will see that there is a tick in the **show** row for each of your chosen fields. You can click on this to remove it from the **MathsGp** column.

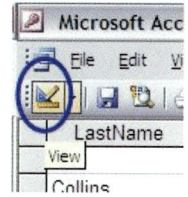

Figure 8.8:
Returning to the design view of the query.

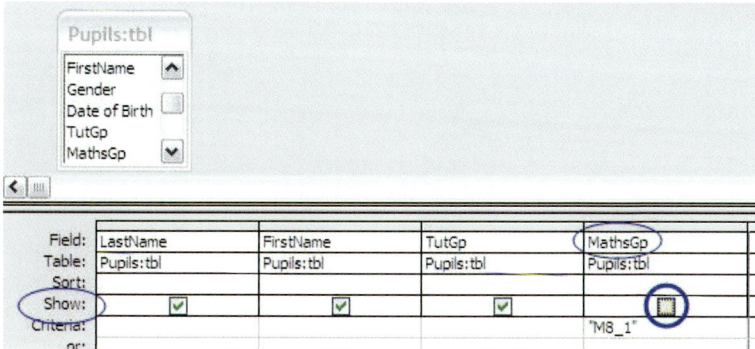

Figure 8.9: *Deselecting **MathsGp** so that this field does not show when you run the query.*

If you run the query again you will see that although the records shown are exactly the same as before, the MathsGp column is no longer shown. Compare Figures 8.7 and 8.10.

LastName	FirstName	TutGp
Bibi	Shamir	8AA
Collins	Steven	8AA
Davies	Lee	8AA
Coates	Gary	8DT
Kaur	Narinder	8DT
Whitehouse	Thomas	8DT
Jacques	Steven	8EW
Whitehouse	Adam	8EW
Windsor	Emma	8EW
Ali	Nazim	8GM
OReilly	Matthew	8GM
Vincent	Joanne	8GM
Corden	Daniel	8JW
Howells	David	8JW
Lloyd	Adam	8JW
Mackay	Gary	8LJ
Parker	Sarah	8LJ
Carter	Tanya	8RS
Thompson	Abigail	8RS
Rahman	Rahma	8SB
Bennett	Adam	8SG
Downing	Caroline	8SG
Girn	Manjinder	8SG
Post	Kelly	8SG

Figure 8.10: *The query with **MathsGp** not showing.*

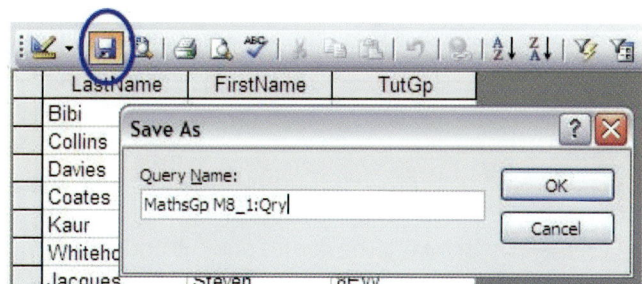

Figure 8.11: *Saving a query.*

If you have created a query that you will want to use again, you can save it so that it can be easily run in the future without having to create it again. Simply click on the **Save** icon on the toolbar and enter a name. Figure 8.11 shows this query being saved as **MathsGp M8_1:qry**.

Activity 1: Creating simple queries...

In this activity you will:

- create queries using design view
- set search criteria
- set sort criteria
- run queries
- save queries
- create evidence of the queries you make.

▶ Load the **School Data Activity 1.mdb** database.

▶ If you have not done so already, read through pages 97–101 and create a query to create a list of names and tutor groups of pupils in Maths group M8_1.

▶ Save your query.

If this query was to be evidence for your assessed portfolio you would need to create **two** screenshots – one of the **design screen** and one of the **result** of the query. You should also print the **result** of the query and provide this as evidence alongside the two screenshots. It is best to wait until your query is working before you do this.

▶ Create a screenshot showing the **design screen** of your final query. It should look like Figure 8.9.

▶ Paste your screenshot into a new page in your word processor.

▶ Create a screenshot showing the **result** of your final query. It should look like Figure 8.10.

▶ Paste this onto your word processor page.

▶ Add a suitable title and a sentence of explanation showing what you were looking for. The file **Portfolio evidence for a query.jpg**, provided in the online resources for this chapter, gives an example of what your final page might look like.

Now carry out the following queries. Create a page of evidence for each.

1 Find all the names and tutor groups of pupils in English group **E7_1**. Sort this list in order of last name.
2 Create a list of pupils in tutor group **9SE** showing their names and gender. Sort this list in order of gender, with boys first.
3 Create a list showing the names and full addresses of pupils who live in **Reed Road**. Sort the list in order of house number.

You can find all these queries in the version of the database called **School Data Activity 2.mdb**.

Parameter queries

In Activity 1 you created a query to find all the pupils in Maths group M8_1. However, the user of the database might want a class list for *any* Maths group, not just that one.

You *could* create and save a new query for each Maths group, but this would be very time-consuming and the user would be left with a huge number of queries to look through each time.

Access allows you to create **parameter queries**, where you can set the structure of the query, choosing the fields to be shown and the field(s) to be searched and sorted on, but leaving the actual criteria to be filled in by the user. This is done by entering an instruction inside square brackets **[ ]** in the **Criteria** box.

Key terms

Parameter

Data that is passed to a query when it is run, rather than set in the query itself.

In the query for pupils in Maths group M8_1, we would set up the query exactly as before, but instead of writing **M8_1** in the **Criteria** box for **MathsGp**, we would write an instruction inside square brackets, e.g. **[Enter the Maths Group required]**. This allows the user to choose *any* Maths group and send it to the query as a **parameter**.

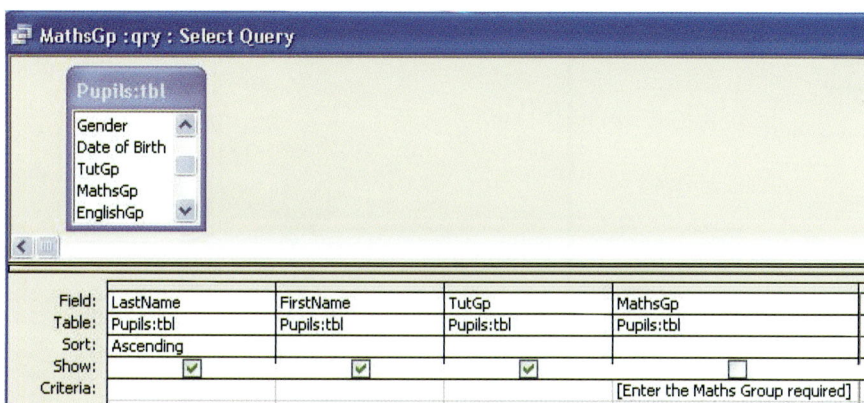

MathsGp :qry : Select Query

Pupils:tbl

Gender
Date of Birth
TutGp
MathsGp
EnglishGp

Field:	LastName	FirstName	TutGp	MathsGp
Table:	Pupils:tbl	Pupils:tbl	Pupils:tbl	Pupils:tbl
Sort:	Ascending			
Show:	☑	☑	☑	☐
Criteria:				[Enter the Maths Group required]

Figure 8.12: A parameter query to search for a particular Maths group.

When this query is run, a box opens up showing the instruction that was entered between the square brackets. This tells the user to enter the Maths group required. When a group is entered then the query will search for that one.

Enter Parameter Value [?][X]

Enter the Maths Group required

[   ]

[OK] [Cancel]

Figure 8.13: Running a parameter query.

By using parameter queries, we can save much more flexible queries, so that a range of searches can be carried out.

In the **School Data** database, we might set three parameter queries to search for a particular Maths group, a particular English group and a particular Tutor group – these would allow a range of class lists to be produced. We might also set up parameter queries to search for pupils by first name and by last name, to help teachers find information about pupils. We could also set up a more flexible parameter query to search for a particular street, rather than the very specific **Reed Road** search you created in Activity 1.

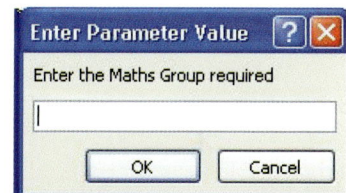

Activity 2: Parameter queries...

In this activity you will:

● create and save some parameter queries
● test your queries with a range of data.

▶ Load the **School Data** database that contains the queries you saved in Activity 1. Alternatively you can load the **School Data Activity 2.mdb** file.

▶ Choose the query you created to find the pupils in Maths group M8_1 and open it up in **Design view**.

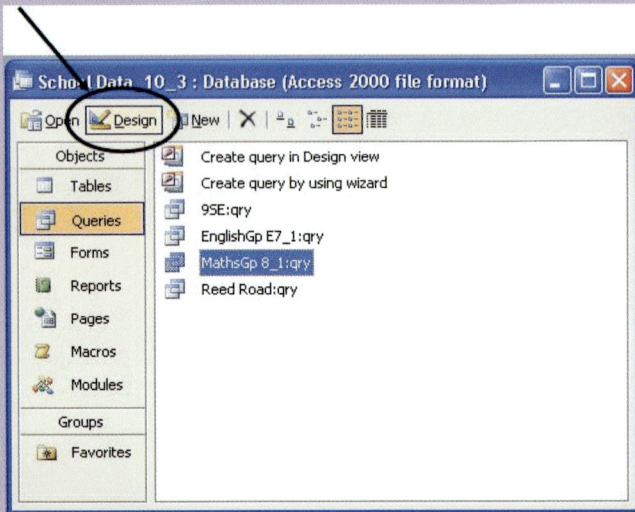

Figure 8.14: Opening a query in Design view.

▶ Alter the **Criteria** box in the **MathsGp** column so that it asks the user to input the particular group required, as shown in Figure 8.12 above.

▶ **Run** your query a few times, entering different groups each time.

▶ When you are happy that your query is working, save it using **File/Save As**, so that you can give it a more appropriate name, such as **MathsGp:qry**.

You should now be able to use the queries you created in Activity 1 to create the following:

1 A query that allows the user to create a list for any English group.
2 A query that allows the user to create a list for any Tutor group.
3 A query that allows the user to find all the pupils who live in a particular street.

You can find all these queries in the version of the database called **School Data Activity 3.mdb**.

Now that you have created the more flexible parameter queries you no longer need the more specific ones you created in Activity 1.

▶ Right click on your query to find the pupils in **9SE**, then choose **Delete**.

▶ Delete the other queries you created in Activity 1.

More complex queries

Often we want to find records in a database that meet more than one criterion. For example, a car dealer might want to search the customer database to find all the customers who bought a certain model of car during a particular month. A librarian might want to search a library file for all books on a particular topic that are suitable for a particular age range. In the **School Data** file that we have been using, we might want to find all the pupils who are in both Maths group M8_1 and English group E8_1.

You can set as many criteria as you like in the design view of a query. Figure 8.15 shows the design of a query to find all the pupils who are in **both** Maths group M8_1 **and** English group E8_1. You will see that the records will be sorted in order of last name and that last name, first name, gender and tutor group will be shown.

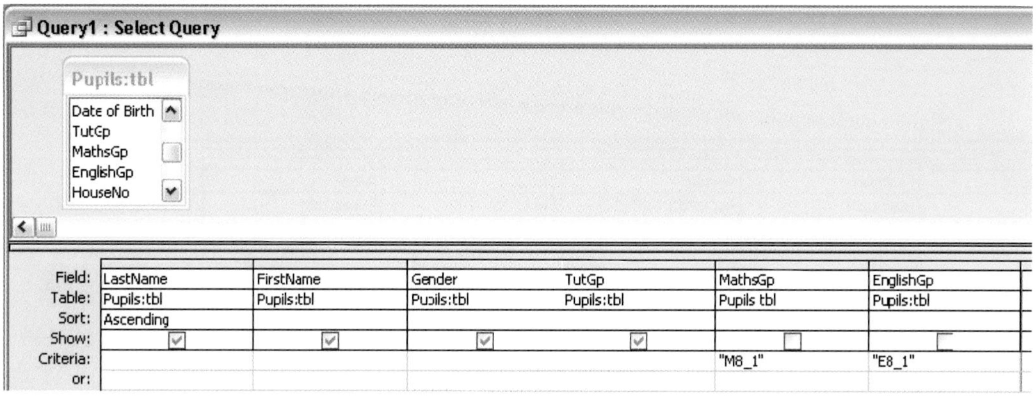

Figure 8.15: *Query to find pupils who are in both Maths group M8_1 and English group E8_1.*

Whenever you put more than one search on the **Criteria** row the computer will search for records that meet **all** the criteria set.

One or more of the criteria can be parameters, to allow the user to select the specific data required. For example, you might want to create a general query that allows the user to search for pupils who are in both Maths and English groups specified (see Figure 8.16).

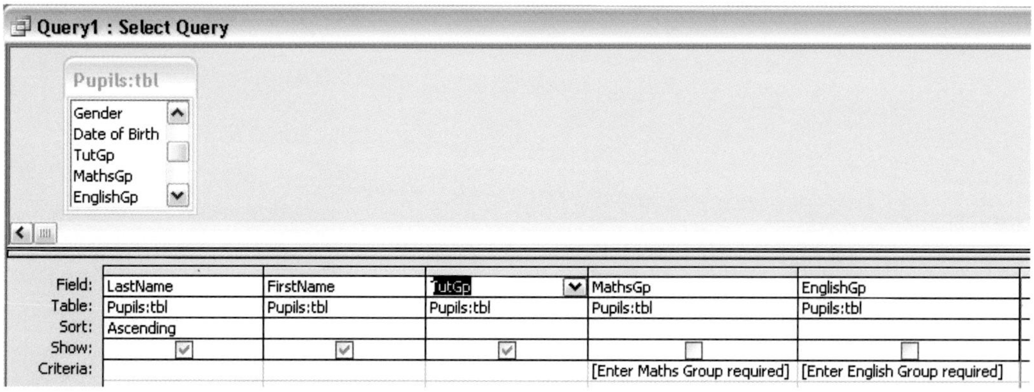

Figure 8.16: *Multiple criteria with parameters.*

If you have more than one question, then they will be asked in the order in which they have been put into the design table, from left to right.

Sometimes you might not want to match the whole of a field. For example, you might want to find all the Year 10 boys who live in West Ruxton. Here you need to set three criteria. The **Area** field needs to be "West Ruxton" and the **Gender** field needs to be "M". However, there isn't a field that just shows the year group, although this information is contained in the tutor group name in the **TutGp** field. In order to find everyone in Year 10 we use the criterion **10***. This means we want to find all the entries that start with **10**. The * means that there may be other characters after the 10. Figure 8.17 shows what you would enter into the design grid for this query.

Field:	LastName	FirstName	Gender	TutGp	Area
Table:	Pupils:tbl	Pupils:tbl	Pupils:tbl	Pupils:tbl	Pupils:tbl
Sort:	Ascending				
Show:	☑	☑	☑	☑	☑
Criteria:			"M"	10*	"West Ruxton"

Figure 8.17: *A query to find all Year 10 boys who live in West Ruxton.*

This query can be thought of as **Gender = "M" AND Area = "West Ruxton" AND TutGp = Like 10***. The **AND**s mean that **all** of the criteria need to be true.

Suppose we want to find all the pupils who are **either** in Maths group M9_1 **or** M9_2. This is a different sort or search – we don't want just the records where **both** of these things are true – in fact there won't be any pupils who are in both Maths groups at once! Instead we want those who are in one group **OR** another.

We can write **OR** in a box as one of the criteria.

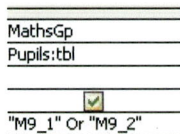

MathsGp
Pupils:tbl

☑
"M9_1" Or "M9_2"

Figure 8.18: *Using **OR** as one of the criteria.*

You can pass a parameter to one or both sides of an **OR**, as shown in Figure 8.19.

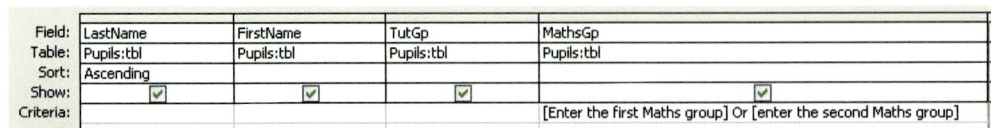

Field:	LastName	FirstName	TutGp	MathsGp
Table:	Pupils:tbl	Pupils:tbl	Pupils:tbl	Pupils:tbl
Sort:	Ascending			
Show:	☑	☑	☑	☑
Criteria:				[Enter the first Maths group] Or [enter the second Maths group]

Figure 8.19: *Using parameters in an **OR** query.*

⊘ NOTES

When you enter 10* Access will automatically change this into Like "10*".

A user cannot use the * in a parameter search.

If the two criteria you want in an **OR** search are in different fields, you need to use a different **Criteria** row for each one. For example, suppose we want to find all the pupils who are **either** in Maths group M9_1 **or** English group E9_1. To do this, we enter the Maths group in one row and the English group in the other (see Figure 8.20).

Field:	LastName	FirstName	TutGp	MathsGp	EnglishGp
Table:	Pupils:tbl	Pupils:tbl	Pupils:tbl	Pupils:tbl	Pupils:tbl
Sort:					
Show:	✓	✓	✓	✓	✓
Criteria:				"M9_1"	
or:					"E9_1"

Figure 8.20: *Finding pupils who are in Maths Group M9_1 OR English group E9_1.*

You can combine **AND**s and **OR**s. For example, Figure 8.21 shows a query to find the pupils who are either boys from tutor group 9JS who live in East Ruxton or girls from tutor group 9RB who live in East Ruxton.

Field:	LastName	FirstName	Gender	TutGp	Area
Table:	Pupils:tbl	Pupils:tbl	Pupils:tbl	Pupils:tbl	Pupils:tbl
Sort:					
Show:	✓	✓	✓	✓	✓
Criteria:			"M"	"9JS"	"East Ruxton"
or:			"F"	"9RB"	"East Ruxton"

Figure 8.21: *Combining ANDs and ORs in a query.*

You can also sort on more than one field. For example, most class lists will be sorted in order of last name, but if any two pupils have the same last name, these will then need sorting in order of first name. This needs a sort firstly on **LastName** and then on **FirstName**. If you choose more than one field to sort on, Access will sort in order (left to right) that you have put the fields in the design table. Figure 8.22 shows a sort in order of last name, then first name.

Field:	LastName	FirstName
Table:	Pupils:tbl	Pupils:tbl
Sort:	Ascending	Ascending
Show:	✓	✓
Criteria:		

Figure 8.22: *Sorting by LastName then by FirstName.*

If you ever need to alter the order in which fields appear in your design table, you can drag them to a different place by clicking on the small box immediately above the field name.

Field:	LastName	FirstName	TutGp	MathsGp	
Table:	Pupils:tbl	Pupils:tbl	Pupils:tbl	Pupils:tbl	
Sort:	Ascending				
Show:	✓	✓	✓	☐	
Criteria:				[Enter the Maths Group	
or:					

Figure 8.23: *Selecting and dragging a field.*

Activity 3: More complex queries...

In this activity you will:

- create a query that searches using multiple criteria
- create a query that sorts on two criteria.

▶ Load the **School Data** file that contains the queries you saved in Activity 2. Alternatively you can load the file **School Data Activity 3** from the online resources.

Query 3A

▶ Create the query shown in Figure 8.15 to find all the pupils who are in **both** Maths group M8_1 **and** English group E8_1. The output should show the last name, first name, gender and tutor group of the pupils found. The records should be sorted in order of last name.

▶ Test your query by running it.

▶ Return to the **Design view** of your query and alter it so that both Maths and English groups are prompted for, as shown in Figure 8.16.

▶ Test your new query.

▶ **Save** your final query using a suitable name.

Query 3B

▶ Create and test a query to find all the Year 10 boys who live in West Ruxton, as shown in Figure 8.17.

▶ Change your query to find all the boys from tutor group 10MM who live in West Ruxton.

▶ Change your query so that a tutor group, gender and area are all passed as parameters to the query.

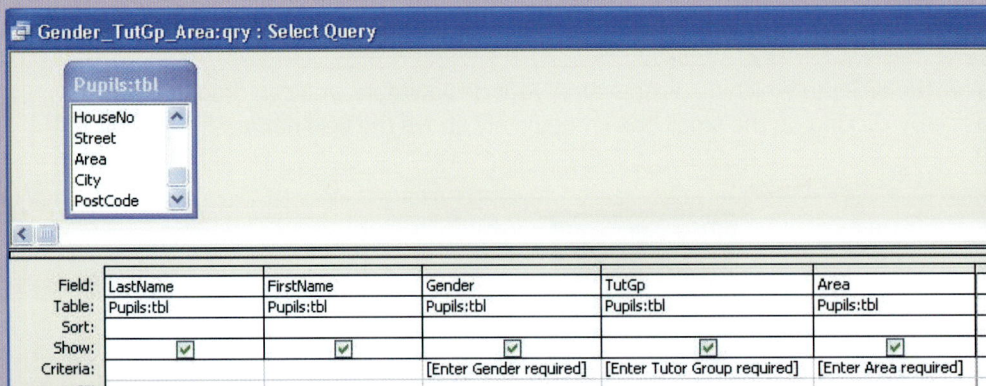

Gender_TutGp_Area:qry : Select Query

Pupils:tbl
HouseNo
Street
Area
City
PostCode

Field:	LastName	FirstName	Gender	TutGp	Area	
Table:	Pupils:tbl	Pupils:tbl	Pupils:tbl	Pupils:tbl	Pupils:tbl	
Sort:						
Show:	✓	✓	✓	✓	✓	
Criteria:			[Enter Gender required]	[Enter Tutor Group required]	[Enter Area required]	
or:						

Figure 8.24: *Parameter query on gender, tutor group and area.*

▶ When you have tested your final query, save it using a suitable name.

Query 3C

▶ There is a way of using a parameter query to find just part of a field, such as year group, but this has to be set in the query itself. Try editing your query as shown in Figure 8.25.

Field:	LastName	FirstName	Gender	TutGp	Area
Table:	Pupils:tbl	Pupils:tbl	Pupils:tbl	Pupils:tbl	Pupils:tbl
Sort:					
Show:	☑	☑	☑	☑	☑
Criteria:			[Enter Gender required]	Like [Enter Year required] & "*"	[Enter Area required]
or:					

Figure 8.25: *Parameter query on gender, year and area.*

The **Like** indicates to the computer that we are not looking for an exact match, then the **&** indicates that there are two parts that we are looking for – one part passed as a parameter by the user, then any number of characters afterwards, indicated by the *****.

▶ Test your new query, then use **Save As** to save it as a separate query to the tutor group one you saved before.

Query 3D

▶ Create and test a new query, to find all pupils who are **either** in Maths group M9_1 **or** M9_2, as shown in Figure 8.18.

▶ Edit your query so that both the groups are passed as parameters by the user, as shown in Figure 8.19.

▶ Now set it to sort on **both** last name **and** first name, as shown in Figure 8.22.

▶ When you have tested your new query, save it using a suitable name.

You can find all these queries in the version of the database called ***School Data Activity 4.mdb***.

Reports

Queries will produce output in table form, which can be printed if required. However, apart from choosing the fields to be output, you have little control over the final printout. **Reports** allow you to create well-formatted printouts, with suitable layout and titles. They can also be used to produce very specific types of printout, such as address labels.

Reports can also be created using data directly from tables, although it is more common to create a query with the output you require, then create a report based on this query.

To create a report, first click on **Reports** in the **Objects** panel of the main database window. When you first click on this there are no reports available, but you have the choice to create a new report in design view or by using the wizard.

Although it is best to create queries in design view, reports can most easily be created using the wizard. This gives a few choices of design, covering most normal requirements.

To see how to create a report, we will use an example from the ***School Data*** database. When you choose **Create report by using wizard** you are first asked to choose the table or query on which to base the report. For this example, we will choose **MathsGp:qry**.

*Figure 8.26: Choosing the **MathsGp:qry** query from the drop-down list in the wizard.*

You are then asked to choose the fields to include on your report. Very often you have already selected the fields in your query, so you can click on the **Select all fields** button which is indicated in Figure 8.27. However, if you only want some of the fields, you can click on them one at a time and choose the **Select this field** button.

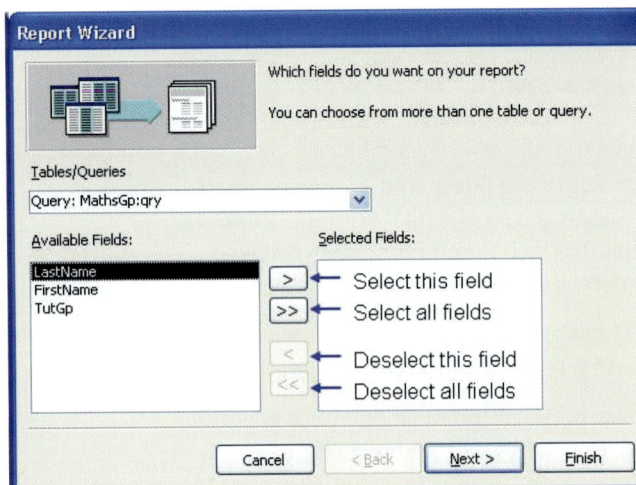

Figure 8.27: Selecting the fields to include on a report.

By choosing fields one at a time, you can also change the order in which they will appear on the report. When you have chosen the fields you want, click on the **Next** button.

The next screen asks if you want any grouping levels. This allows the records to be printed in groups. Usually you won't need to select anything here, so you would just click on **Next**.

You are then asked if you want to sort by any fields. Although you have already set the sorting you need in your query, you are advised to select these again at this stage. This is not a difficult or time-consuming job and it can prevent problems when creating more complex queries later. When using sort in the report wizard the fields will be re-ordered – if you wish to maintain the field order, you can do this by sorting in design view.

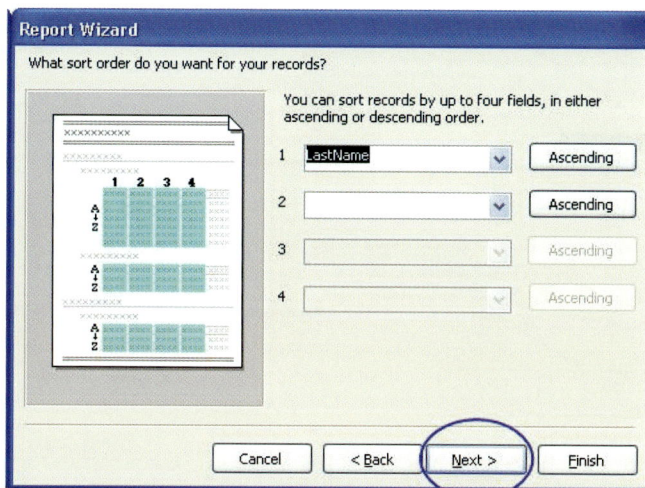

Figure 8.28: *Creating a report using the wizard: selecting the sort order.*

The next screen offers you a choice of ways of presenting your report – as a table (**Tabular**), in a single column (**Columnar**) or with each record underneath the other, spread out across the table (**Justified**). Look at the files ***Report_columnar.jpg***, ***Report_tabular.jpg*** and ***Report_justified.jpg*** provided with the online resources for this chapter – these show the three different options for the MathsGp report. You will probably agree that **tabular** is the one that you will use most often. When you have chosen the type of report you click on **Next**.

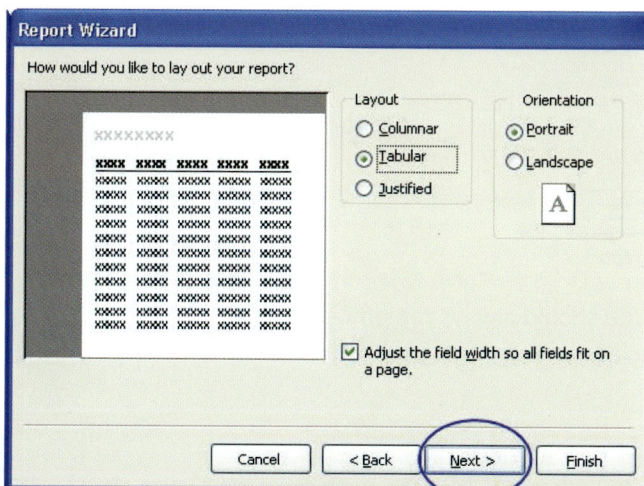

Figure 8.29: *Creating a report using the wizard: selecting the layout.*

The next screen gives more formatting choices with some different fonts, colours and lines. You can click on each one to see the basic format, then choose the one you want and click on **Next**.

Figure 8.30: *Creating a report using the wizard: selecting the formatting.*

The last screen asks you to name your report. It is good practice to choose a name ending in **:rpt**.

Figure 8.31: *Creating a report using the wizard: naming the report.*

The report shows you how many pages there are. You should always remember to check this before printing your report.

Now let's go back and look at one of the options we skipped over regarding grouping levels. Figure 8.32 shows what this report would have looked like if we had chosen to group the records on tutor group (see bottom of page 110).

MathsGp: qry

TutGp	LastName	FirstName
8AA		
	Collins	Steven
	Davies	Lee
	Bibi	Shamir
8DT		
	Coates	Gary
	Kaur	Narinder
	Whitehouse	Thomas
8EW		
	Jacques	Steven
	Whitehouse	Adam
	Windsor	Emma

Figure 8.32 Report grouped on tutor group.

Activity 4: Creating reports...

In this activity you will:

- create and print a report using the results of a query
- investigate the range of standard reports.

▶ Load the *School Data* file that contains the queries you saved in Activity 3. Alternatively you can load the *School Data Activity 4.mdb* file.

▶ Follow the steps above to create and print a report based on your **MathsGp:qry** query.

▶ Now create a report for each of the queries you have saved. Experiment with different styles and formats for each one, so you can see what each one offers.

▶ Print out **one** report using each different style. Label them to show the style chosen, then store them safely – you will be able to use these later to remind you of the different styles available.

Normally if you were creating reports for a database you would stick to the same style for each one. However, at this stage you should be investigating all the different styles.

Relational databases

The **flat-file** databases we have worked with so far have their limits – they can only deal with data that can be stored in a single table.

Very often we might want to link information about different types of item. For example, a librarian needs not only to store data about books but also about borrowers. This could be done by creating two separate databases – one for the books and one for the borrowers. However, if the librarian wishes also to record details about the books currently on loan to borrowers, there is also a need to link these two sets of data together.

A **relational database** is one where there is more than one table of data, with links between the different tables. In the library database example, a relational database would make it possible to link borrowers to the books they have borrowed.

Consider the **School Data** database we have been working with in this chapter. This stores data about the pupils in a school, including some of the classes they are in. A school would also need to store details about the teachers in the school. This would be different from the data about the pupils, and so would need to be in a different table.

You have already used the **School Data** database to produce class lists. If the data from the pupils table was linked to a table of data about teachers, then it would be possible to print class lists that included the name of the teacher, or to find out who an individual pupil's Maths teacher is.

You might think that it would be possible to add the teacher details to the pupils' records. For example we might add two new fields – **Maths teacher** and **English teacher**. However, if a teacher left the school and was replaced, we would then need to edit hundreds of pupil records. Also, if we wanted to store any additional data about teachers, such as telephone number, we would not want to have to enter this into hundreds of pupil records.

The main principle of relational databases is that they allow you to structure your data so that you don't have to enter the same data more than once. For example, you can store teacher details, including their telephone numbers, in a separate teacher table, so you only have to enter the details about each teacher once. Unnecessary duplication of data, which should be avoided, is called **data redundancy**.

Key terms

Relational database

A database consisting of a number of tables, linked together.

Activity 5: The structure of a relational database...

In this activity you will:

- use a relational database with more than one table
- look at the basic structure of a relational database
- use forms to add, edit and delete records in a relational database.

▶ Open the database **School Data Activity 5.mdb**. This contains a pupil table like the database you looked at in the previous activities, but has additional tables to allow teacher details to be added.

▶ Open the **Pupils:tbl** table. You will see that this is the same as the table used in the previous activities, but now the **EnglishGp** and **MathsGp** fields are missing.

▶ There is a **+** sign to the left of each record. Click on this for one of the pupils. This will **expand** the record to show details held on another table about this pupil: the Maths and English groups they are in.

		Number	LastName	FirstName	Gender	Date of Birth	Tut(
▶	+	4000	Baker	Leanne	F	01/05/1991	11HB
	+	4001	Butler	Ashley	M	15/07/1991	11HB
	+	4002	Butler	Samantha	F	01/09/1990	11HB
	+	4003	Davies	Kay	F	18/05/1991	11HB
	+	4004	Green	Daniel	M	26/07/1991	11HB
	+	4005	Hicks	Jodie	F	02/03/1991	11HB

Figure 8.33: *Clicking on the + sign expands a pupil record.*

▶ Open the **Teachers:tbl** table. This gives basic details of each teacher. For this example, only the teachers whose main subject is either Maths or English are included.

▶ Expand some of the teachers' records to show the groups they teach.

Teachers:tbl : Table

		Teacher ID		Title	First Name	Last Name	Main Subject
–	AJ			Mr	Alan	Jewkes	English

		ID	Subject
▶	+	E10_1	English
	+	E11_1	English
	+	E7_1	English
	+	E7_8	English
	+	E9_1	English
	+	E9_8	English
*			

		Teacher ID	Title	First Name	Last Name	Main Subject
+	AK		Mrs	Anna	Keeley	Maths
+	AM		Dr	Alex	Munroe	Maths
+	CK		Mr	Chris	Kent	Maths
+	EW		Mrs	Ellen	Wilkes	Maths

Figure 8.34: *An expanded teacher record.*

▶ Look at the two tables **PupilGroups:tbl** and **TeachingGroups:tbl**. You will see that these tables have been designed to show which groups pupils and teachers belong to. The information you found when you expanded the pupil and teacher records has come from these extra tables.

Although there is one other table (**Subjects:tbl**), which we will consider at the end of this chapter, these four tables form the main structure of the *School Data* relational database.

▶ Click on the **Relationships** icon on the toolbar. This shows how the tables are linked together.

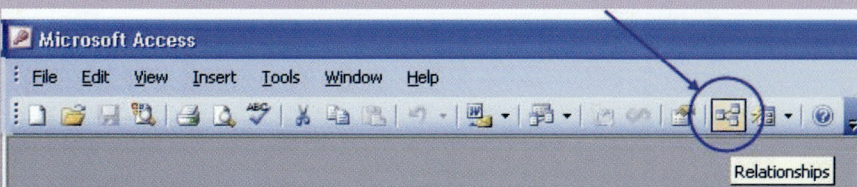

Microsoft Access

File Edit View Insert Tools Window Help

Relationships

Figure 8.35: *Showing the relationships.*

You can see that the four main tables are linked together by telling the computer which fields are the same. For example, the **Number** field in **Pupils:tbl** is the same as the **PupilNo** field in **PupilGroups:tbl**. This allows the software to link data from one table to another.

▶ Click on **Forms** in the **Objects** panel to see the forms that are available in this database. Double click on **Pupils:frm** to open it.

The form shows the data from **Pupils:tbl** and also the relevant records from **Pupil-Groups:tbl**. This allows easy entry of data about each pupil using a single form, even though it is to be stored in two separate tables.

The data about groups is held in a **subform** – a 'form within a form'. This has its own controls to allow you to easily scroll between records and add new records, although as there are only two records in the subform at present, these controls are not really needed.

▶ Click on some of the controls at the bottom of the subform and at the bottom of the main form, until you are happy you understand what each of them does.

Now you are going to use the form Pupils:frm to make some changes to the data.

▶ Add a new record for Hayley Farmer, who has joined tutor group 8SG. She has been put into Maths group M8_1 and English group E8_2. Her address is 2 Roseberry Drive, Rayton, Northingham, NT5 8RG. Her date of birth is 2nd May, 1994. She has been allocated a pupil number of 7224.

▶ Mustafa Haider has changed English group from group E10_7 to E10_6. Update the database with this change. Use the **Filter by form** tool on the toolbar to find Mustafa Haider's record. (If you are unsure how to do this, refer to the online resource activity *I Forms.doc*).

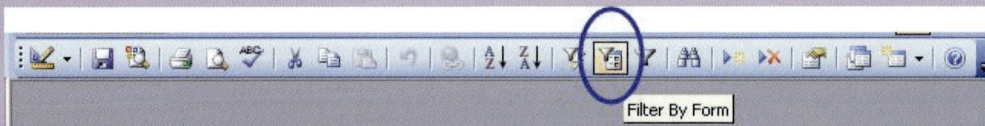

*Figure 8.36: The **Filter by form** button.*

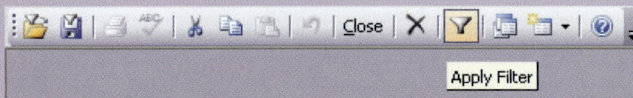

*Figure 8.37: Once you have entered the filter information, click the **Apply filter** button.*

▶ Emma Martin from tutor group 7BA has moved out of the area and left the school. Delete her record.

When you delete a pupil's record the usual 'Are you sure?' message reminds you that you are not only deleting a record from the **Pupils** table but also from another table (the **PupilGroups** table). While you always need to be very careful when deleting records from a database, you should be able to click on **Yes**.

Microsoft Office Access

⚠ Relationships that specify cascading deletes are about to cause 1 record(s) in this table and in related tables to be deleted.

Are you sure you want to delete these records?

[Yes]   [No]   [Help]

***Figure 8.38:** Deleting a pupil causes records to be deleted from more than one table.*

▶ Close down **Pupils:frm** and open the table **Pupils:tbl**. You should be able to find the new record you created for Hayley Farmer.

▶ Open the table **PupilGroups:tbl**. Here you should be able to find the **two** records you created for Hayley Farmer – one for her Maths group and one for her English group. You should also be able to see the record you updated for Mustafa Haider. You should find no records for Emma Martin (pupil number 8066).

▶ Close down the tables and open the form **Teachers:frm**.

▶ Use **Filter by form** to find Miss Beale's record. You will see that although English is her main subject she also teaches one Maths class. This database structure allows this to be recorded just like all her other classes.

At the moment this database only has details of Maths and English teachers. However, the structure allows other subject teachers and groups to be added.

▶ Add records for two French teachers, as shown in Figures 8.39 and 8.40.

Teachers:frm

Northingham Community College

Teacher ID PK

Title Mr   First Name Peter   Last Name Knowles

Main Subject French

Groups taught:

Group:	Subject:
F8_1	French
F7_2	French
F9_4	French
F10_1	French
F11_2	French
F7_5	French
F8_8	French
F9_6	French

Record: ◀◀ ◀ 9 ▶ ▶▶ ▶* of 9

Record: ◀◀ ◀ 8 ▶ ▶▶ ▶* of 16

***Figure 8.39:** New record for Mr Knowles, French teacher.*

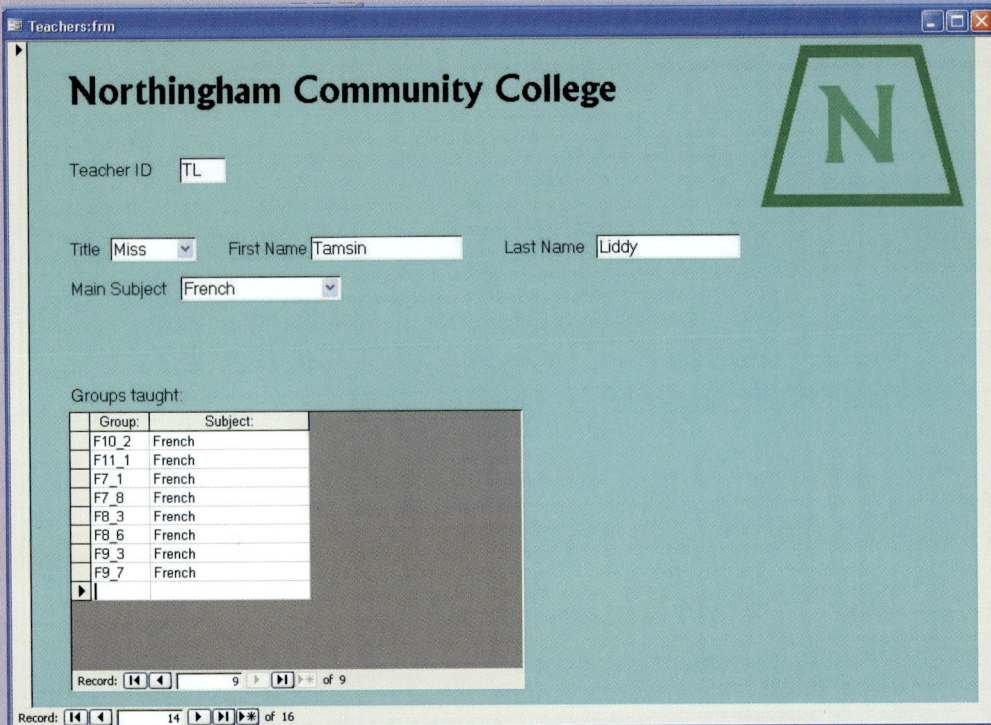

Figure 8.40: New record for Miss Liddy, French teacher.

▶ Open up the tables **Teachers:tbl** and **TeachingGroups:tbl** to see the new records you have added to each of these tables.

You should see that this structure is much more flexible than the flat-file database you used at the beginning of this chapter. Not only does it link pupils and teachers to classes, but it is now possible to add details of other groups — not just Maths and English.

Links between tables

Figure 8.41 shows the links between the tables in the **School Data** database.

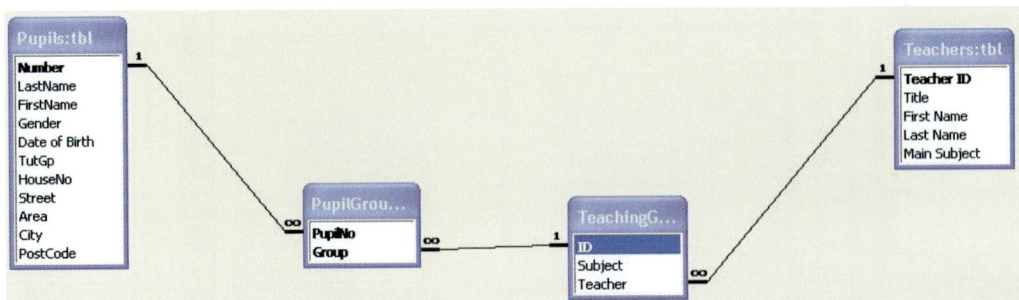

*Figure 8.41: Links in the **School Data** database.*

This shows that each of the tables is linked to one of the others by one common field, which is the most usual type of link:

- The **PupilNo** field in **PupilGroups:tbl** links to the **Number** field in **Pupils:tbl** – this is the unique key field in that table: the field used to identify each pupil. In this way, any item of data needed about the pupil can be found from **Pupils:tbl**, without needing to copy it into **PupilGroups:tbl**.
- The **Group** field in **PupilGroups:tbl** links to the **ID** field in **TeachingGroups:tbl** – this is the unique key field in that table: the field used to identify each group. For example, M11_1 is the unique identifier for Year 11 Maths group 1. In this way, any item of data, such as the subject, can be found from **TeachingGroups:tbl**.
- The **Teacher** field in **TeachingGroups:tbl** table links to the **TeacherID** field in **Teachers: tbl** table – this is the unique key field in that table: the field used to identify each teacher. In this way any item of data from **Teachers:tbl**, such as the teacher's name, can be attached to information from **TeachingGroups:tbl**.

Using these links it is possible to, for example, find the name of the teacher who teaches a particular pupil for a particular subject, even though this information is in different tables that are not directly linked to each other. It is these links that allow the creation of subforms so that data can be entered into more than one table from a single form.

Look closely at the lines between the tables. You will see that these are labelled with a **1** and a **∞**. The symbol **∞** is used to represent the word 'many'. For example, Figure 8.42 shows the relationship between **Teachers:tbl** and **TeachingGroups:tbl**. It shows that for every **one** teacher in **Teachers:tbl** there could be **many** (i.e. more than one) records in **TeachingGroups:tbl**. This is because each teacher will teach a number of different groups. This sort of relationship, where **one** record in one table can have **many** related records in another table, is called a **one–to–many** relationship.

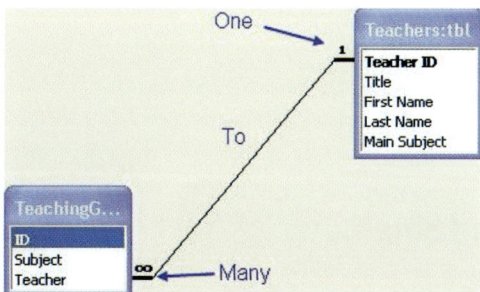

Figure 8.42: The one-to-many relationship between *Teachers:tbl* and *TeachingGroups:tbl*.

One-to-many relationships are the most common relationships to be found in a relational database.

There are two other possible relationships between sets of data:

- **One-to-one** relationships. This is where **one** record in one table corresponds to **one** record in another table. For example, each pupil has only one last name and one date of birth. This sort of relationship is usually contained in a single table. For example, the pupils' last names and dates of birth are contained within **Pupils:tbl**.
- **Many-to-many** relationships. This is where **many** records in one table correspond to **many** different records in another table. For example, each pupil belongs to **many** teaching groups, but each teaching group also has **many** pupils. Database software cannot deal with this type of relationship, so we have to design our database structures with **one-to-many** relationships. This is why there is the **PupilGroups:tbl** table. This simply acts as a link between the tables **Pupils:tbl** and **TeachingGroups:tbl**. Each pupil is in **many** groups, so there is a **one-to-many** relationship between **Pupils:tbl** and **PupilGroups:tbl**. And each teaching group has many pupils, so there is a **one-to-many** relationship between **TeachingGroups:tbl** and **PupilGroups:tbl**.

Take another look at the data inside these four tables to help you understand these relationships.

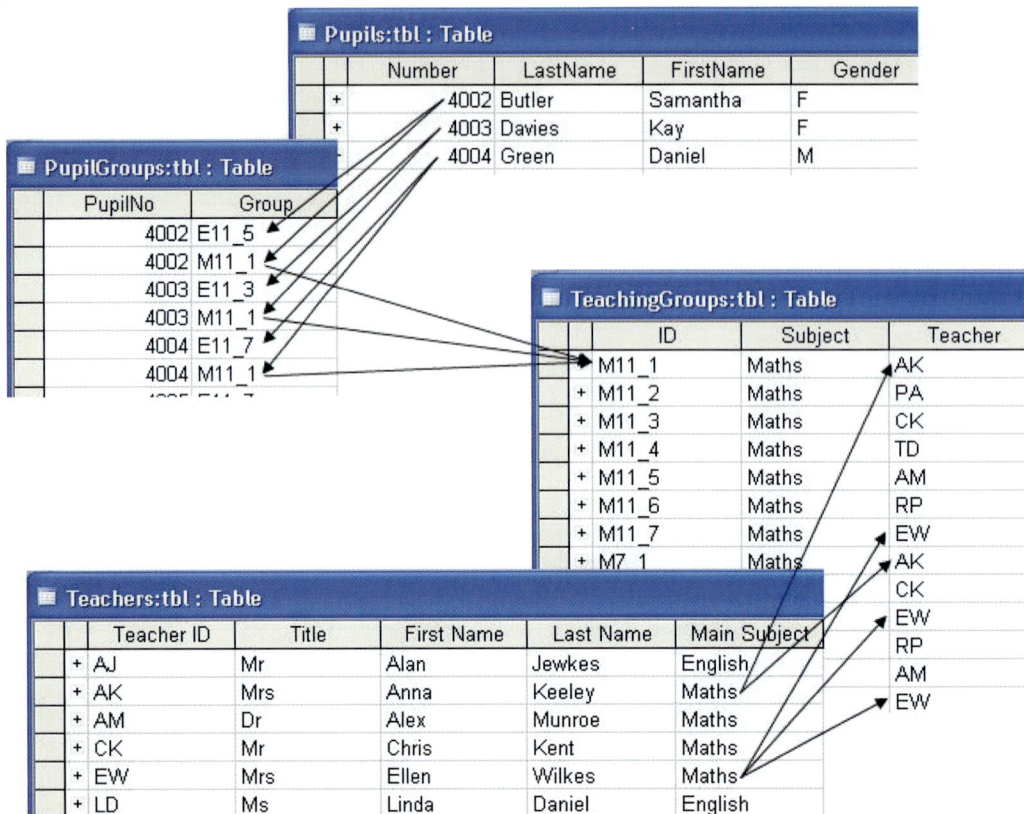

Figure 8.43: One-to-many relationships between tables.

Activity 6: Using the relationships between tables...

In this activity you will:

- create a query linking the data from different tables
- create a report to show data from different tables.

▶ Open the database you used in Activity 5. Alternatively you could use the database **School Data Activity 6.mdb** provided with the online resources for this chapter.

Earlier in this chapter you created queries from the single-table database to create lists of the names and tutor groups of pupils in particular Maths and English groups. Because all groups, regardless of the subject, are now in the same field in **PupilGroups:tbl** we can replace these queries with a single query to create a class list for any group.

▶ Open the **Queries** window and select **Create query in Design view** as before.

▶ Add the **Pupils:tbl** table as you did before, also the **PupilGroups:tbl**, then click on **Close**.

▶ Double click to select **LastName**, **FirstName** and **TutorGp** from **Pupils:tbl** and then select **Group** from **PupilGroups:tbl**.

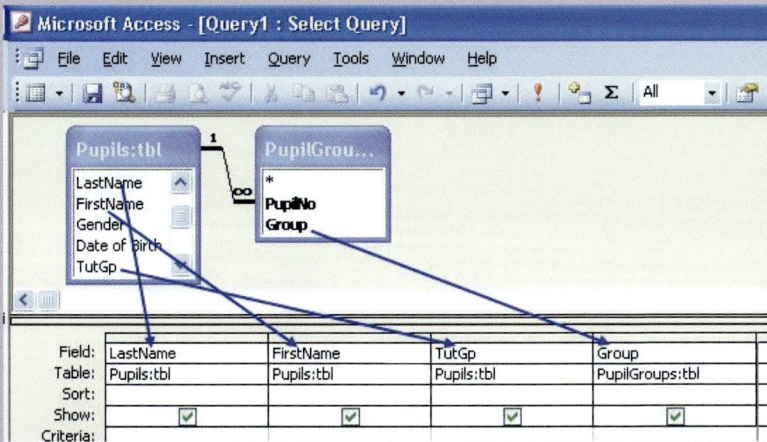

Figure 8.44: *Selecting fields from both tables.*

We now need to enter the search criteria. In this case we want the user to be able to specify a group name.

▶ Add the parameter query as shown in Figure 8.45.

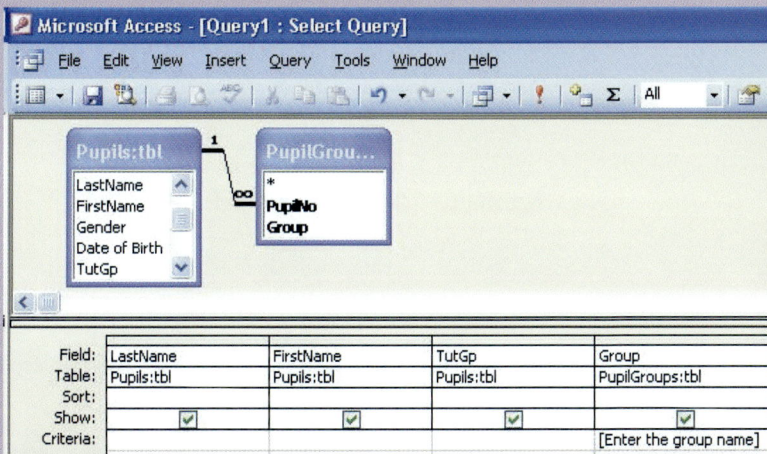

Figure 8.45: *Query with search criteria set so the user enters a group name.*

▶ Now set the query to sort in ascending order by **LastName** and then **FirstName**. Doing this ensures that if two pupils have the same last name they will appear in order of first name, as they would do on a class list.

▶ Run the query for Maths group M8_3 and check the final list. Notice how data from the two different tables is shown. A person using this query would not need to know that the **Group** is held in a different table from the rest of the pupil information.

▶ Click on the **Save** icon and save the query as **ClassList:qry**.

A school might find it useful to print class lists with the name of the teacher as well. The query can be extended to include this. The name of the teacher is stored in **Teachers:tbl**, so this needs to be added to the query:

▶ Return to the **Design view** of your query **ClassList:qry**.

▶ Right click in the top of the window, where the tables are shown, and choose
Show Table...

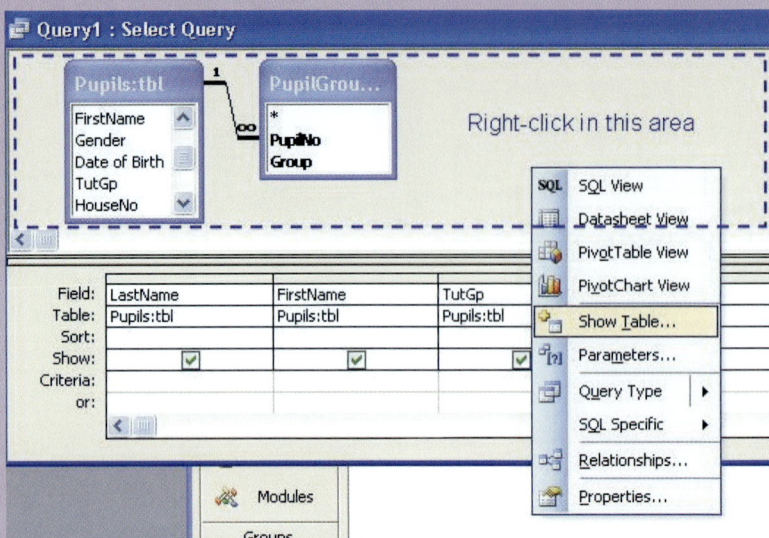

Figure 8.46: *Adding another table to a query design.*

▶ You cannot just add **Teachers:tbl** as this is not linked directly to the tables you are
already using, so you also need to add **TeachingGroups:tbl**. It does not matter in
what order you add the tables but you might like to drag them to a position where
you can see them and the links clearly.

▶ You can now add the fields **Title**, **FirstName** and **LastName** from the **Teachers:tbl**
table.

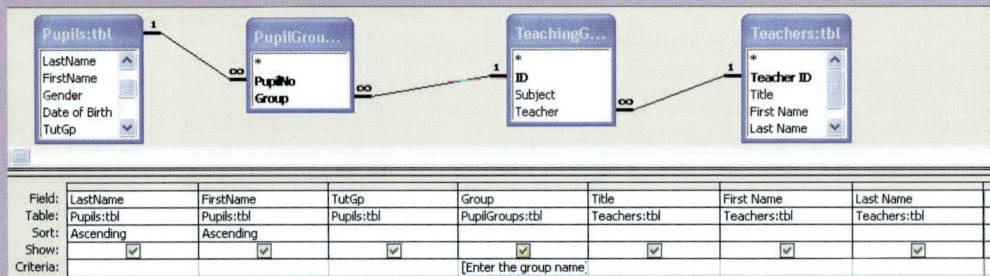

Figure 8.47: *Final query design.*

▶ Test your new query, then close it down,
saving the changes.

Queries are limited in how they can display the
information. Most of the time you should create a
report to show the results of the query:

▶ Select the **Reports** tab and choose **Create
report by using wizard**.

▶ Choose your **ClassList:qry** query and select
all fields using the **Select all fields** button as
shown in Figure 8.27.

⊘ **TIP**

**You must add sufficient
tables to a query so
that links are shown
between all of the
tables, even if there
are tables that you
don't want to actually
use in the query.**

▶ When you click on **Next** there is a new dialogue box, because you are using data from more than one table. You are asked to select different ways of viewing the data. Choose **by Teachers:tbl**, as this will give the name of the teacher at the top, with all the pupils for that teacher underneath. This will avoid printing the name of the teacher more than once as the query did.

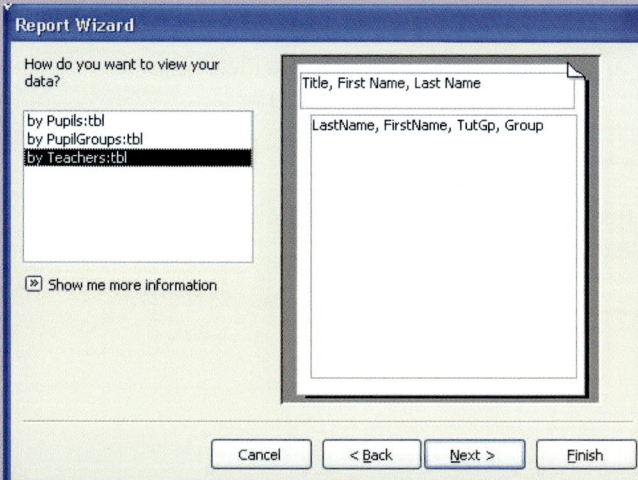

Report Wizard

How do you want to view your data?

by Pupils:tbl
by PupilGroups:tbl
by Teachers:tbl

Title, First Name, Last Name

LastName, FirstName, TutGp, Group

☒ Show me more information

| Cancel | < Back | Next > | Finish |

*Figure 8.48: Selecting to view the data by **Teachers:tbl**.*

▶ There is no need to add any grouping levels, so you can now click on **Next**

▶ At the next stage, select **LastName** then **FirstName** to sort on, then click on **Next**.

▶ At the next stage, choose one of the **Align left** options, as this will list all the pupils at the left of the page. You might want to try out the other options later, to compare results.

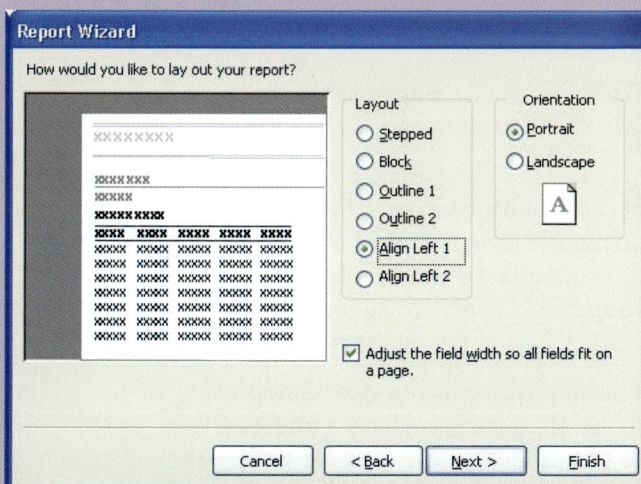

Report Wizard

How would you like to lay out your report?

XXXXXXX

XXXXXXX
XXXXX

XXXXXXXXX
XXXX XXXX XXXX XXXX XXXX
XXXX XXXX XXXX XXXX XXXX
XXXX XXXX XXXX XXXX XXXX
XXXX XXXX XXXX XXXX XXXX
XXXX XXXX XXXX XXXX XXXX
XXXX XXXX XXXX XXXX XXXX
XXXX XXXX XXXX XXXX XXXX

Layout
○ Stepped
○ Block
○ Outline 1
○ Outline 2
◉ Align Left 1
○ Align Left 2

Orientation
◉ Portrait
○ Landscape

A

☑ Adjust the field width so all fields fit on a page.

| Cancel | < Back | Next > | Finish |

*Figure 8.49: Choose **Align Left 1** or **2**.*

> **⊗TIP**
>
> There are many dialogue boxes when creating a report. If you are not sure what option to take, experiment! It is easy to delete a report and create a new one if you find it doesn't show the data as you wanted.

▶ Select a style of your choice, then give the report the name **ClassLists:rpt** and click on **Finish**.

▶ Test your report to find group **M8_3**. You should see already that this is more appropriate than the simple query output, as the teacher's name is shown only once, at the top of the list. You will see how to further improve reports in Chapter 13.

A closer look at tables

Tables are the basic elements of any database – they are where the data is stored. We might create forms, queries and reports to make accessing the data easier for the user but all of these eventually acquire their data from the tables. You saw in Activity 5 how any changes made in a form are reflected in the underlying tables and in Activity 6 how the data from these tables can be processed and presented in queries and reports.

In this last section of this chapter we will look at the structure of the *School Data* tables and the reasons for designing them in the way they are. You may find some of these ideas a little hard at first, but don't worry – more detail about this will be given in the next chapter, when you come to design a new database. It will be helpful if you have already looked at the structure of an existing database.

Whenever you set up a database the first thing you need to do is plan and create the tables. There are a number of questions that need to be asked:

- What data needs to be stored?
- What tables are needed?
- What fields are needed for each table?
- How will the tables be linked?
- What type of data will be stored in each field?
- What checking methods can be used to minimise data entry errors?

What data needs to be stored?

This first stage involves thinking about all the individual items of data needed. You might list these according to the main groups of data. For example, when planning the *School Data* database we could have come up with two lists. We know we need to store data about pupils and teachers, so we would produce one list for each. For example:

- pupils: name, address, date of birth, gender, tutor group, subject groups
- teachers: name, main subject, groups taught.

What tables are needed?

By splitting up the data into two groups we already know we need a **pupils table** and a **teachers table**. We then need to look at all the data we need to store and see if any of this would be repeated between the tables.

If we look at the list of pupil details that we need, we can see that each pupil has only one name, address, date of birth, gender and tutor group but will be in a number of different groups for different subjects. This tells us that there is a **one-to-many** relationship between pupils and teaching groups, so **subject groups** need to go into another table. This new table will need to contain the subject group and a link field to the pupil table.

Looking at the teacher details, we can see that each teacher will have only one name and main subject but will teach a number of different groups. Here again we have a **one-to-many** relationship, so the **teaching groups** need to be in another table. This new table will need to contain the teaching group and a link field to the teacher table.

We might wonder if these two extra tables might be the same. If this were the case then we would need a link to the pupil table, the group name and a link to the teacher table. However, as we have already seen, the relationship between pupils and teachers is many-to-many, so these cannot be in the same table.

What fields are needed for each table?

By deciding on the data to be stored we have already considered some of this question.

For pupils we need name, address, date of birth, gender and tutor group. Most of this data will be stored in single fields, but we must decide whether name and address each have a single field or are split into separate fields, as has been done in the **School Data** database. If you ever might want to search/sort on just part of the data (e.g. first or last name or area), then it is best to split them into separate fields. In this situation it is possible that we might want to search on any part of the name or address. We might also want to create a mail-merged letter, with the address split over a number of lines.

A similar decision is needed for teachers' names. Here we might want some flexibility, so that we could, for example, refer to **Mr Alan Jewkes**, **Mr Jewkes** or **Alan Jewkes** depending on the situation. Again, therefore, we would want to split up the name.

Each table also needs a **key field** (also called a **primary key**) – the unique field used to identify the record. In the case of pupils and teachers, we cannot use their names, as these may not be unique, so we need another field. School pupils are already given a unique *admissions number* when they join a school, and teachers are given a unique identifier for the timetable, usually a set of initials, so it seems sensible to use these as the key field. In many cases there is no obvious unique identifier, so the software can create a key field automatically.

This leads to the following fields for the **Pupils** table:

- **Admissions number** (this is shown in bold to show that it will be the primary key)
- Last name
- First name
- Gender
- Date of birth
- Tutor group
- House number
- Street
- Area
- Town/City
- Postcode.

The following fields will be required for the **Teachers** table:

- **Timetable initials**
- Title
- First name
- Last name
- Main teaching subject.

In the **Teaching groups** table, we need the name of the teaching group and a link to the teacher table. This link will be the primary key from the **Teachers** table, as it needs to identify the particular teacher's details for each group. It may be useful also to include the subject as a separate field. Therefore the fields will be:

- **Group name**
- Subject
- Teacher timetable initials.

The table containing the subject group and the link to the **Pupils** table is slightly different. We already have a table with information about the groups, so all we need here is a link to it. This sort of table is referred to as a **junction table** – its sole purpose is to link two other tables which are in a many-to-many relationship (there are many pupils in each group and each pupil is in many groups). The two fields *together* form the primary key – if you wrote them out as one long code, then each one would be unique. This leaves the last table with the following fields:

- **Group name**
- **Pupil admissions number**.

We really need a name for this table that gives us some indication of its contents. In the **School Data** database it is called **Pupil groups**.

How will the tables be linked?

When deciding on the fields above we have already considered how the tables need to be linked.

We know that we need to link the **Teachers** table to the **Teaching groups** table. For *one* record in the **Teachers** table there may be *many* records in the **Teaching groups** table. The first table (**Teachers**) is on the *one* side and we call this the **parent** table. The second table (**Teaching groups**) is on the *many* side and we call this the **child** table. We always link the primary key from the **parent** table to a corresponding field in the **child** table.

This means that between the **Teachers** and **Teaching groups** tables we would make a link from the **Timetable initials** in the **Teachers** table to the **Teacher timetable initials** in the **Teaching groups** table.

Similarly we need to link the **Pupils** table to the **Pupil groups** table. There will be *many* (more than one) records in the **Pupil groups** table for each *one* pupil, because each pupil is in more than one teaching group. This means that the **Pupil** table will be the parent and the **Pupil groups** table will be the child. We therefore need to link the **admissions number** from the pupil table to the **pupil admissions number** in the **Pupil groups** table.

It is often useful to draw these relationships on a diagram. If we did this at this stage we would see that there is a gap in the links (see Figure 8.50).

Teachers	Teaching groups	Pupils	Pupil Groups
Timetable initials	Group name	**Admissions number**	Group name
Title	Subject	Last name	**Pupil admissions number**
First name	Teacher timetable initials	First name	
Last name		Gender	
Main teaching subject		Date of birth	
		Tutor group	
		House number	
		Street	
		Area	
		Town/City	
		Post code	

Figure 8.50: Beginning to plan the links.

This diagram helps us see that the final link needed is between **Group name** in the **Teaching groups** table and **Group name** in the **Pupil groups** table. For each *one* record in the **Teaching groups** table there will be *many* records in the **Pupil groups** table, as there are many pupils in each teaching group. Therefore **Teaching groups** will be the parent table and **Pupil groups** will be the child table. This means that we need to link the **Group name** from the **Teaching groups** table to the **Group name** in the **Pupil groups** table, as shown in Figure 8.51.

Teachers	Teaching groups	Pupils	Pupil Groups
Timetable initials	**Group name**	**Admissions number**	**Group name**
Title	Subject	Last name	**Pupil admissions number**
First name	Teacher timetable initials	First name	
Last name		Gender	
Main teaching subject		Date of birth	
		Tutor group	
		House number	
		Street	
		Area	
		Town/City	
		Post code	

Figure 8.51: *The final links for the **School Data** database.*

What type of data will be stored in each field?

When you set up a computer database you must not only specify the data to be stored but you must also tell the computer what type of data it is. Computers store numbers and text in different ways. Calculations can only be performed on numbers, so if you want the computer to be able to do this you must tell it that the data is a **number**. Sometimes you might have something that is made up of numeric digits that you do not want to use in calculations – for example, telephone numbers. Telephone numbers often start with the digit **0**, but if you type a number starting with **0** the computer will ignore it, so we would tell the computer that a telephone number field was **text**.

The most common data types are:

- **Text**.
- **Number**
- **Date/Time**
- **Currency**
- **AutoNumber**
- **Yes/No**

You might like to think of the computer memory as a huge warehouse getting ready to store data. By setting the field types you are telling the computer what sort of boxes to get ready to store the different fields you want. We will look at all these data types in more detail in Chapter 9.

As well as the data type, at this stage we would decide on the **Field Names** – the titles/column headings for each field. These can be thought of as the labels on the storage boxes.

In addition to the *type* of field, you also need to give further details such as the number of characters required in a text field. This is like telling the warehouse manager how big each box needs to be.

It is important that any fields to be linked must be given the same data type in each table.

You can see the settings for the fields in each table in the **School Data** database by looking at the table in **Design View**. Make sure you have **Tables** selected in the **Objects** panel. Then select the table you want and click on **Design**.

The top of the design view shows a list with the name of each field and the data type chosen for each.

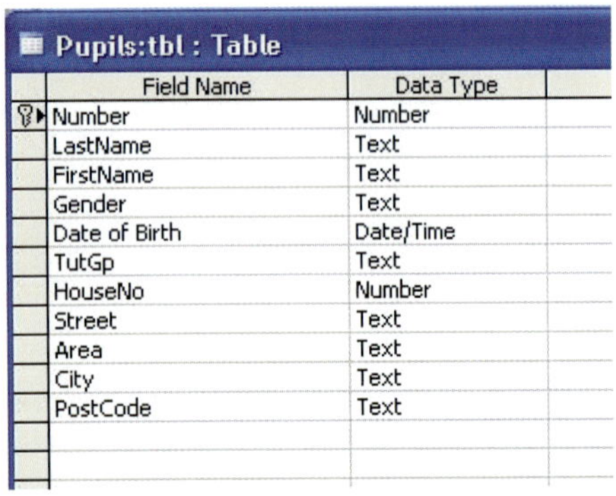

Field Name	Data Type	
Number	Number	
LastName	Text	
FirstName	Text	
Gender	Text	
Date of Birth	Date/Time	
TutGp	Text	
HouseNo	Number	
Street	Text	
Area	Text	
City	Text	
PostCode	Text	

Pupils:tbl : Table

Figure 8.52: *The top of the table **Pupils:tbl** as seen in Design View.*

The bottom of the design view shows other settings for each field. In particular the size of the field.

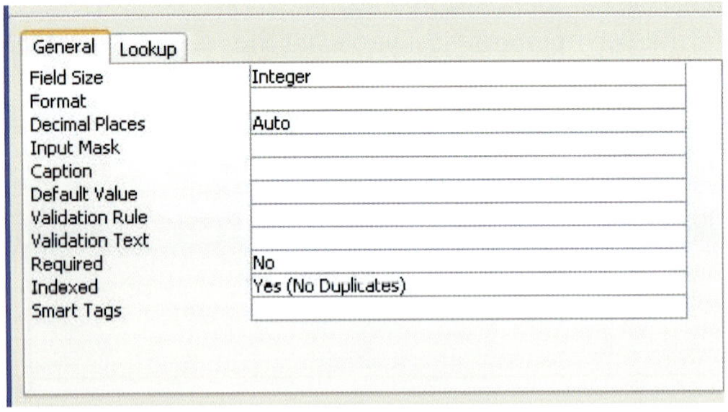

General	Lookup
Field Size	Integer
Format	
Decimal Places	Auto
Input Mask	
Caption	
Default Value	
Validation Rule	
Validation Text	
Required	No
Indexed	Yes (No Duplicates)
Smart Tags	

Figure 8.53: *The bottom of the table **Pupils:tbl** as seen in Design View.*

You might like to spend some time looking at the settings for the tables in the **School Data** database. More details of these settings will be given in the next chapter, when you will start to design your own database.

What checking methods can be used to minimise data entry errors?

It is very easy to make a typing error when entering data into a computer. Once inaccurate data has been entered it is often difficult to spot. Although a human could be expected to notice if a record suggested that a school pupil was 111 years old, a computer cannot do this automatically. Therefore we set limits to as many fields as we can, to tell the computer what sort of data to accept in a field. These limits are called **validation checks**.

We might, for example, tell the computer that a value entered into a numeric or currency field has to be within a certain range. For example, in a table about employees in a company, it might be possible to set a check on the salary, which must be within certain limits.

Microsoft Access allows us to specify **validation rules** such as this. Again, we will deal with this in more detail in the next chapter. However, there is one special type of validation rule that has been used in the **School Data** database. This is a **lookup** rule.

We use a **lookup** rule if a field can only have a certain number of possible entries. For example, gender can only be **M** or **F**. When setting up **Pupils:tbl** the option **Lookup Wizard** was chosen from the **Data type** column. The two options **M** and **F** were then typed in and the computer automatically reset the **Data Type** to **Text**. That is why you can choose M or F from a drop-down list on the **Pupils** form.

You may have forgotten the fifth table in the **School Data** database. Nothing has been said yet about the **Subjects:tbl** table. This does not form part of the main data, but is used as a lookup table for fields in other tables.

There are two tables containing fields with data about subjects taught in the school — **Teachers:tbl** has the field **Main Subject** and **TeachingGroups:tbl** has the field **Subject**. Both of these have been created to lookup data from **Subjects:tbl**, again allowing drop-down boxes to be used for data entry.

By creating the lookup table as a separate table, it is easier for a user to change the options. If the school started to teach Spanish, for example, the new subject could easily be added.

You can see details of the lookup options for a field by showing the design view for the table, selecting the field and then clicking on the **Lookup** tab at the bottom of the page.

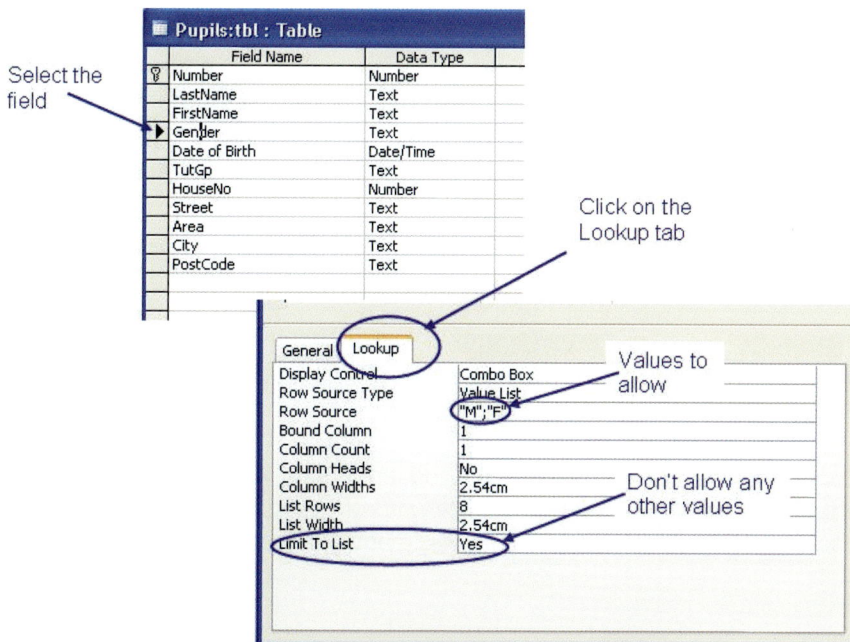

Figure 8.54: *Viewing the lookup options for the gender field in* **Pupils:tbl**.

Another way of reducing data entry errors in Microsoft Access is to create an **input mask**. This defines the format of the data to be entered. For example, we know that a postcode has to be two capital letters followed by one or two numbers, then a space, then a number, then two capital letters. An input mask will allow only the right kind of characters to be entered, and will even convert lower case letters to capitals, so that the user doesn't have to worry about these. Access provides ready-made input masks that can be chosen for dates and times. You can also define your own to ensure, for example, that capital letters are inserted in the correct places. These input masks are entered as codes, which can look quite complicated but the simplest ones are just chosen from a list, so they are actually very easy to include in a table design. Perhaps the most useful one is for a postcode:

>LL09\ 0LL

The **>** will turn all letters after it into capitals

The **L**s each represent one letter

The **0**s each represent one numeric digit

The **9** represents an optional numeric digit, that may or may not be there

The **** means that the character after it (a space) has to be there.

Unfortunately the automatic mask provided by Microsoft Access for postcode is incorrect – it cannot cope with postcodes that do not have two numbers after the letters (so it will accept WV34 2TY but not WV3 2TY). You may find it useful to copy the above code if you need an input mask for a postcode field.

You can see the fields where an input mask has been used by looking at the detail in the bottom section of the design view.

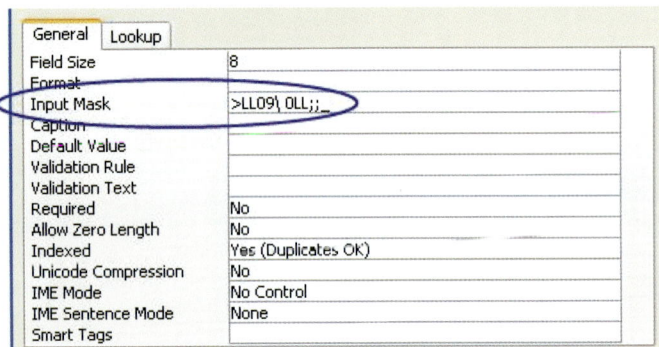

General Lookup	
Field Size	8
Format	
Input Mask	>LL09\ 0LL;;
Caption	
Default Value	
Validation Rule	
Validation Text	
Required	No
Allow Zero Length	No
Indexed	Yes (Duplicates OK)
Unicode Compression	No
IME Mode	No Control
IME Sentence Mode	None
Smart Tags	

Figure 8.55: *Showing the input mask for postcode.*

More detail about how to create different types of validation check and input mask will be given in Chapter 9. For now you just need to be aware that there are ways of checking that data input into a database is reasonable. A good database will have as many of this type of check as possible.

➔ *Assessment Objective 1*

Design a Relational Database to Meet the Needs of an Organisation

Overview:

This chapter will lead you through the stages involved in designing a database to meet the needs of an organisation. This includes investigating and identifying the requirements; designing the table structures, including field names, primary keys, field types, field lengths, validation and input masks; and designing the links between the tables. You will also design forms for the input of data.

This assessment objective is concerned with only the **design** of your database – the actual creation of the database is assessed in Assessment Objective 2, which we will look at in Chapter 10.

In order to complete the activities in this chapter you will need access to a number of additional files. These files are contained in the Chapter 9 Resources zip file which can be downloaded from the OCR Nationals in ICT (Units 6 & 7) Student Resources page on the Payne-Gallway website: www.payne-gallway.co.uk.

How this assessment objective will be assessed...

- A word-processed page detailing the user requirements – what the database needs to be able to do and who will be using it
- Handwritten and/or word-processed designs for each table, showing field names, primary keys, field types, field lengths, input masks and validation for each field
- A design on paper showing the relationships between the tables
- A design on paper for each data entry form to be included

Merit and **Distinction** candidates are required to include designs for more items, such as validation, combo boxes, input masks and more forms. The key to the higher grades is the detail that you include in your designs.

Skills to use...

In this assessment objective you will not have to demonstrate any skills in the use of database software, rather you need to demonstrate your understanding of the structure of a relational database.

How to achieve...

Pass requirements

P1 You will identify the user and purpose of the database.

P2 You will create a design that includes basic details of table structures, including primary keys, field names, field types and field lengths.

P3 You will create a design for the relationships between the tables.

P4 You will design at least one form for the entry of data.

P5 Although the design may not be the most efficient, it will allow the database to function to meet the identified purpose.

Merit requirements

M1 You will identify the user and purpose of the database.

M2 You will create a design that includes details of table structures, primary keys, field names, field types, field lengths, combo boxes and validation rules.

M3 You will create a design for the relationships between the tables.

M4 You will create a design for a data entry form for each table.

M5 Most of the choices shown in the designs will be appropriate and the database as designed will meet the identified purpose well.

Distinction requirements

D1 You will give details of the user and purpose of the database.

D2 You will create a design that includes comprehensive details of table structures, primary keys, field names, field types, field lengths, combo boxes, validation rules and at least one input mask.

D3 You will create a design for the relationships between the tables.

D4 You will create individual designs for data entry forms for each table.

D5 All of the choices shown in the designs will be appropriate and the database as designed will meet the identified purpose well.

Key terms

Design

Whenever the term **design** is used in this chapter, it refers to a design drawn out by hand or by the use of a word-processing or graphics package. Printouts from database software are **NOT** considered to be designs.

Scenario

For your portfolio you will need to negotiate a scenario with your teacher. The remaining chapters in this book will guide you through the process of creating a database and achieving all the assessment objectives for the following scenario.

Mal Thomas owns a car hire business. He has a number of cars, with a range of different models, which he hires out. He wants a computer database to store details of his cars and his customers, including the cars they hire.

You must **not** use this scenario for your own portfolio, as the guidance given in this book exceeds the help that you are allowed to receive for your assessed assignment. However, you should be able to use this guidance to help you make decisions about your own scenario and to find out what evidence you need to include in your portfolio.

Stage 1: defining the problem

The first thing you need to do, before you can design your database, is find out as much as you can about *exactly* what your user needs from the database. Usually, as in the scenario given above, the problem given at first is very vague.

> ⊘NOTE
>
> **You will be creating a database for someone else to use. We will refer to this person as 'the user'. The OCR specification sometimes refers to this user as 'the audience' for the database.**

You need to find out as much as possible about the problem. Try asking the following questions.

- Exactly why does the user want a computer database? The only reason for storing data is that you want to retrieve it later. What is the user hoping to do with it?
- What details does the user think need to be stored on the database?
- How much data does the user want to store?
- What information does the user want to be able to retrieve from the database?
- What types of printout would the user like the database to create?
- How familiar is the user with computers and database software?

Ideally you would find out the answers to these questions by discussing the needs with the user. If you are designing a database for an imaginary user, then you will need to think through the questions carefully yourself.

After finding out details of the problem, you are ready to write the introductory page for your portfolio. Here is an example of what you might write about the database for Mal Thomas.

I have been asked by Mal Thomas to create a database to help him run his car hire business. He has 25 cars, of different models. Every morning he needs to have ready the cars that are going out that day. He would like to be able to print out a list every morning of these cars. He would also like to be able to print out a list of cars that are due back in that day, so that he can check them off as they arrive.

Sometimes cars are not brought back when they are due. Mal would like to print the name and telephone number of the customers on the list of cars due back, so that he can contact them easily if necessary.

Mal would also like to be able to use the database to quickly search his stock of cars for a list that meet a customer's requirements. For example, customers often request a particular make, model, engine size and/or body type (hatchback, saloon, estate, 4 x 4, etc.). This would be particularly useful when his assistant, who is not as familiar as he is with the cars, is answering queries.

Mal also runs promotional events and would like to invite selected customers to these. For example, he might want to invite all customers who have hired a 4 x 4 in the past year to an evening promoting a new 4 x 4 model he has just acquired. He hopes that his database will allow him to produce lists of customers to invite, as well as mailing labels so that he can easily mail out invitations and leaflets.

The information Mal wants to store about his cars is: registration number, make, model, year of manufacture, engine size, number of doors, colour, body type.

The information he wants to store about his customers is: full name, telephone number, mobile telephone number, address and details of any cars hired – which car and the dates hired from and to.

Mal has 25 cars and currently has details of about 100 customers. He expects the number of customers to rise.

Mal has the following makes of cars: BMW, Ford, Vauxhall, Renault, VW and Toyota.

Mal and his assistant are familiar with using computers but have never used a database before, so they would like the system to be easy to use.

If you are dealing with a real-life problem, you may find that the user wants a lot of different things. For the purpose of your portfolio you only need to create a relational database with a minimum of **three** queries and reports. You are therefore advised to 'slim down' the user requirements if necessary – if you start off by defining a very wide and complex problem you will then be penalised if you don't meet all the needs you identify.

A good problem that would enable you to gain up to a **Distinction** would be one that needs two or three different tables, with three or four specific needs that will require queries, including parameter queries, using more than one table and searching and sorting on more than one field.

Stage 2: table structure

In designing the table structure, we will consider the questions we raised in the 'A closer look at tables' section of Chapter 8, on pages 124–130.

What data needs to be stored?

Using the information about the problem we can see that we need to store the following two sets of data:

- customers: full name, telephone number, mobile telephone number, address and details of the car(s) hired – which car(s) and the dates hired from and to
- cars: registration number, make, model, year of manufacture, engine size, number of doors, colour, body type.

What tables are needed?

We need a table for **customers** and a table for **cars**.

In the customer table each customer will have only one full name, telephone number and address but they might hire cars more than once, so all the other details will need to go into another table. This could be thought of as the **Hire** table, containing details of car hires: what car is hired and the dates hired from and to. This table will also need a field that corresponds to the primary key of the customer table.

In the cars table we can have all of the details given in the list above, as each car will have only one registration number, make, model, etc.

What fields are needed for each table?

Here you need to consider how you will split the data into fields for each table. You also need to ensure there is a unique **primary key** for each table, so that each record can be identified.

Customer table

- There is currently no unique key field, so we will need to add a field to be the primary key. This can be called **CustomerNo**
- Name will be best split into **Title**, **FirstName** and **LastName**, as this gives us more flexibility for creating address labels, etc.
- Telephone number
- Mobile telephone number
- Address will be best split into the different lines as they would appear on an address label. There is no real need to split house number from street, so we can have **Address1**, **Address2**, **Address3**, **Address4** and **PostCode**. This is a little more flexible than using more precise names such as **Street**, **Area**, **Town/City** and **County**, although many database systems do use these.

Car table

- The registration number is unique to every car, so this can be the primary key. This can be called **RegNo**
- Make
- Model
- Year of manufacture
- Engine size
- Number of doors
- Colour
- Body type

Hire table

- There is no unique field, so we will need to add a field to be the primary key. This can be called **HireNo**
- Customer ID
- Registration number
- Date the car went out
- Date the car came back in

How will the tables be linked?

There is a **many-to-many** relationship between the **Customer** table and the **Car** table, as a customer might hire more than one car and a car will be hired by more than one person. The **Hire** table acts as a junction between these two, so we will need a link from the **Customer** table to the **Hire** table and from the **Car** table to the **Hire** table. Each of these relationships will be **one-to-many**.

You need to draw a relationship diagram for your portfolio to show the tables, with the links between them. Figure 9.1 shows a suitable diagram for this example scenario.

Customer table	Hire table	Cars table
Customer number	**Hire number**	**Registration number**
Title	Customer ID	Make
First name	Registration number	Model
Last name	Date hired from	Year of manufacture
Telephone number	Date hired to	Engine size
Mobile telephone number		Number of doors
Address2		Colour
Address3		Body type
Address4		
PostCode		

Figure 9.1: *Relationships diagram for Mal's Car Hire database.*

It is not unusual to have difficulty deciding on the tables and links at first. It is a good idea to discuss a number of ideas with other people, including your teacher, before you settle on your final decision.

What type of data will be stored in each field?

At this point you need to consider each field in turn and decide on the data type that you will choose to use.

Before we consider our requirements for Mal's Car Hire database, we will spend a little time looking at the alternative data types we can use in Microsoft Access. Some of these were introduced at the end of Chapter 8, but a full list and details of each are given below.

If you load an Access database (for example, you could open any of the **School Data** databases provided in the online resources for Chapter 8), you can click on a table and look at it in **Design View**.

If you click in an empty cell in the **Data Type** column you will see a drop-down menu. Clicking on this will show all the data type choices that Access offers.

There are a number of other options that can be set for each field, shown in the **Field Properties** box at the bottom of the screen. Some of these are related to validation and input masks, which we will look at in the next section. Some are options that are beyond the needs of this qualification and are therefore not considered here.

Figure 9.2: *Choices of data type in Access.*

The first option in the properties box is **Field Size** – this is important to the efficiency of data storage. In Chapter 8 we compared setting up fields for data to preparing boxes in a warehouse for objects of different sizes. It would be very wasteful of storage space if we just used enormous boxes for everything, regardless of the amount of space each object needs. When setting up a database, choose a field size that is big enough to contain the largest item of data you could imagine needing, but no more.

For some fields the **Format** option is also important. A summary of the different data types is given below, including **Field Size** and **Format** options where they are appropriate for your project.

- **Text** is the most common data type. It can contain any string of characters, including letters, numbers and special characters such as spaces, punctuation marks, etc. A text field can contain up to 255 characters, which is usually more than enough! When you first choose a text field the **Field Size** is set to 50 characters, but you can change this to fit the data you will be entering.
- **Memo** is available if you ever want a text field that needs to contain more than 255 characters. It is unlikely that you will need to use a memo field.
- **Number** is for any field that will only contain numbers, where you might want to do calculations, sort in numeric order or search for values that are 'more than…' or 'less than…'. If the values are money, then it is best to use **Currency** (see below). If you set a field as **Number** you can choose between different **Field Sizes**:
  - **Byte** for whole numbers between 1 and 255.
  - **Integer** for whole numbers between -32,768 and +32,768.
  - **Long Integer** for even larger whole numbers.
  - **Single** can be used if you might need to store numbers that are not whole numbers, with figures after a decimal point. This format will allow up to seven significant figures, e.g. 1234.567, 0.1234567, 1,234,567,000.

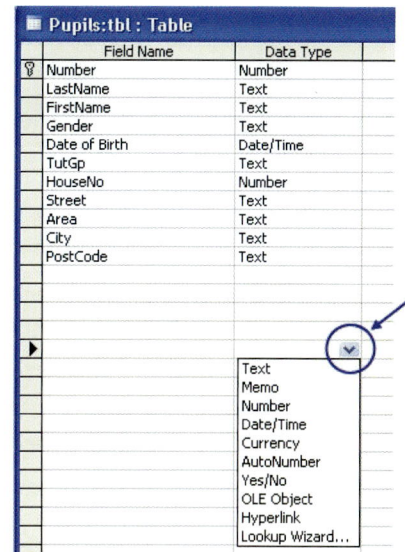

— If you need more significant figures than this use **Double**. But bear in mind that **Double** uses twice as much storage space as **Single**, so you shouldn't use it unless you need it.

— **Decimal** sounds like the best format to use for decimal numbers, but this option uses the most storage space of all the options and so is not recommended. If you do choose **Decimal**, then you need to alter the **Scale** option to set the maximum number of decimal places that can be stored.

When you first choose a number field, the **Field Size** will be set to **Long Integer**, but you can change this. For most normal use you will probably choose either **Integer** for whole numbers or **Single** for numbers which are not whole numbers.

> **⨁TIP**
>
> **If you are unsure of whether or not a field should be text or numeric, then ask the following questions:**
>
> **Could there be any characters in this field that are not numeric digits, e.g. letters, spaces...?**
>
> ● **If the answer is yes, then the field must be text.**
>
> **Will I ever want the computer to perform calculations with the number, or find records where the field is 'more than' or 'less than' an amount?**
>
> ● **If the answer is yes, then the field must be numeric.**

● **Date/Time** is used, as you might expect, to store dates and/or times. Using **Date/Time** fields will allow you to search for dates before or after specified times. You should always use this type of field to store a date or time.

You do not have to choose a field length for this type of field, but you should choose the **Format** that best suits you from the drop-down list at the bottom of the screen, as shown in Figure 9.3.

General	Lookup		
Format			▼
Input Mask	General Date	19/06/1994 17:34:23	
Caption	Long Date	19 June 1994	
Default Value	Medium Date	19-Jun-94	
Validation Rule	Short Date	19/06/1994	
Validation Text	Long Time	17:34:23	
Required	Medium Time	05:34 PM	
Indexed	Short Time	17:34	
IME Mode	No Control		
IME Sentence Mode	None		
Smart Tags			

Figure 9.3: Format *options for a Date/Time field.*

● **Currency** is used for money. It allows you to enter numbers and see them displayed with a £ sign and 2 decimal places. You do not have to choose a field length and the format is automatically set to British currency if your computer's regional settings are correctly set to UK.

!TIP

If you find that dates and currency are not shown correctly, it is likely that your computer's regional settings are set to the United States (US) rather than the United Kingdom (UK). These can be changed by clicking on the Start menu of your computer and going to the Control Panel. If you are using a network, these settings are likely to be controlled by your network manager.

- **AutoNumber** is a special type of number field, in which Access automatically creates a unique number for each record. You should use **AutoNumber** if you want a primary key to be automatically created. The field length will automatically be set to **Long Integer** and you should not change this.
- **Yes/No** is used most often if you have a field where the only options are 'yes' or 'no'. You might use the **Yes/No** data type, for example, if you want a field to show whether an invoice has been paid or not.
- **OLE Object** is used to insert objects that have been created by other applications. The most common use is to insert pictures or photographs. For example, a company personnel database might include a photograph of each employee. There are no field size options for this type of field. Although including photographs may sound appealing, it can lead to huge file sizes with consequent slow access, so it is not recommended.
- **Hyperlink** provides an option to put a link to another file or web page into a record. There are no field size options. It is unlikely that you will want to use this type of field.
- **Lookup Wizard** is provided as a data type option, although it is not really a different type of data. It allows you to set a list of possible entries that can be used in the field. For example, a gender field would be set to accept only **M** or **F**. You can either type in the options when you set up the field or you can link them to another table, as was done with the **Subjects:tbl** of the *School Data* database. When you have entered your options, the software sets the data type to **Text** unless you have set the options to link to another table in the database, in which case it sets the data type to match the field used for the options. When the field is set you can choose the **Field Size** options just like any normal text or number field.

!TIP

Although you can create a table without changing the field size or format of the fields you set, in order to achieve a Distinction in Assessment Objective 1 you need to show that all your choices are appropriate. If you do not carefully consider field types and sizes for each of your fields you will not be able to be awarded a Distinction. Even for a Pass you need to show some consideration of field sizes in your plan.

Activity 1: Investigating data types...

In this activity you will:

- create a new Access table
- investigate different data types
- set field size and formatting as appropriate for different data types.

▶ Load Microsoft Access and choose to **Create a new file...**. Choose the **Blank database...** option.

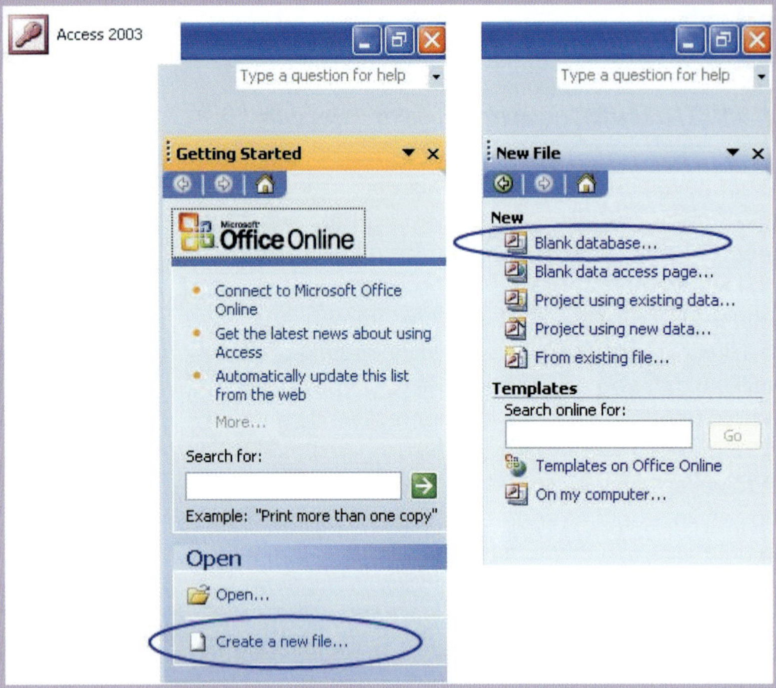

Figure 9.4: *Creating a new database.*

▶ You will then be asked where to save the file. This may seem strange, as you have not created anything yet, but as Access saves everything as you do it, you need to save the blank file now.

▶ The first thing you need to do when you set up a database is create the tables. Choose to **Create table in Design view**.

You will see a blank design screen where you can enter your fields and choose field types and sizes. For this activity you simply need to investigate the different options available – you are not actually setting up a real database.

For each field you can choose a **Field Name** and **Data Type**, which are compulsory, and a **Description**, which is optional. It is good practice to enter a short description for each field. For this activity we will use simple field names that reflect the type of data they can contain.

▶ Create a field called **AutoNumber**, and set it to the **AutoNumber** field type. You would usually use this field type for a primary key. Enter a suitable description, such as the one shown in Figure 9.5.

Figure 9.5: Adding an **AutoNumber** field.

It is usual to have the primary key as the first field in a table. However, you also need to show the computer that it is the key field:

(▶) Select the field by clicking on the small box to the left of the field name, then click on the **Primary Key** button on the toolbar.

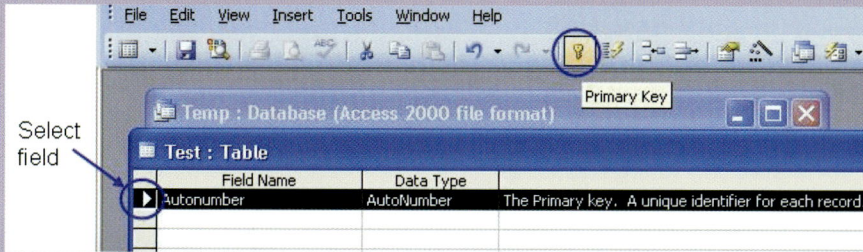

Figure 9.6: Setting the primary key.

(▶) Add another field called **Text**. Make it a **Text** field and change the **Field Size** to **10**.

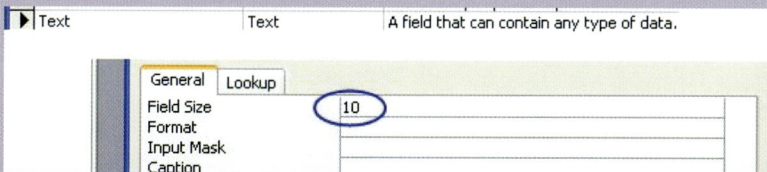

Figure 9.7: Adding a text field with a length of 10 characters.

(▶) Add a field called **Whole Number** and make it a **Number** field. Make this an **Integer**:

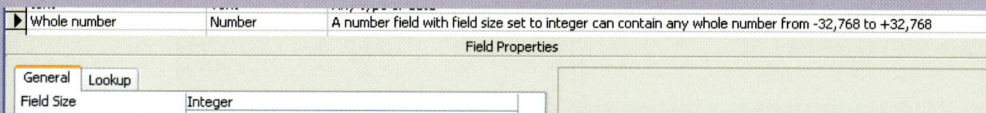

Figure 9.8: Adding a numeric field for whole numbers.

(▶) Now add another numeric field called **Decimal Number** and set this to **Single**.

(▶) Add another field called **Date** and set it to the **Date/Time** data type. Choose a suitable format for entering dates.

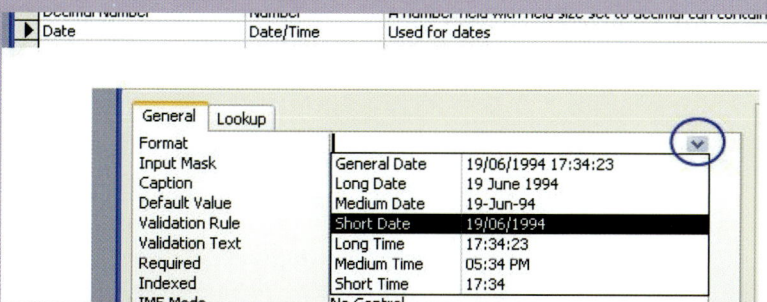

Figure 9.9: Adding a field to contain dates and setting the date format.

▶ Add another field and set it to **Currency** data type. There are no further options to set for this type of field.

Field Name	Data Type	Descript
Autonumber	AutoNumber	The Primary key. A unique identifier for each record.
Text	Text	A field that can contain any type of data.
Whole Number	Number	A number field with field size set to integer can contain any whole number from -32,768 to +32,768
Decimal Number	Number	A number field with field size set to decimal can contain any number
Date	Date/Time	Used for dates
Currency	Currency	A field to contain amounts of money

Figure 9.10: *Adding a currency field.*

▶ Add a **Yes/No** field. Again there are no further options to set.

▶ Add a field called **Picture** and set it to **OLE Object**. You will be using this to see how you can add a picture, such as a photograph, to a record. There are no other options to set for this type of field.

▶ Picture	OLE Object	A field that allows you to include a picture

Figure 9.11: *Adding a field for a photograph.*

The final field type you will set up in this test is a drop-down box of choices for the user, also known as a combo box.

▶ Add a final field with the field name **Choices** and choose **Lookup Wizard...** for the field type. This will then take you through a series of choices.

▶ First you will be asked where the lookup list will be. Choose **I will type in the values that I want**.

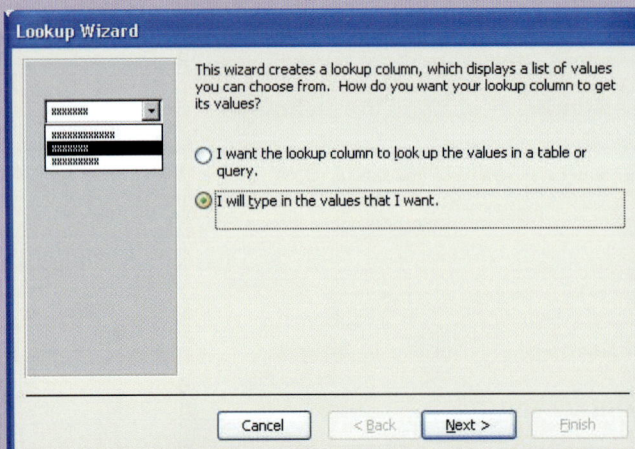

Figure 9.12: *Choosing to type in the values for the lookup list.*

▶ You will then see a dialogue box where you can type in the values that will be allowed for this field. Enter them as shown in Figure 9.13. Do not press **Enter** after each one – use the mouse to click into the next row, or press the **Tab** key.

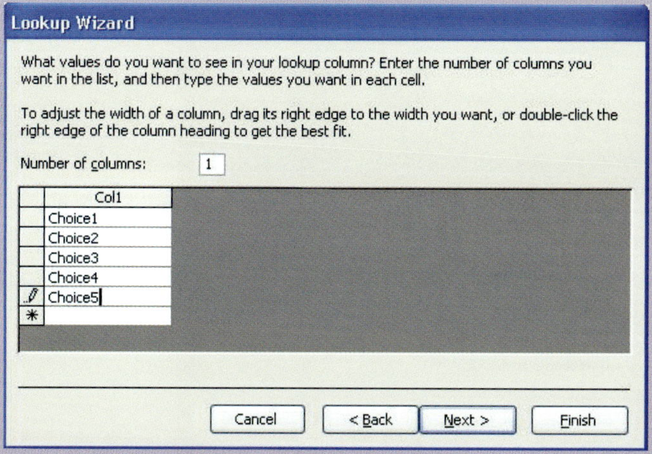

Figure 9.13: *Entering the values for the lookup list.*

▶ You will then be asked to confirm the field name, then click on **Finish**.

▶ You will then see that the field has been set back to **Text**. Set the **Field Size** property to **7**, since all of the options you have entered are seven characters long.

▶ You can see the choices you have entered if you click on the **Lookup** tab at the bottom of the screen in the **Row Source** box.

▶ To make sure the user cannot enter anything apart from an item on the list you entered, change the **Limit To List** option from **No** to **Yes**.

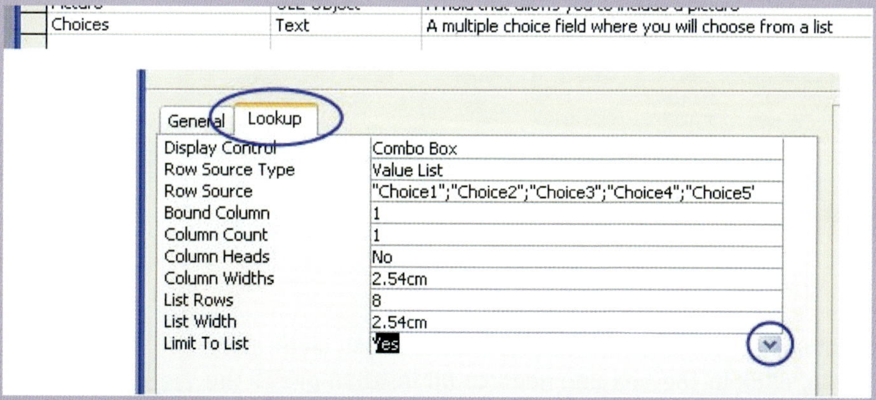

Figure 9.14: *Setting the lookup field to only accept entries from the list of options you have entered.*

▶ When you have set all the fields, click on the **View** icon to leave the design view. You will be asked to save your table. It does not matter what you call it, since it is just a test table.

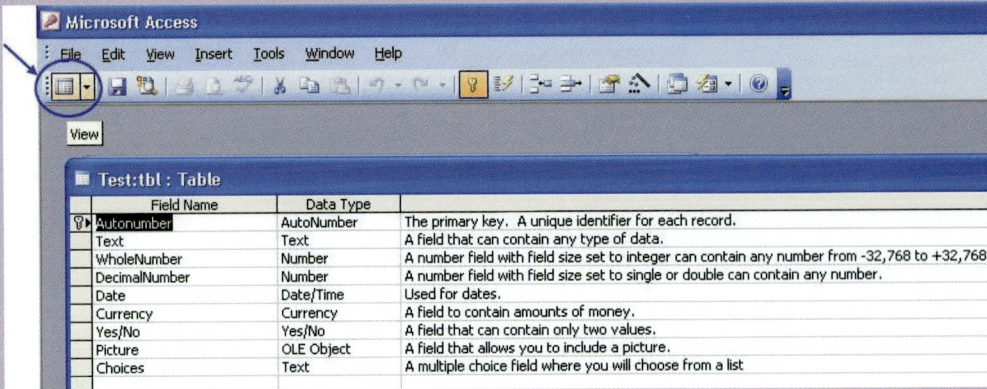

Figure 9.15: *Switching from **Design View** to **Table View**.*

Experiment with entering data into the different field types. Try entering a range of different data items to test the sort of data that can be entered.

The easiest way of entering a picture into the picture field is to copy and paste it from another application. This avoids problems that can be caused by different picture formats. You will not see the actual picture in the table, but it will be shown on a form or report.

⊘TIP

You can always move to and from Design View by using the View icon at the left of the toolbar. This changes according to the view you are in.

Design view

Form view

Table view

Figure 9.16: *Some test data entered into the table.*

	Autonumber	Text	Whole Number	Decimal Numbe	Date	Currency	Yes/No	Picture	Choices
	1	abcdefghij	17	0.1234567	01/01/2007	£2.50	☑	Picture	Choice2
	2	abc12345	24000	123.4567	31/12/2005	£125,890.00	☐	Picture	Choice1
	3	NAME	0	1234567	01/01/1980	£0.01	☑	Picture	Choice3
	4	Two words	0	1.1	21/05/2060	200,000,000.00	☐	Picture	Choice4
▶	(AutoNumber)		0	0		£0.00	☐		

⊘TIP

There are lots of options to choose from when setting up fields. If you want more information about any of these, click in the box you need to fill in, then press the F1 key.

What checking methods can be used to minimise data entry errors?

A well-planned database will include as much automatic error checking as possible. To be awarded more than a **Pass** you will need to consider this in your plan.

There are three main ways of trying to minimise data entry errors that you need to know about for your portfolio:

- **combo boxes** (drop-down boxes): these are a form of data entry that are set using the **Lookup Wizard** in the **Data Type** option – you have already set up one of these in Activity 1
- **validation checks**: setting acceptable limits for data – for example, in Mal's Car Hire database the number of doors can only be between 2 and 5
- **input masks**: setting rules for the type of characters that can be entered into a field.

You can also set a **default value** for a field, which will be entered automatically, to minimise typing.

Validation checks

Validation checks are set by adding a **Validation Rule** to the **Field Properties** box at the bottom of the design view of a table. You can also add an error message to be displayed if a user enters data that does not match your rule.

Use **>** (greater than) and **<** (less than) signs, together with **And** and **Or** to create validation rules for numbers (including currency and dates), for example:

- **>0** means 'must be greater than 0'
- **<250** means 'must be less than 250'
- **>0 and <250** means 'must be greater than 0 and less than 250', i.e. 'must be between 1 and 249'
- **<5 or >10** means 'must be either less than 5 or more than 10', i.e. 'must not be between 5 and 10'
- **>=01/01/2007 And <=31/12/2007** means 'must be greater than or equal to 01/01/2007 and less than or equal to 31/12/2007', i.e. 'must be a date in 2007'. There are some useful functions that you can use when setting validation on dates. **Date()** represents today's date (see Figure 9.17). **Month(Now)** and **Year(Now)** represent the current month and year.

We can use **Or**, **Not**, ***** and **?** to add checks to text fields. For example:

- **M Or F** is an alternative way of allowing only 'M' or 'F', rather than using the **Lookup Wizard**. This method would not provide a combo box for data entry.
- **A*** means that the data entered must start with **A**.
- **A* Or B*** means that the data entered must start with either **A** or **B**.
- **A?????** means that the data must start with **A** and then have another 5 characters.
- **NOT Word** means that any data can be entered *except* the word **Word**.

⊙TIP

* and ? are called wildcard characters. They are used to show that any character can be entered.

* means any number of characters, so use this when the number of characters will vary

? means any one character, so you need to put in the exact number of question marks for the characters required.

Whenever you enter a validation rule, you should enter a suitable error message in the **Validation Text** box – this will be shown if a user enters incorrect data. For example, Figure 9.17 shows a suitable validation rule and text to ensure that a date entered is not in the future:

Figure 9.17: *Validation set to ensure a date is not in the future.*

You can also add one validation rule for the whole table. This allows you to compare two fields. For example, in Mal's database the date the car was returned has to come *after* the date the car was taken out. This can be entered by clicking on **View** on the menu bar and choosing **Properties**. The validation rule can then be entered by putting the field names inside square brackets. Figure 9.18 shows a validation rule for a table that ensures that a date in a field called **DateReturned** is the same or comes after a date in a field called **DateOut**.

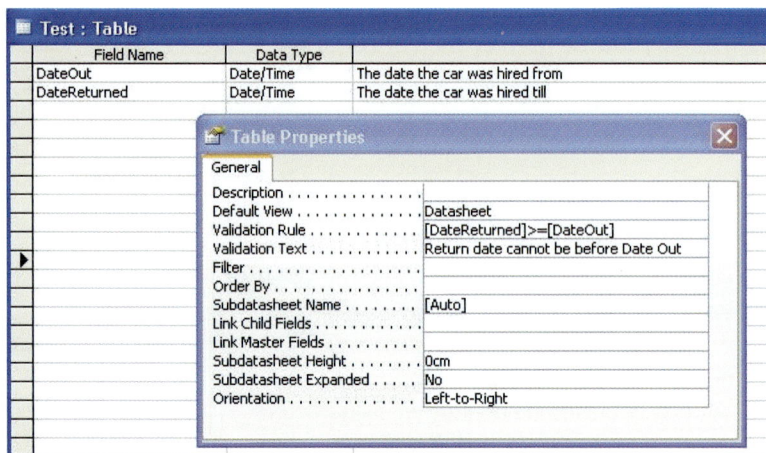

Figure 9.18: *Setting a validation rule for a table.*

Input masks

Input masks are set by adding a code to the **Input Mask** section of the **Field Properties** box at the bottom of the design view screen. These codes define the type of character that can be added. For a **Distinction** in this assessment objective you need to include at least one input mask, which will probably be for a postcode or a telephone number. The relevant codes are:

- postcode: **LL09\ 0LL**
- city telephone number (e.g. 0121 378 2135) – **0000\ 000\ 0000**
- regional telephone number (e.g. 01902 174161 or 01344 54763) – **00000\ 000009**

If you prefer to enter your own input masks, the codes that can be used are shown below. If you think that looks too complicated, don't worry – you will almost certainly be able to use one of the codes given above and still satisfy the requirements for a **Distinction**.

- **0** – a single numeric digit, which must be entered
- **9** – a single numeric digit, which may or may not be entered
- **#** – a single numeric digit or a **+** or **-** sign, which may or may not be entered
- **L** – a single letter of the alphabet, which must be entered
- **?** – a single letter of the alphabet, which may or may not be entered
- **A** – a single character (a letter or a numeric digit), which must be entered
- **a** – a single character (a letter or a numeric digit), which may or may not be entered
- **&** – any character or space, which must be entered
- **C** – any character or space, which may or may not be entered
- **<** – converts any letters that are entered after it to lower case
- **>** – converts any characters that are entered after it to upper case
- **** – used before a character in a mask to show that this character should appear in the final data (in the masks for postcode and telephone numbers shown above, it is used before a space).

One useful mask is **>L<??????????????**, which could be used in a 15-character long text field, to make sure that the first letter is always a capital and the rest lower case. By changing the number of **?**s you can make this appropriate for fields of different lengths. This can be useful, for example, in a field for a product name, where the input mask will convert any characters typed, so making data entry quicker (you don't have to worry about the shift key for capitals) and the data entered will look more consistent. However, be careful when using this – you might be tempted to use it for a **FirstName** field for a person, but some people might have a double first name, such as **Sally-Ann**. Similar problems could arise if you used it for a **LastName** field.

Default values

Default values are not required for your portfolio but they are very easy to create, by filling in the **Default Value** in the **Field Properties** box. This is a value that will come up automatically for every new field. For example, in the *School Data* database it might have been useful to set the default value for the **City** field, since almost all the pupils in the school come from the same city. The default value will appear automatically for each new entry added to the table, so there is less data to enter for each pupil, but it *can* be changed if necessary.

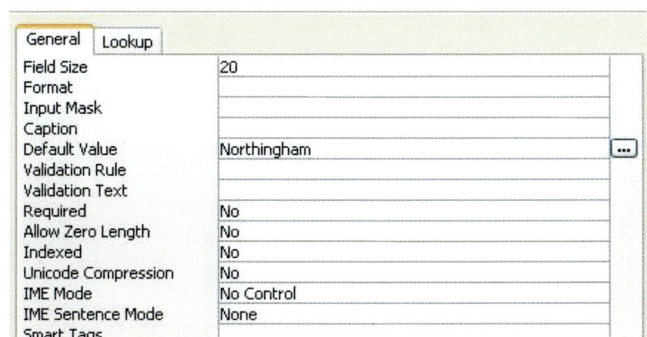

General	Lookup	
Field Size	20	
Format		
Input Mask		
Caption		
Default Value	Northingham	[...]
Validation Rule		
Validation Text		
Required	No	
Allow Zero Length	No	
Indexed	No	
Unicode Compression	No	
IME Mode	No Control	
IME Sentence Mode	None	
Smart Tags		

Figure 9.19: Setting a default value.

Planning field types and checking methods

You can plan your field types and checking methods at the same time, by considering each field in turn. You can download a database planning sheet from the online resources for this chapter, which you can use to plan out the detail of each table. It is called **Database table planning sheet.doc**. There is space on this sheet to plan eight fields, but any unwanted rows can be deleted and more can be added by copying and pasting additional rows to the table.

You will see that there are two rows for each field – one to insert the details required and a second, shaded row to add any other comments, such as the purpose of the field and identifying the primary key. For a **Distinction** you need to produce 'detailed designs which include comprehensive details of table structures, primary keys, field names, field types, field lengths, combo boxes, validation rules and at least one input mask'. This extra row gives you the space to add any extra detail you think is necessary. You can add explanations to show *why* you have made particular decisions. This makes it much more likely that your teacher will be able to agree that you have made appropriate choices. For a **Pass** you will only need to identify the primary key and leave the rest of these shaded rows blank.

Activity 2: Planning a database…

In this activity you will:

- look at what makes a good database plan
- consider an appropriate field structure for the three tables in Mal's Car Hire database.

Completed database table planning sheets for the three tables for Mal's database are available with the online resources for this chapter. They are called:

Planning sheet customer table.doc

Planning sheet cars table.doc

Planning sheet hire table.doc

Open up these three files, or look at printouts of the tables. You will be able to see how the planning sheets can be filled in to show all the details needed to create the tables.

Look carefully at the decisions for data type, field size/formatting and validation/combo box/input masks. Detailed explanations of these choices have been included on the planning sheets.

You will use these plans in the next chapter when you actually create this database.

Input forms

The final thing you must design is an input form. For a **Pass** you need only design a form for one table. For a **Merit** you must design a form for *each* table. For a **Distinction** your designs must be customised, so that they will involve more than can be automatically created using the form wizard.

Before you can design your own forms you need to explore a little to see what is possible.

Activity 3: Creating input forms...

In this activity you will:

● use the form wizard to create input forms for tables.

▶ Open the test database you created in Activity 1. Alternatively you can open the file **Temp1.mdb** provided in the online resources for this chapter.

▶ Click on **Forms** in the **Objects** panel and choose **Create form by using wizard**. Although you can create a form from scratch, it is easier to use the wizard and make any changes you need later.

▶ The first thing you need to do is choose the table you want to enter data into, then the fields you want to enter. This is done in the same way as creating a report. Here we have only one table, so we simply have to choose to include all the fields, then click on **Next**:

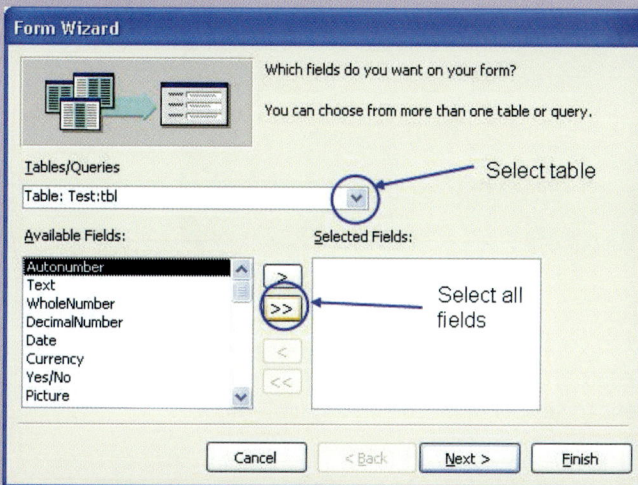

Figure 9.20: *Choosing the table and fields.*

You are then asked to choose the layout of your form. The two that allow you to show each record on a separate form are **Columnar** and **Justified**:

Figure 9.21: *Columnar form layout.*

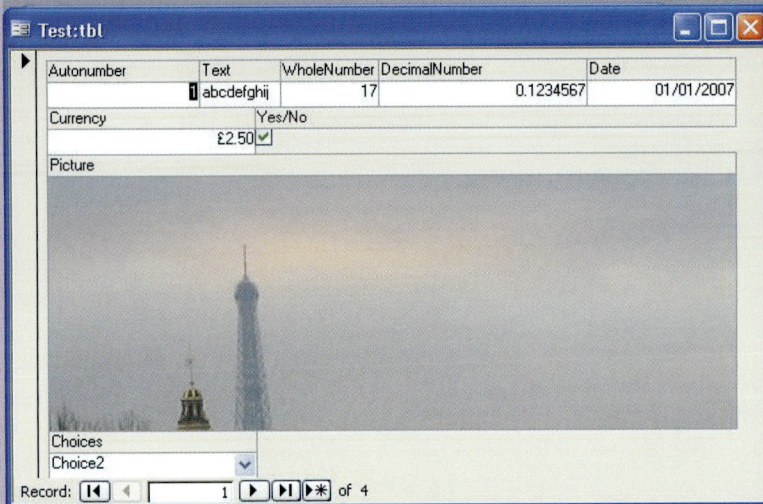

***Figure 9.22:** Justified form layout.*

▶ Choose either **Columnar** or **Justified** layout and click on **Next**.

▶ You are then given a choice of styles. Choose one and click on **Next**.

▶ You then are asked to give your form a name. Call it **Test:frm** then click on **Finish**. (The **frm** suffix is good practice to show that this is a form.)

Designing forms: Pass candidates

To gain a **Pass** in this unit you can rely on the wizard to create your forms. However, you still have to design one to meet the requirements of Assessment Objective 1. You do not need to draw out a design on paper for this. It will be sufficient to simply state the layout (columnar or justified) and style choices that you will make.

You can see a suitable design for Mal's database forms in the downloadable resources for this chapter. It is called ***Form Design Pass.doc***.

You might like to print out a form, so you can use it as a reference when designing your own for your portfolio. Make sure you label it to show the choice of style and format that it shows. You could also create a few forms, using different layouts and styles, so that you have a few to choose from.

If you are aiming only for a **Pass** in this objective you can omit the next section of this chapter and move straight onto the **Portfolio builder** section on page 160.

Designing forms: Merit/Distinction candidates

To gain a **Merit** or **Distinction** you need to design your own forms. It is still easier to start with the wizard, then alter the form to match your own design.

Compare the form you created in Activity 3 with the ones you used in Chapter 8. You will see that the designer of the **School Data** database forms changed a number of things:

- increased the size of the form
- added a background colour
- added a title
- added a logo
- changed the font size for the fields
- changed some of the labels on the fields
- changed the position of fields.

Such changes can easily be made using the **Design View** of a form, once it has been created using the wizard.

Forms can also be made easier to use by adding buttons for common tasks. For example, you can add buttons to move to the next record, add a record, delete a record and/or print a form. Although Access already provides icons for all these things, adding buttons to the forms themselves can make them much more obvious and therefore easier for the user.

Activity 4: Editing the design of a form…

In this activity you will:

- change the size of a form
- change the background colour
- add a title and a logo
- change the font, size and position of fields
- change field labels
- change the format of a picture field
- add control buttons.

▶ Load the file you created in Activity 3. Alternatively you can use the file **Temp2.mdb** provided with the resources for this chapter. It has a form that has been created with a **Columnar** layout.

▶ Click on **Forms** in the **Objects** panel, then click on the form you created in Activity 3 (or **Test:frm** in **Temp2.mdb**) and choose **Design** view.

▶ Drag the bottom right-hand corner of the window down and to the right, to make the window bigger. You might also find the form easier to manage if it is in the top left-hand corner of your Access window. Drag it using the title bar at the top.

▶ Move to the top of the **Form Footer** bar and drag it down towards the bottom of the window to increase the size of the form. Then drag the right-hand edge of the background to the edge of the window:

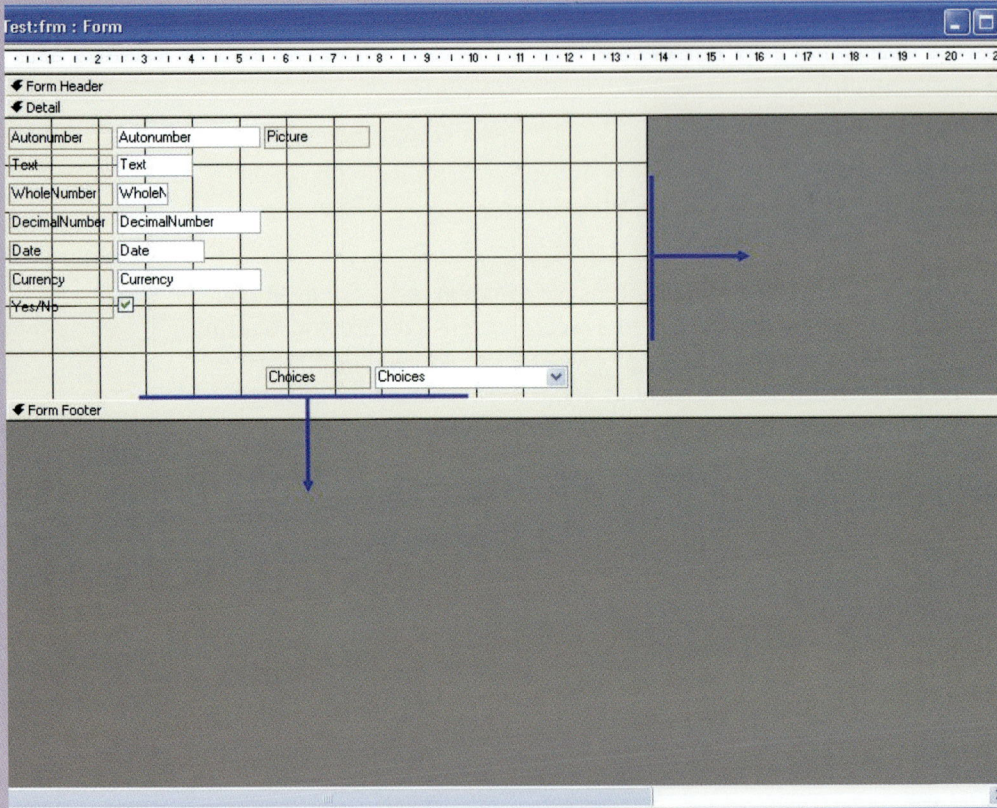

Figure 9.23: *Dragging the edges to make the form bigger.*

▶ If you click and hold on one of the fields you will find that you can move it around. Move the fields around to spread them out and leave room for a title. You can use the grid to help you keep the fields in line with each other.

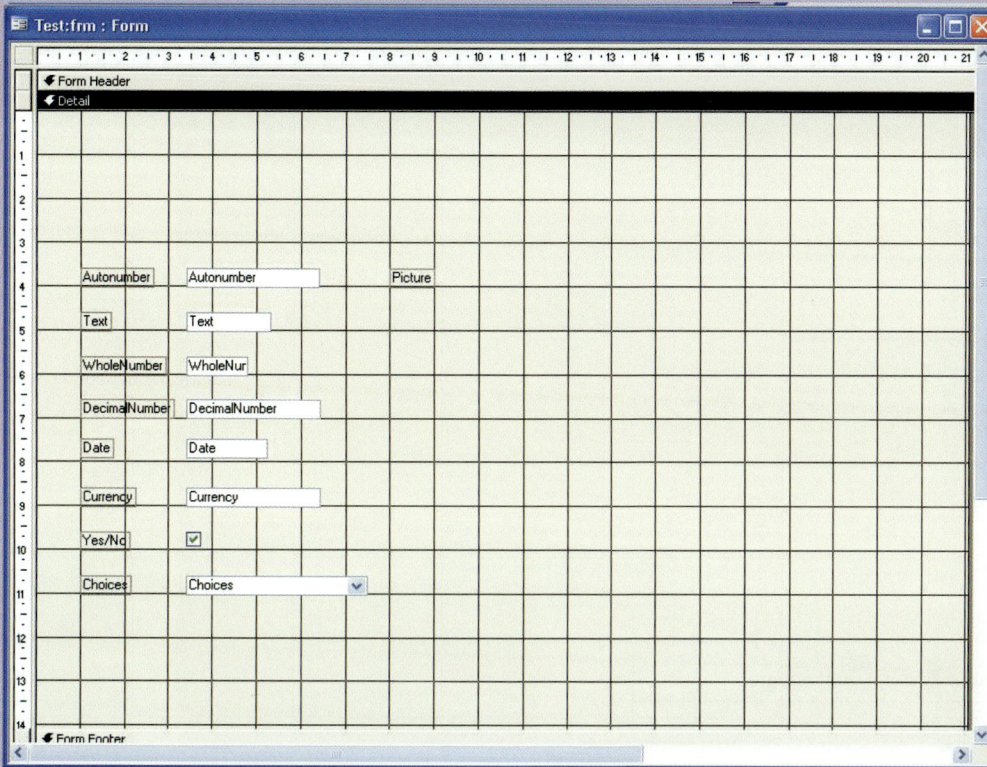

Figure 9.24: *Move the fields to spread them out.*

When a field is selected you can change its font and font size. However, it is quicker to do this if you select all the fields at the same time.

▶ Drag over all the fields to select them all. If possible, avoid selecting the picture box. Now choose a larger font, say 12 point, and a different font if you wish.

You will now need to make the boxes bigger to make room for the larger font. You *can* drag out each box individually but it is easier and more consistent to do them all together.

▶ With the fields still selected, right click on one of them and choose **Properties**.

▶ Make sure the **Format** tab is selected and change the **Height**. You might want to experiment with a few different heights, but 0.6 cm is about right for most fonts at 12 point.

Figure 9.25: *Setting the height of the boxes to 0.6 cm.*

▶ Click on an empty part of the form to deselect the fields, then click on **one** field to select it. You should then be able to experiment moving and resizing the whole field, the label and the data entry box.

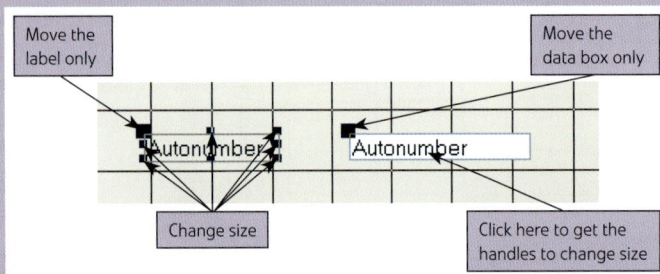

Figure 9.26: *Moving and resizing the field label and data box.*

▶ You will need to make some of the label and data entry boxes wider to make room for the larger text. You might also like to change some of the labels – they don't have to be the field names, they can be longer, more helpful labels to help the user. If you have a picture field you might not even want a label – if you select **just** the label you can delete it with the delete key, but be careful not to delete the picture frame too.

> **⊘TIP**
>
> Don't forget you can use the Undo button if you make a change you don't like!

▶ You may have noticed that the pictures you entered have been cropped to fit into the picture frame. You can alter the size of the picture frame, just like any other box on the form, but you can also change the way pictures fit into the frame. Right click in the picture frame and choose **Properties**, then make sure the **Format** tab is selected and change the **Size Mode** to **Zoom** using the drop-down list.

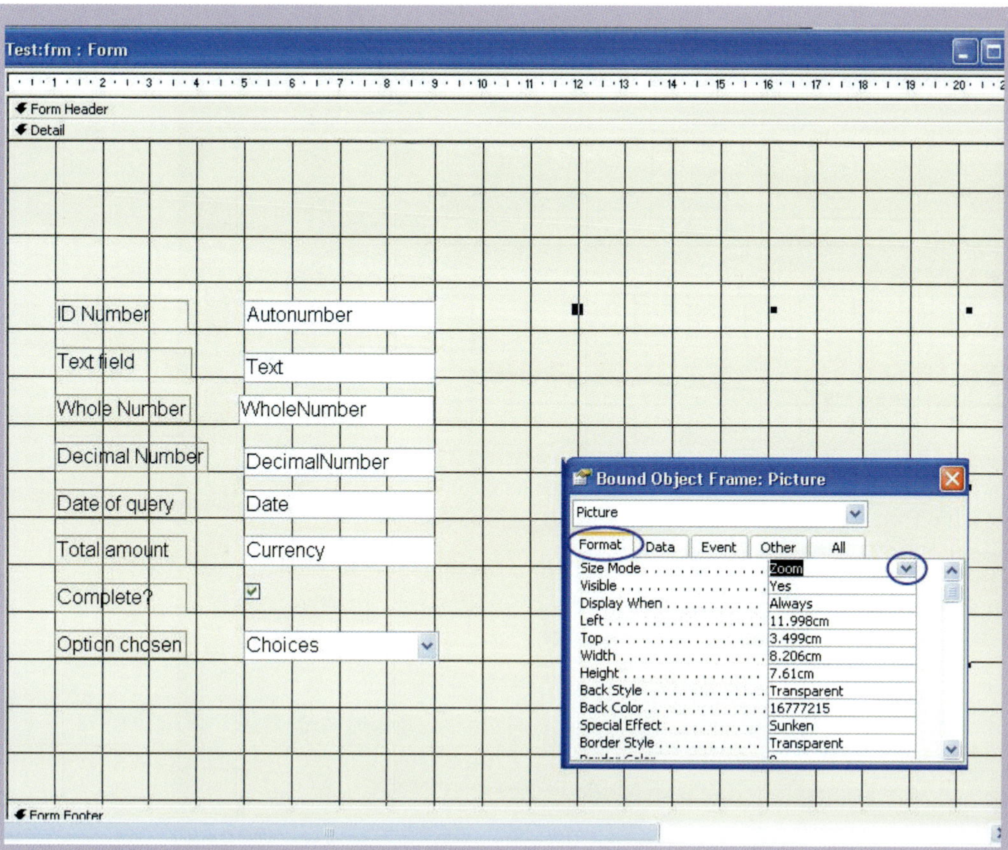

Figure 9.27: *Setting the picture to fill the frame.*

▶ Use the **View** button on the left of the toolbar to move back to **Form View** and see the effect of your changes. When you have seen this, return to **Design View** again.

▶ To add a title and buttons, you need the **Toolbox**. If this is not already visible, right click on an empty part of the screen and choose **Toolbox**.

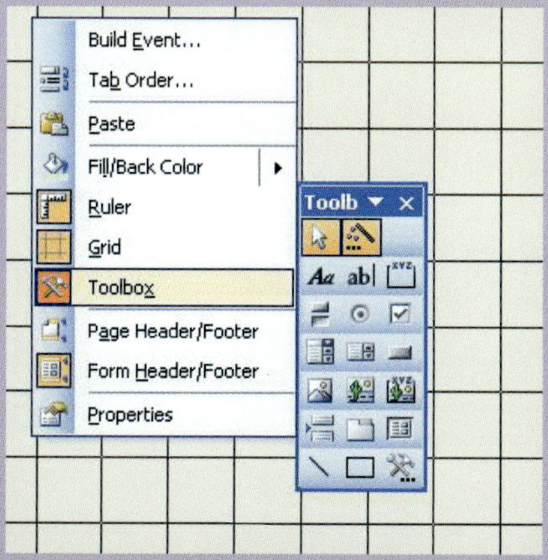

Figure 9.28: *Viewing the **Toolbox**.*

▶ Choose the **Label** tool (at the top of the **Toolbox**) and drag out a box at the top of the form for a title. Type in a suitable title, then click out of the box.

▶ Click onto your title again and you should be able to change the font, size, alignment, font colour and background using the normal tools on the main formatting toolbar.

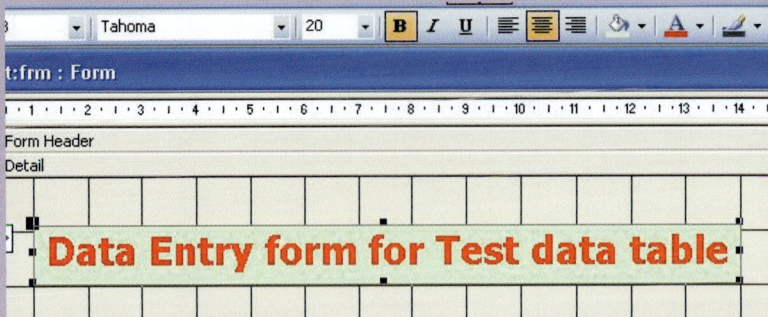

Figure 9.29: Formatting the title.

If you are creating a form for a company you might want to include a logo.

▶ Click on **Insert** from the menu bar and choose **Picture** for a picture from a file on your computer or **Object** for a piece of clipart. If you are looking for clipart you then need to scroll down and choose **Microsoft Clip Gallery**. You can now find and insert a picture.

▶ If the picture is not the size you want, drag the handles of the box it is in, until it is the right size. Then right click on the picture and choose **Properties**. Choose the **Format** tab and choose **Zoom** from the **Size Mode**, as you did before with the picture frame.

▶ You can change the background colour of your form by right clicking on an empty space and choosing **Fill/Back Color**.

▶ Experiment a little with the layout options until you are happy with the layout of your form. (You can move between the **Design View** and **Form View** of your form at any time using the **View** button.)

▶ Leave about 2 cm empty at the bottom of the form, as we are going to use this for buttons.

When you are entering data into a form you usually move from one field to another with the **Tab** key or the **Enter** key. The order that the computer takes the fields in is called the **tab order**. If you have changed the order of the fields on the form you should also change the tab order, otherwise the insertion point will jump about from one field to another in an unpredictable way.

▶ To do this, click on **View** on the menu bar and choose **Tab Order**. You can then drag the fields up and down into a sensible order.

You are now going to add some buttons to your form.

▶ Choose the **Command Button** tool from the **Toolbox**, and drag out a button at the bottom of your form. We will use this as a button for moving to the next record.

*Figure 9.30: Selecting the **Command Button** tool in order to create a button.*

▶ You will then be shown a dialogue box, from which you can choose the action to be carried out by your button. Scroll down the categories to see the options, then choose **Go To Next Record** and click on **Next**.

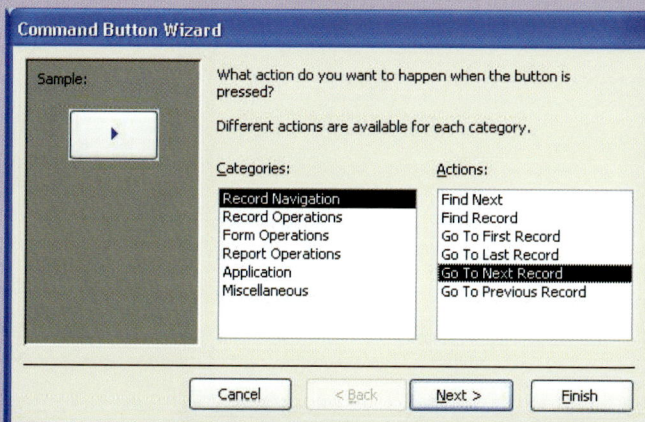

*Figure 9.31: Choosing the **Go To Next Record** option for the button.*

▶ You will then be asked whether you want text or a picture on your button. Since the purpose of buttons is to make using the form easier for inexperienced users it is often best to choose **Text**, unless the picture is very obvious, such as a printer. Choose **Text** for this button, then click on **Next**.

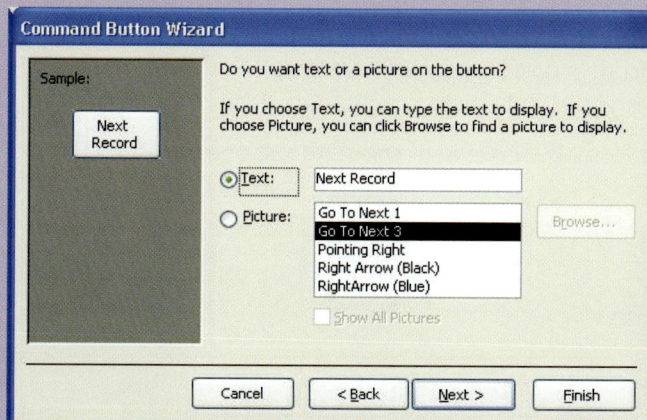

Figure 9.32: Choosing button text.

▶ Give the button a meaningful name (in this case 'Next Record'), then click on **Finish**.

▶ Switch to **Form View** and test your button, then switch back to **Design View**.

▶ Complete your form by adding more buttons for the features a user might want the most. For example: Previous Record, Add New Record, Delete Record, Print Record. You might also like to try Find Record and see what it does.

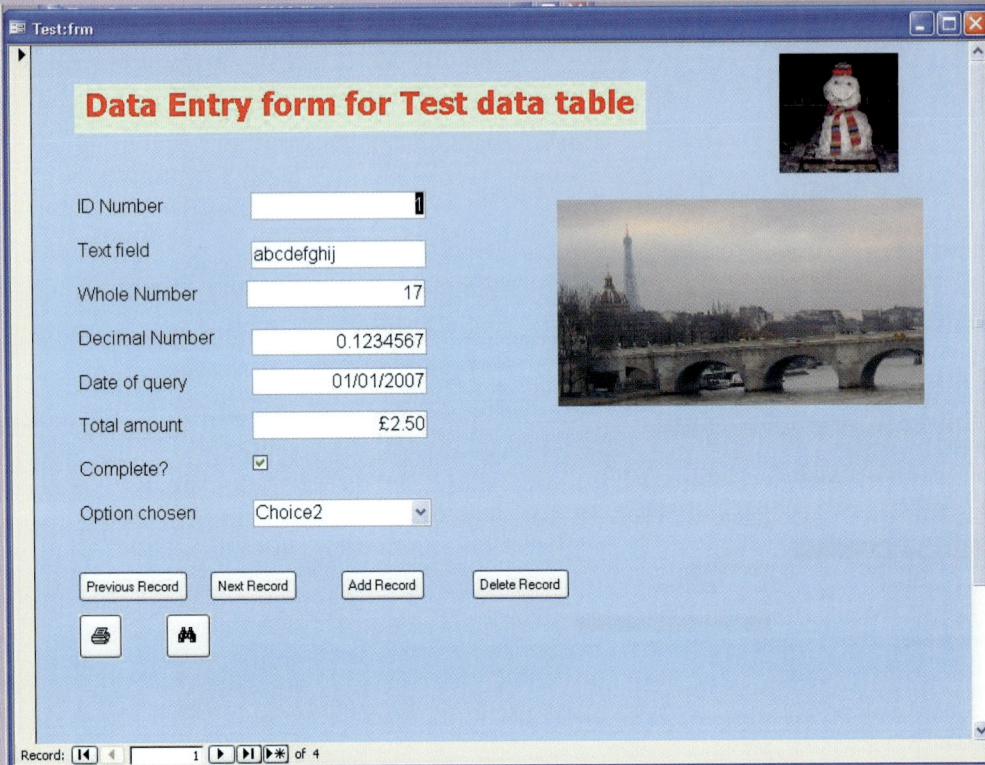

Figure 9.33: *Example of a completed form.*

The file ***Form Design MD1.doc***, provided with the downloadable resources for this chapter, is an example of a suitable design for the forms needed for the three tables required in Mal's Car Hire database.

Subforms

In Chapter 8 you saw how data could be entered into more than one table at a time, by using a subform. It is not necessary to create a subform in order to succeed, even at **Distinction** level, in this unit. However, you may wish to include them in your work.

Subforms are created in the same way as any other form, but instead of choosing just one table at the start of the Wizard, you choose two.

Activity 5: Creating a form with a subform...

In this activity you will:

● create a form with a subform to enter data into more than one table.

▶ Open the database *School Data Activity 6 complete.mdb* provided with the online resources for Chapter 8. We will use this to create a copy of the form you used to enter pupil data.

▶ Click on **Forms** and choose to **Create form by using wizard**.

▶ Select **Pupils:tbl** and select all the fields. Don't click on **Next** yet.

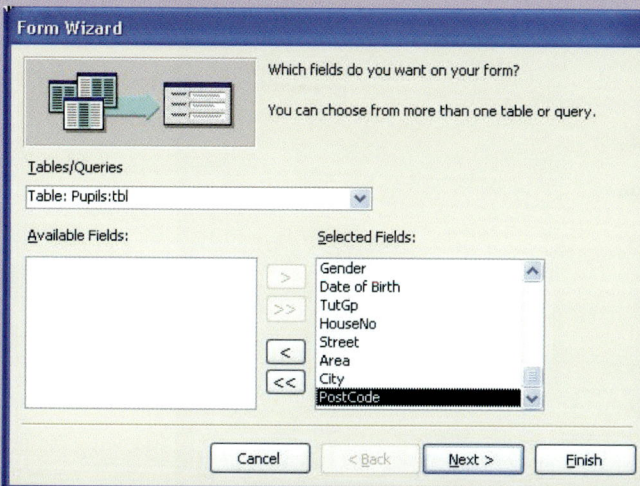

Figure 9.34: *Selecting all fields from **Pupils:tbl**.*

▶ Now choose **PupilGroups:tbl**. There is no need to select the **PupilNo** field, since this is already present. Just select the **Group** field, then click on **Next**.

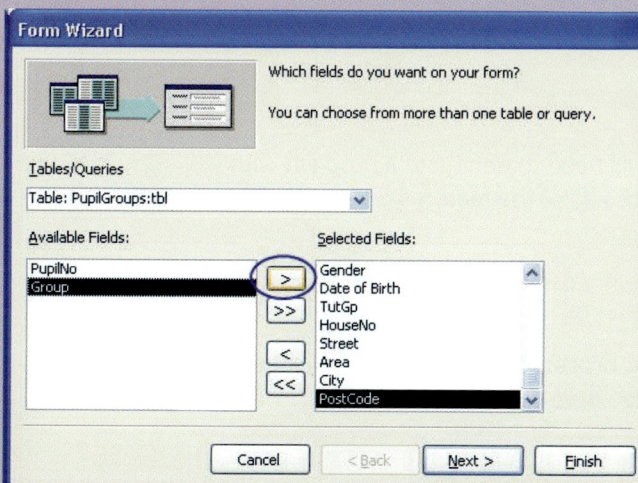

Figure 9.35: *Selecting the remaining field from **PupilGroups:tbl**.*

▶ You will then be asked to confirm that you want to group your data by **Pupils:tbl** as a **Form with subform(s)**. This is correct – you want a form for every record in **Pupils:tbl**, so just click on **Next**.

▶ On the next screen, confirm that you want the subform in **Datasheet View**, by clicking on **Next**.

▶ You will then be asked to select a style. Choose one from the list, then click on **Next**.

▶ You will then be asked to name your form and subform. Give them names that will avoid overwriting the existing forms, then click on **Finish**:

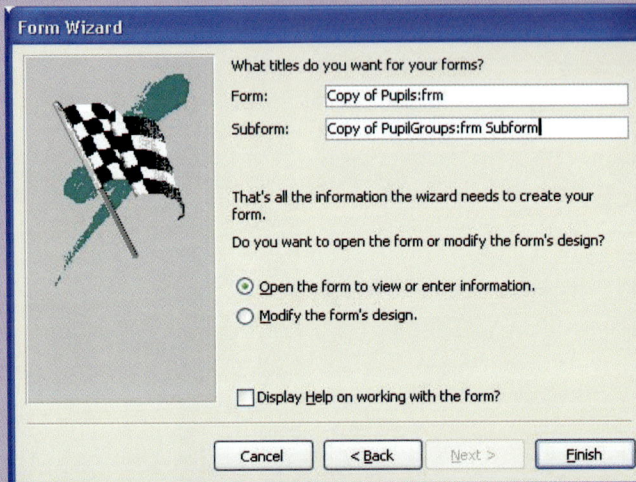

Figure 9.36: *Naming the form and subform.*

You have now created a form with a subform. If you want some more practice in editing a form design you might like to see if you can make it match the original.

The file ***Form Design MD2.doc***, provided with the downloadable resources for this chapter, is an alternative design for the forms needed for Mal's database, making use of a subform.

Portfolio builder

When you are working for your own portfolio you will need to negotiate a problem with your teacher. It is important that this allows you to use all of the features detailed in the 'How to achieve' section at the beginning of this chapter.

Your first task will be to write an explanation that clearly defines the problem, as described on pages 133–134 of this chapter.

You should then follow through the decision-making process in this chapter. You should make rough notes as you work through the first three questions.

● What data needs to be stored?
● What tables are needed?
● What fields are needed for each table?

The next question is:

● How will the tables be linked?

You need to think this through carefully, and then a diagram to show the tables and links between them, similar to the one shown in Figure 9.1.

You should then complete a **Database table planning sheet** for each of your tables in order to answer the final two questions.

● What type of data will be stored in each field?
● What checking methods can be used to minimise data entry errors?

You need to make sure that you include details of all the field names, data types and field sizes that you will use. You must also set the primary key for each table. For a **Merit** you must also include combo boxes and validation rules and for a **Distinction** you must include at least one input mask.

When you have a design it is a good idea to check it again against the 'How to achieve' section at the beginning of this chapter.

When you have designed your tables you then need to produce a design for your forms. For a **Pass** this might simply be a statement of the style and format that you will choose from the wizard.

For a **Merit** or **Distinction** your form designs should be a set of drawings (by hand or computer art/design package) to show the layout you will use for *each* table. It must *not* be simply a printout of a completed form – this cannot be considered a design. Your design should show:

● the size of the form
● the background and text colours
● the position of the fields and the labels to use for them
● the font and size to use
● any additional items, such as title, logo
● any buttons, and the style for these – text or graphic.

You will see why it is not a good idea to choose an over-complex problem requiring many tables – two or three tables are enough. The more tables you create the more designs you need to produce.

Example designs are provided with the Chapter 9 downloadable resources.

● **Form design P.doc** is an example of a **Pass** level design.
● **Form design MD1.doc** and **Form design MD2.doc** provide two alternative sets of designs, each of which would be sufficient to gain a **Merit** or **Distinction**.

When you think you have completed all your designs you need to make sure that your portfolio contains:

1 your own explanation of the task and the user requirements
2 a diagram showing the relationships between your proposed tables
3 a printout of your database table planning sheet for each table
4 a design for your forms.

CHAPTER (10)

➔ *Assessment Objective 2*
Construct the Database According to the Design

. . . .

Overview:

In this chapter you will actually create the database for Mal's Car Hire that we designed in Chapter 9. You will set up the three tables, create the forms and enter some sample data.

There are very few new skills to learn here – you have already learned most of what is necessary in the previous two chapters. You will learn a little more about using the lookup wizard and more about the process of linking tables.

As you work through this example project, you will be producing the type of evidence that will be required for this objective in your own portfolio when you come to work on your own database.

In order to complete the activities in this chapter you will need access to a number of additional files. These files are contained in the Chapter 10 Resources zip file which can be downloaded from the OCR Nationals in ICT (Units 6 & 7) Student Resources page on the Payne-Gallway website: www.payne-gallway.co.uk.

How this assessment objective will be assessed...

The most important evidence you will be producing will be the database itself. You will need to produce a database that works, with a minimum of two related tables, each containing a minimum of 20 records. You must have at least one form for data entry and the database must reflect the design you produced for Assessment Objective 1.

If you need to change your design as you create it, that is fine, but you must write about any changes that you make, giving your reasons. There is a lot of difference between someone who improves on an original design and someone who simply ignores the design!

Skills to use...

- Setting up database tables, setting field names, data types, field lengths, validation, combo boxes and input masks
- Setting a primary key for each table
- Linking tables
- Creating and customising forms for the input of data

How to achieve...

Pass requirements

P1 You will construct a relational database that works, with a minimum of 20 records in each table.

P2 A form will be used to enter data into at least one table. This might be created using a wizard.

P3 The database will mostly reflect the design submitted for AO1.

Merit requirements

M1 You will construct a relational database that works, with a minimum of 20 records in each table.

M2 Forms will be used to enter data into all tables. These might be created using a wizard but some editing will have taken place.

M3 The database will reflect the design submitted for AO1.

Distinction requirements

D1 You will construct a relational database that works, with a minimum of 20 records in each table.

D2 Forms will be used to enter data into all tables. These will all be customised, including additional buttons.

D3 The database will match exactly the design submitted for AO1. Any improvements will be documented.

Creating the table structures

The first stage in creating the database is to set up the tables according to your design. You should start a new Access database, then choose to **Create table in Design view**. You should then use your **Database table design sheets** to enter the field names, data types, field lengths, descriptions, validation, lookups (to set combo boxes) and input masks that you have designed.

Activity 1: Setting up the tables for Mal's Car Hire database...

In this activity you will:

● use the designs from Chapter 9 to set up the three tables for Mal's Car Hire database.

You will need to use the three files of table designs developed in the last chapter. These are provided in the Chapter 10 downloadable resources and are called **Planning sheet customer table.doc**, **Planning sheet cars table.doc** and **Planning sheet hire table. doc**. You may like to print these.

▶ Start by looking at the design for the **Customer** table.

▶ Load Microsoft Access and choose **Create a new file...** and **Blank database...** as you did in Chapter 9 Activity1. Save the file with an appropriate file name – it will be Mal's Car Hire.

▶ Choose to **Create table in Design view**.

▶ You will be taken to the **Design View** of a blank table. Here you should enter the details of the fields needed for the **Customer** table, which are summarised in Figure 10.1.

Field Name	Data Type	Field Size / Format	Validation etc
CustomerNo (primary key)	Autonumber	Long Integer	None
Title	Text	Length 4 characters	Lookup from Mr/Mrs/Miss/Ms/Revd/Dr Don't restrict to this list.
FirstName	Text	Length 20 characters	None
LastName	Text	Length 20 characters	None
TelNo	Text	Length 15 characters	None
MobNo	Text	Length 15 characters	None
Address1	Text	Length 30 characters	None
Address2	Text	Length 30 characters	None
Address3	Text	Length 30 characters	None
Address4	Text	Length 30 characters	None
PostCode	Text	Length 8 characters	Input mask: >LL09\ 0LL

Figure 10.1: *Fields for the Customer table.*

▶ Enter the first field name: **CustomerNo** and select the **AutoNumber** data type. Add a suitable description in the right-hand column.

▶ Click on the **Primary Key** icon to make this the primary key for the table.

▶ The next field **Title** needs to be set so that it can be looked up from a list. Remember that, although the field type will be text, you need to choose **Lookup Wizard** in the data type column in order to set the options.

▶ Choose **I will type in the values that I want** and on the next screen of the wizard enter the list shown in the table in Figure 10.1.

▶ When you have finished the wizard, don't forget to set the **Field Size** to 4 and enter a description. When you enter values in the lookup wizard it doesn't automatically restrict entries to this list, which is what we want, so there is no more to do for this field.

▶ Enter the rest of the fields according to the plan, adding a suitable description for each one.

▶ The last field **PostCode** has an input mask. Enter this exactly as it is shown on the plan – **>LL09\ 0LL** – in the **Input Mask** line in the **Field Properties** box for this field.

▶ When you have entered all the fields, check your table against Figure 10.1, then save it as **Customer:tbl**.

When you have finished a table you should consider what skills you have used and how you should provide evidence of these.

Here you have entered all the details of the fields, most of which can be shown by a screenshot of the top of the screen. However, you have also set alternatives so that the **Title** field can be entered using combo boxes and you have set an input mask for **Post-Code**.

You could create screenshots of these three items and put them together onto a word-processed page as shown in *Table structure evidence.jpg* which is provided in the Chapter 10 downloadable resources.

▶ Close down your **Customer:tbl** table.

▶ Now take the design for the **Cars** table, summarised in Figure 10.2.

Field Name	Data Type	Field Size / Format	Validation etc
RegNo (Primary Key)	Text	7 characters	Input mask: >AAaaaaa
Make	Text	15 characters	Combo box – Lookup from another table – BMW, Ford, Renault, Toyota, Vauxhall, VW. Limit entries to this list.
Model	Text	15 characters	None
Year	Number	Integer	Validation: <=Year(Now)
EngineSize	Number	Single	Validation: >=0.8 And <=4
NoDoors	Number	Byte	Combo box – Lookup from 2, 3, 4 or 5. Limit entries to this list.
Colour	Text	15 characters	None
Body	Text	10 characters	Combo box – Lookup from another table - Saloon, Estate, 4x4, Hatch, sports. Limit entries to this list.

Figure 10.2: Fields for the Cars table.

Two fields in this table – **Make** and **Body** – are planned to be lookups from another table. This means you need to create these tables first. There is no need to be concerned about the designs of these tables, as long as they contain the values we need. Although you could create the table in design view, it is easier for simple tables such as these to create them simply by entering data.

▶ Choose **Create table by entering data**.

▶ Enter the options for the **Make** field into the first column.

▶ Close down the window and save when prompted as **Makes:tbl**. The software will give a message trying to persuade you to allow it to set a primary key. This is not necessary in this type of table, so choose **No**.

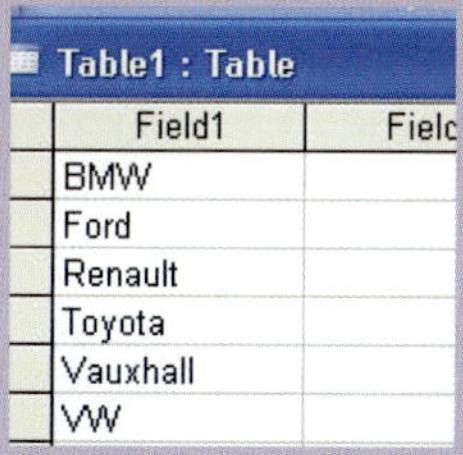

Figure 10.3: Entering the options for the Makes lookup table.

▶ Create a table for the body types in the same way. Call this **BodyType:tbl**.

▶ Now you have created the two lookup tables needed you can create the **Cars** table. Choose **Create table in Design view**.

▶ Enter the field name **RegNo** and set this as a text field with a field size property of 7 characters. Enter the input mask **>AAaaaaa** as on the plan. This will make sure all letters entered are capitals and will require at least 2 characters, with up to 5 more.

▶ Add a suitable description for the **RegNo** field.

▶ Use the **Primary Key** icon to set this as the primary key for the table. 🔑

▶ Enter the next field name – **Make**. Although this field type will be text you need to choose **Lookup Wizard** in the data type column in order to set the options. This time choose to look up the values from another table.

Figure 10.4: *Lookup table for **Body Type**.*

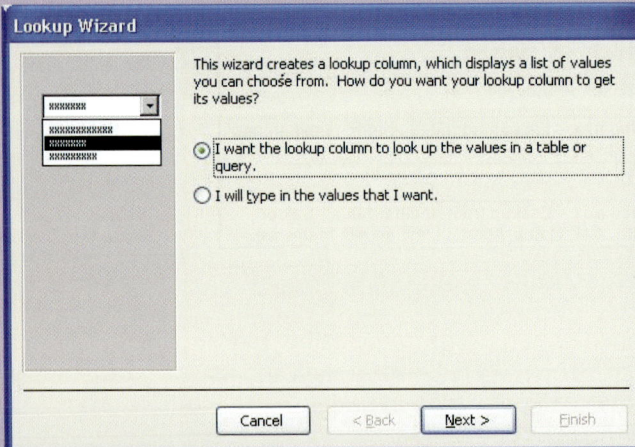

Figure 10.5: *Choosing to look up values from another table.*

▶ Choose **Makes:tbl**, then select the only field available.

▶ You are then asked if you want the table sorted. Although you typed in the list in alphabetical order, it would be useful if the lookup table was always in order, even if Mal added extra makes to **Makes:tbl**. Choose to sort on Field1 (the only field).

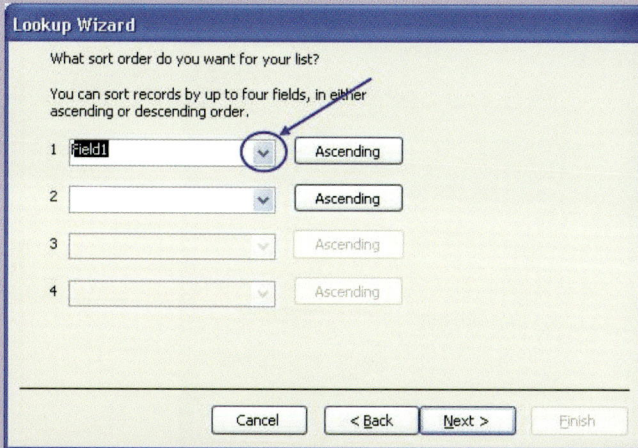

Figure 10.6: *Choosing to have the lookup column sorted.*

▶ You will then be shown a preview of your lookup table. This should look fine, so you simply need to click on **Next**.

▶ Next you will be asked for the name of the lookup column. Keep it as **Make** by clicking on **Finish**.

▶ Access now needs to create a link between the cars table you are creating and **Makes:tbl**. You will be asked to save the main table you are creating. Call it **Car:tbl**.

▶ The Make field will now be set back to **Text**. Set the **Field Size** to 15 and enter a description.

▶ We want values to be restricted to the lookup table, so that errors will be reduced. Click on the **Lookup** tab in the **Field Properties** section at the bottom of the screen and set **Limit To List** to **Yes**.

▶ Enter the details for the **Model** field, with a suitable description.

▶ Enter the details for the **Year** field, with a suitable description. Choose **Integer** as the field size and type the validation code **<=Year(Now)** into the **Validation Rule** box and a suitable error message in the **Validation Text** box.

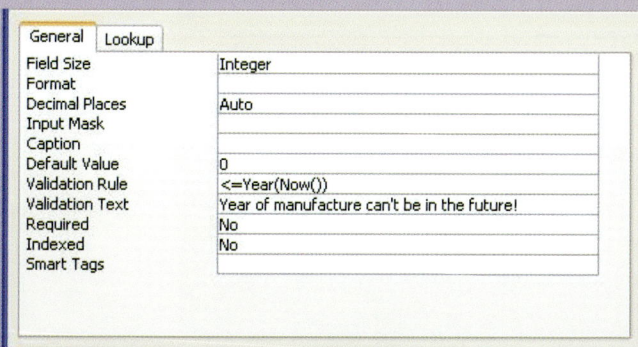

Figure 10.7: *Setting validation for the Year field.*

▶ Enter the details for the **EngineSize** field, adding your own description and validation text:

General	Lookup	
Field Size	Single	
Format		
Decimal Places	Auto	
Input Mask		
Caption		
Default Value	0	
Validation Rule	>=0.8 And <=4	
Validation Text	Engiine size must be in litres, between 0.8 and 4	
Required	No	
Indexed	No	
Smart Tags		

*Figure 10.8: Properties for the **EngineSize** field.*

▶ Use the **Lookup Wizard** to create the options for the next field, which is **NoDoors**. Choose **I will type in the values that I want**, as you did for **Title** in **Customer: tbl**. Don't forget to change the data type to **Number**, the field size to **Byte** and set the lookup option to **Limit to list**.

Car:tbl : Table

	Field Name	Data Type	
🔑	RegNo	Text	Registration number, entered with no spaces. As this is unique it is also the primary key
	Make	Text	Make of car. If Mal starts to buy makes that are not on the list, add to the list in Makes:tbl
	Model	Text	Model of car.
	Year	Number	Year of manufacture
	EngineSize	Number	Engine size, in Litres. Enter just the numeric value, eg 1.6
▶	NoDoors	Number	The number of doors.

General	Lookup	
Field Size	Byte	
Format		
Decimal Places	Auto	
Input Mask		
Caption		
Default Value	0	
Validation Rule		
Validation Text		
Required	No	
Indexed	No	
Smart Tags		

General	Lookup	
Display Control	Combo Box	
Row Source Type	Value List	
Row Source	2;3;4;5	
Bound Column	1	
Column Count	1	
Column Heads	No	
Column Widths	2.54cm	
List Rows	8	
List Width	2.54cm	
Limit To List	Yes	

*Figure 10.9: **Field Properties** settings for **NoDoors**.*

▶ Add the last two fields – **Colour** and **Body**. Use the **Lookup wizard** to link the **Body** field to **BodyType:tbl** in the same way as you set the **Model** field.

▶ Save your table, then produce some screenshots to show the options you have set, before closing down the table. Don't worry that all the options in the Lookup section won't be visible on your screenshots – there will be enough evidence to show that you have created them.

▶ You now need to create the final table: **Hire:tbl**. The design is summarised in Figure 10.10.

Field Name	Data Type	Field Size / Format	Validation etc
HireNo (Primary Key)	Autonumber	Long Integer	None
CustomerID	Number	Long Integer	Lookup from CustomerNo field of customer table.
RegNo	Text	7 characters	Lookup from RegNo field of cars table.
DateOut	Date	Eg 01/01/2007	None
DateBack	Date	Eg 01/01/2007	None
Set a validation rule for the whole table, which checks to make sure that DateBack >= DateOut			

Figure 10.10: Fields for the Hire table.

▶ Choose to **Create table in Design view**.

▶ Create the **HireNo** field as **AutoNumber** and set it as the primary key, adding an appropriate description.

▶ Create a field called **CustomerID** and use the **Lookup Wizard** to link this to **Customer:tbl**. When you are asked to choose fields, choose **CustomerNo**, **Title**, **FirstName** and **LastName**. Although we only want the **CustomerNo** to be inserted into this table, having the other fields on view will make it easier for Mal to select the right customer – he won't have to remember their ID number.

▶ Choose to sort the list on **LastName**, then **FirstName**, to make it even easier for Mal to find the customer he wants.

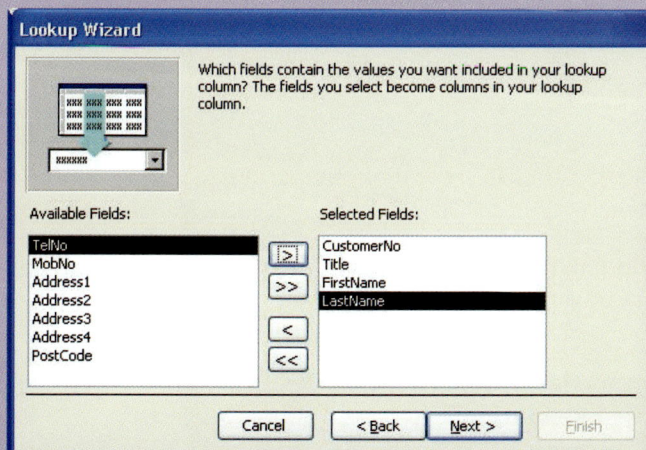

Figure 10.11: Choosing the fields from Customer:tbl in the lookup wizard.

▶ Although Access recommends hiding the key column, that is not what we want. It is the key column – **CustomerNo** – that we want entered into this field. Deselect this option:

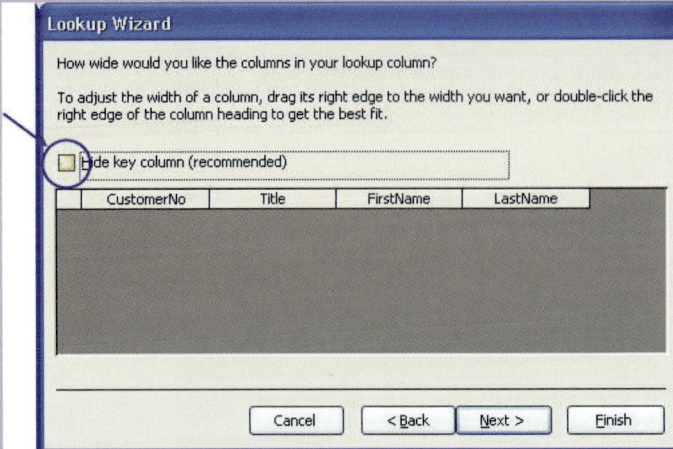

Figure 10.12: Choosing not to hide the key column.

▶ Keep **CustomerNo** selected as the identifying field in the next screen, then **Finish**. Save the table when prompted, calling it **Hire:tbl**.

▶ You should see that Access automatically sets the data type and field size to match the **CustomerNo** field in **Customer:tbl**. You now only need to add a suitable description.

▶ Create **RegNo** as a lookup from **Car:tbl** in the same way. Show **RegNo**, **Make** and **Model**, sort by **RegNo** and make sure that the **RegNo** field is not hidden.

▶ Create the two fields **DateOut** and **DateBack** as planned. Make sure you have a suitable description for all fields.

▶ Save your table and create some appropriate screenshots to show the settings you have used.

The final item on the plan is to create a validation check that makes sure the **DateBack** is later than the **DateOut**. This is not a validation check on a single field, but on the whole table.

▶ Click on **View** on the menu bar and choose **Properties**. This will show properties for the table, including rows for **Validation Rule** and **Validation Text**.

▶ To refer to field names in a table validation rule you have to put them inside square brackets. Enter the rule and text as shown in Figure 10.13.

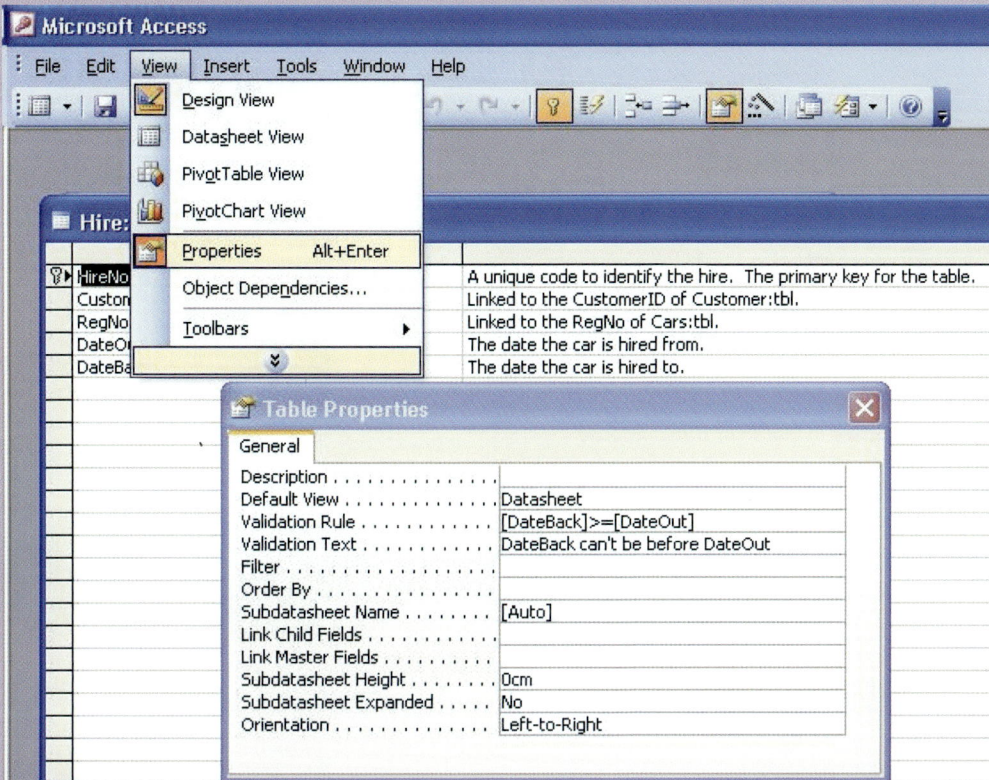

Figure 10.13: Entering a validation rule for the table.

▶ Save your table again and create any screenshots you need as evidence of what you have done, then close down the table.

▶ You can try entering some data into your three main tables by double clicking to open them and typing in data. You might try to test some of your validation checks by entering data you think should not be allowed. You will need to enter at least one customer and at least one car before you can enter anything into the hire table.

▶ If you want to check any of the settings in your tables you can compare them with the file ***Mals Car Hire 1.mdb*** provided with the downloadable resources for this chapter.

Linking the tables

Access automatically linked some of your tables when you used the lookup wizard. To see these links you need to click on the **Relationships** icon on the toolbar.

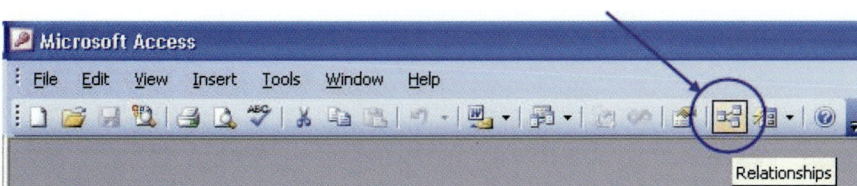

*Figure 10.14: The **Relationships** icon.*

At first it is not easy to see where the relationships are, but you can move the tables around, by dragging on their blue title bars, until they are clearer. You can also drag the bottom of each box down, so that all the fields can be seen:

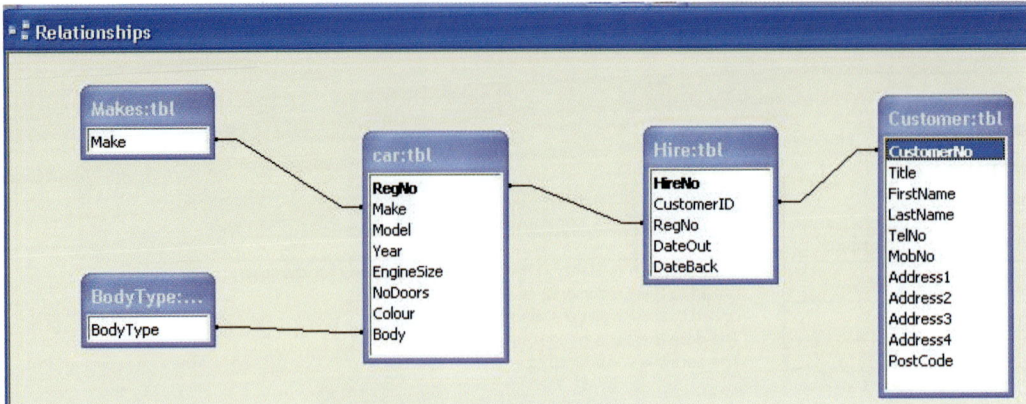

Figure 10.15: *Showing the relationships in Mal's Car Hire database.*

Although the database will work quite well without changing anything, there is nothing to stop Mal entering a non-existent customer number or registration number into the hire table. Access allows us to prevent such errors by setting **referential integrity** on the two main relationships. This is done by double clicking on the relationship line, then checking the three optional boxes as shown in Figure 10.16.

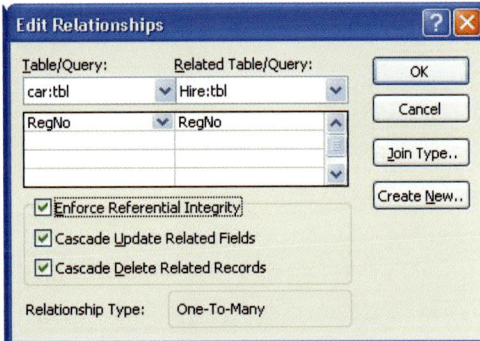

Figure 10.16: *Setting referential integrity.*

Referential Integrity means that Access will not allow you to choose a value in the linked field of the child table that does not exist in the parent table. In the link between **Hire:tbl** and **Customer:tbl** this means that you will be prevented from entering a customer number in the hire table that does not exist in the customer table.

Cascade Update Related Fields means that if you change a value in the linked field of the parent table, this change will be made to any matching records in the child table. Since this is the key field it is very unlikely to happen, but there is no harm in setting it. In the case of Mal's Car Hire, if Mal decided to buy a personalised number plate for one of his cars, he could then change the registration number in the **Car** table and this change would then be made to all linked records in the **Hire** table.

Cascade Delete Related Records means that if you delete a record in the parent table, Access will automatically delete all related records in the child table. In this example, if Mal sold a car and deleted that record from **Car:tbl**, then all hire records for that car would also be deleted. This is the feature that enabled you in Chapter 9 to delete a pupil record and automatically have that pupil removed from all classes. You need to think about whether or not this is what you want, though usually it is advisable.

You should always consider setting these options on the main links in your database. There is no need to alter any links to lookup tables such as **Makes:tbl** and **BodyType:tbl**.

If you haven't already linked the tables using the lookup wizard, you may find that the links are not set automatically. If the links are not already there, you need to create them yourself in the **Relationships** window. First you need to right click on the **Relationships** window and choose **Show All** to see all the tables. Then you can link them by dragging from the link field of the parent table to the related field in the child table.

Activity 2: Viewing and editing relationships...

In this activity you will:

- view the relationships in Mal's Car Hire database
- edit relationships to set referential integrity
- delete a relationship
- set a relationship.

▶ Load the database you created in Activity 1. Alternatively you can use the file provided with the downloadable resources for this chapter called **Mals Car Hire 1.mdb**.

▶ Click on the **Relationships** icon to see the relationships in this file. If you do not see all five tables, right click and choose **Show All**.

▶ Double click on the link between **Car:tbl** and **Hire:tbl**. You should now be able to **Enforce Referential Integrity**, **Cascade Update Related Fields** and **Cascade Delete Related Records** as shown in Figure 10.16.

▶ Double click on the link between **Customer:tbl** and **Hire:tbl** and set the options as before.

You have now set the relationships as they need to be. However, this is a good opportunity to find out how to delete and set relationships too:

▶ Click on the link you have just set and press the **Delete** key. This will allow you to delete the relationship. Confirm the deletion by clicking **Yes** when prompted.

▶ Recreate the relationship by dragging with the mouse from the **CustomerNo** field of **Customer:tbl** to the **CustomerID** field of **Hire:tbl**.

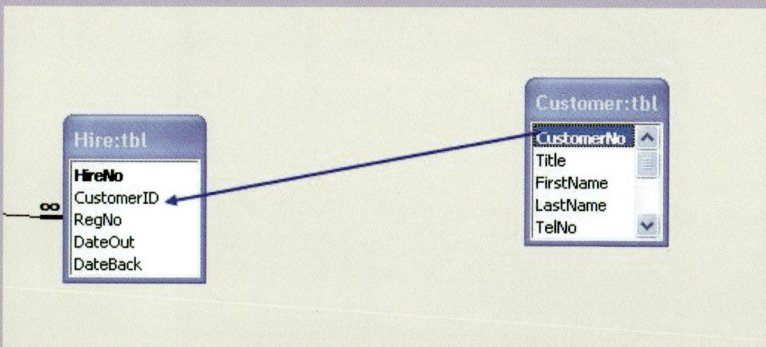

Figure 10.17: Creating a relationship by dragging from one field to the same field in another table.

▶ Set the options as before, then close down the **relationships** window, saving the layout if prompted.

Creating the forms

Now the tables are created you need to create the forms. This is done in the same way as described in the last chapter – first use the form wizard, then edit the layout of the form using design view.

If you are aiming for a **Pass** in this unit you only need to carry out the first part of Activity 3 and create the forms using the wizard. If you are aiming for a **Merit** or **Distinction** you also need to customise each form that you create.

Activity 3: Creating the forms...

In this activity you will:

● create forms for **Mals Car Hire** database, following the designs from the last chapter.

▶ Choose a set of form designs by opening *one* of the following files from the Chapter 10 downloadable resources, according to the level you are aiming for in this unit.
  1. Form Design Pass.doc – this set of designs uses only the form wizard and is at **Pass** level for this unit.
  2. Form Design MD1.doc – this is the simpler of the two sets of form designs that are at **Merit**/**Distinction** level. There is a separate form for each table.
  3. Form Design MD2.doc – this is a more sophisticated set of designs, using two forms only, one with a subform. While it is not necessary to create a subform in order to gain a **Distinction**, you may find this is a neater and more satisfying solution. However, if you found subforms confusing, then you should consider using the MD1 form designs.

▶ Print out the designs you have chosen.

▶ Click on **Forms** in the **Objects** panel and use the form wizard to create a form for **Car:tbl**. Remember to follow the design when choosing fields, layout and style.

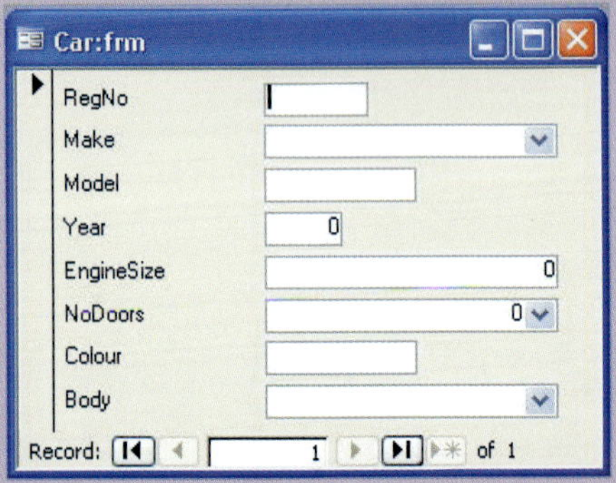

Figure 10.18: Car:frm.

▶ Test your form by entering some realistic details of a car. You might like to copy the data shown in Figure 10.19.

▶ Sometimes you find that a form created by a wizard doesn't leave quite enough space for a field. Here you may find there is not enough space for the registration number.

▶ Click on the **View** button to switch to **Design View**, then click into the **RegNo** box and drag it out a little to the right.

▶ Switch back to **Form View** and you should see that there is now sufficient room in the field.

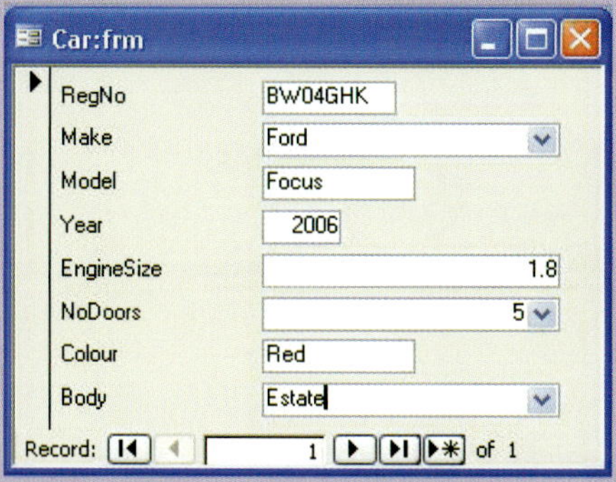

Car:frm	
RegNo	BW04GHK
Make	Ford
Model	Focus
Year	2006
EngineSize	1.8
NoDoors	5
Colour	Red
Body	Estate

Record: ◄◄ ◄ 1 ► ►► ►* of 1

***Figure 10.19:** The finished **Car:frm**.*

▶ Now use the form wizard to create the remaining form(s) on your design sheet.

▶ Test each of your form(s) by entering a record as before.

▶ If you are working to **Pass** level, then you can now create a screenshot of each of your forms. There is no need to complete the rest of this activity. You can compare your final forms with those in the database file **Mals Car Hire 2P.mdb** provided with the downloadable resources for this chapter.

▶ If you have chosen one of the **Merit**/**Distinction** designs, you should now open up each of your forms in **Design View** and alter the layout so that it matches the design. You can use a simple piece of clipart for the logo, or you might choose to use the file **Logo.bmp**, supplied with the resources for this chapter.

▶ You can compare your final forms with those in the database files **Mals Car Hire 2MD1.mdb** (the design with three custom forms) and **Mals Car Hire 2MD2.mdb** (the design with two forms, including one with a subform).

Your forms may not be exactly like the ones contained in these files, but they should be very similar, as you should have managed to create forms that were reasonably close to the designs. For a **Distinction** your forms should match the designs exactly, unless you make a further improvement which you will need to write up.

You should provide a screenshot of each of your final forms, for your portfolio.

⊙TIP

If you find, when creating your tables, relationships and forms, that your designs were not really good enough, or that something was missing, for the purposes of this assessment you can always change your designs, to make sure you don't miss out on the **Distinction** objective of matching your designs exactly. This is not good practice in real situations but it can be the easiest way of meeting this objective.

Entering the data

For your own portfolio database you are required to enter at least 20 records into each table. This data will usually be entered by typing into the forms. This can be a time-consuming activity, so for this practice database some files of data have been provided for you, so that you only have to import them into your database.

You can choose whether to enter your own data or to follow Activity 4 to import the data provided for you.

Activity 4: Importing data into a database...

In this activity you will:

● import data into your database tables.

▶ Open the database file you have been creating. Alternatively you could use one of the **Mals Car Hire 2** files, according to the type of form you want to use.

▶ Click on **File** on the menu bar, then choose **Get External Data** and **Import**.

▶ Change the **Files of type** to **Microsoft Excel**, then locate and import the file **CustomerData.xls** (provided with the Chapter 10 resources).

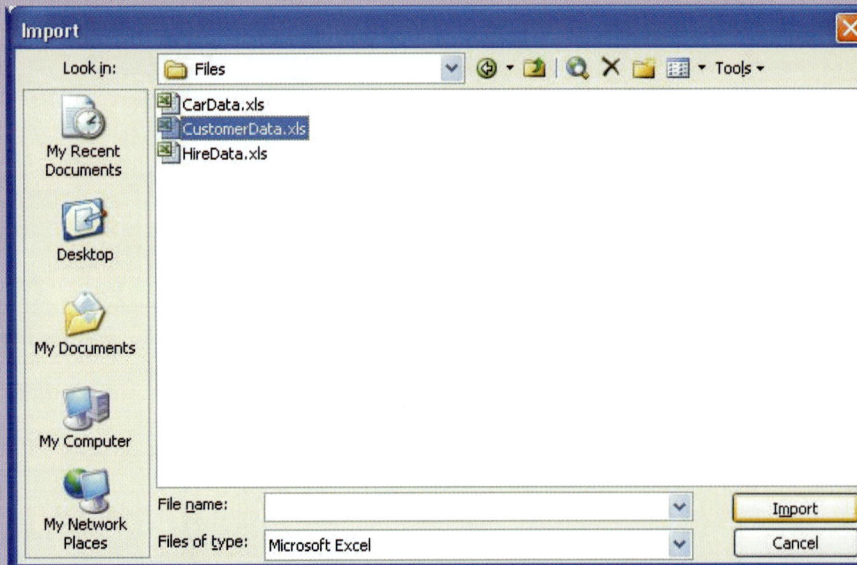

Figure 10.20: Finding the **CustomerData** Excel file.

▶ Choose to show **Sheet 1**, then click **Next**.

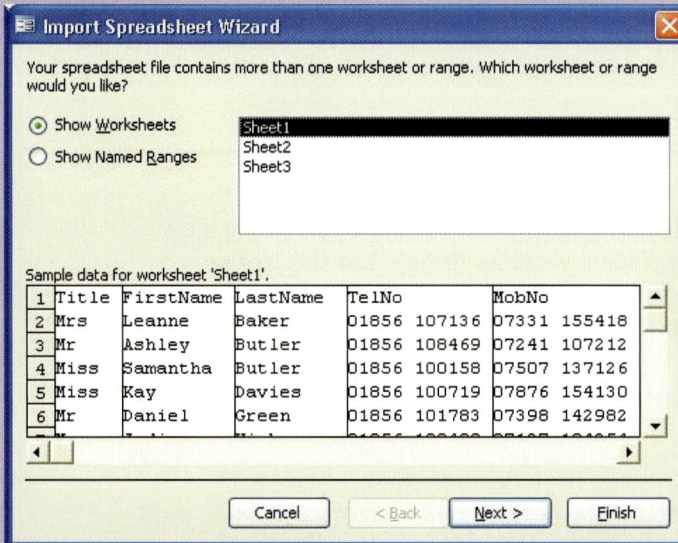

*Figure 10.21: Show **Sheet 1**.*

▶ Choose the **First Row Contains Column Headings** option, then click **Next**.

▶ Choose to store the data **In an Existing Table** and choose **Customer:tbl**.

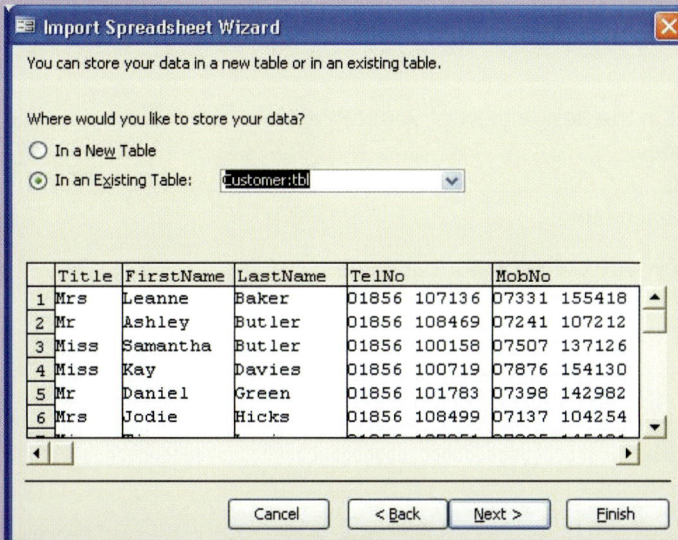

*Figure 10.22: Importing into **Customer:tbl**.*

▶ Click **Next** and then **Finish**.

The data from the file should now be imported.

▶ Follow the same steps to import the Excel file ***CarData.xls*** into **Car:tbl** and ***Hire-Data.xls*** into **Hire:tbl**.

▶ Open up the tables and the forms to see the data you have imported.

You can check the tables by looking at the appropriate file from the downloadable resources for the next chapter (Chapter 11) – one of the ***Mals Car Hire 3*** database files.

Portfolio builder

For your own portfolio you will need to take the designs you created for Assessment Objective 1, which should contain designs for:

- table structures
- relationships
- forms.

You must then follow the steps taken in this chapter to create:

- the tables – setting field names, data types, field lengths and any combo boxes (using the lookup wizard), validation rules and input masks following your design. You should also set the primary key for each table.
- the relationships between the tables, setting referential integrity between your main tables
- forms to enter the data into all of your tables. This may be a separate form for each table or you may use a subform.

When you have created your tables and forms you then need to enter at least 20 records into each table. While it is likely that you will need to type these in, if you have a table of personal details such as the **Customer:tbl** in Mal's Car Hire database, you may find that you can use the file *SampleData.xls* provided with the resources for this chapter. This contains a range of specimen data, with instructions for use to create a spreadsheet you can import, to save you some typing time. It is very important that the column headings in your spreadsheet match the column headings in your database table exactly.

The database you create is really evidence enough for your assessment. However, if you are working as part of a group your teacher will probably need you to create some paper evidence. This should include:

- screenshots to show the options you have set in the design view of your tables
- a screenshot of your final **Relationships** window
- a screenshot showing each of your final forms
- screenshots or printouts showing the data in each table.

There is no need to provide any description of *how* you created your database.

CHAPTER 11

➔ *Assessment Objective 3*

Interrogate the Database

....

Overview:

For this objective you need to create queries that will allow your user to easily find the data s/he needs from your database. These queries should carry out sorts and searches to provide lists of records that meet your user's requirements.

In this chapter you will see how the user's requirements are converted into these queries and how to check with the assessment requirements and add additional queries if necessary.

> In order to complete the activities in this chapter you will need access to a number of additional files. These files are contained in the Chapter 11 Resources zip file which can be downloaded from the OCR Nationals in ICT (Units 6 & 7) Student Resources page on the Payne-Gallway website: www.payne-gallway.co.uk.

How this assessment objective will be assessed...

- You will need to produce two screenshots for each query you create: one to show the design view and one to show the output produced when the query is run. You should also print the results of each query and include these print outs with your screenshots.
- You will also need to add some explanation to each of your screenshots, saying why you have created each query. For a **Pass** this might simply be a statement of what the query is designed to produce, while for a **Merit** you will need to explain why you created each query by referring to your user's requirements. For a **Distinction** you are asked to 'fully justify' the range of queries produced. This means that your explanations must be detailed, and that they should contain some evidence that you thought of alternative queries, showing why you chose the ones you did and why other possibilities were rejected.

Skills to use...

- Creating queries in design view using more than one table
- Setting sort criteria using one and two fields
- Setting search criteria using more than one field
- Setting search criteria using AND, NOT, OR, BETWEEN and parameter queries

How to achieve...

Pass requirements

P1 You will carry out one sort on one table.

P2 You will carry out one query that searches on one criterion.

P3 You will carry out a second query that searches on more than one criterion, using more than one table.

P4 You will describe the purpose of each query.

Merit requirements

M1 You will carry out one sort on one table, using more than one field.

M2 You will carry out a range of queries, including one that searches on more than one criterion.

M3 You will carry out one query that searches using complex criteria – using AND, NOT, OR, BETWEEN or parameters – using more than one table.

M4 All queries used will be appropriate.

M5 You will explain the range of queries used.

Distinction requirements

D1 You will carry out one sort on one table using more than one field.

D2 You will carry out a range of queries, including one that searches on more than one criterion.

D3 You will carry out two queries that search using complex criteria – using AND, NOT, OR, BETWEEN or parameters – using more than one table.

D4 All queries used will be appropriate.

D5 You will fully justify the range of queries used.

Planning and creating queries

The first thing you need to do is refer back to your work for Assessment Objective 1, where you defined the problem (see Chapter 9). A well-defined problem will have listed a number of items that you want to produce from your database. In the problem set out on pages 133–134 we identified the following requirements for Mal's Car Hire system.

● Every day Mal needs to have ready the cars that are going out that day. He would like to be able to print out a list every morning of these cars.

● He would also like to be able to print out a list of cars that are due back in the day, so that he can check them off as they arrive. Sometimes cars are not brought back when they are due. Mal would like to print the name and telephone number of the customers on the list of cars due back, so that he can contact them easily if necessary.

● Mal would also like to be able to use the database to quickly search his stock of cars for a list that meets a customer's requirements. For example, customers often request a particular make, model, engine size and/or body type (hatchback, saloon, estate, 4 x 4, etc.). This would be particularly useful when his assistant, who is not as familiar as he is with the cars, is answering queries.

● Mal also runs promotional events and would like to invite selected customers to these. For example, he might want to invite all customers who have hired a 4 x 4 in the past year to an evening promoting a new 4 x 4 model he has just acquired. He hopes that his database will allow him to produce lists of customers to invite, and to produce mailing labels so that he can easily mail out invitations and leaflets.

In Activity 1 you will consider each of these requirements in turn and create a suitable query for each one.

Activity 1: Creating queries...

In this activity you will:

● create a query to meet each of Mal's requirements.

▶ Load the database you created in Chapter 10. Alternatively you can load one of the files provided in the downloadable resources for this chapter: *Mals Car Hire 3P.mdb*, *Mals Car Hire 3MD1.mdb* or *Mals Car Hire 3MD2.mdb*. These all contain the same data but have different form designs.

Query 1

Mal's first requirement is for a list of cars that are going out on a particular day, so that he can get them ready for customers. You need to think about this and decide what fields would be useful for him. There is no absolute right answer for this – in real life you might go back to Mal and ask him for more details. However, it is essential that the **RegNo** is included, as this is the field that will uniquely identify each car. It would be reasonable to suggest that if the list also includes the **Make**, **Model** and **Colour** of the car, these details will make finding the right car much easier. These all come from **Car:tbl**. The other field that will be needed in the query is the **DateOut** from **Hire:tbl**, as this will be needed to search.

You then need to think about search and sort criteria. Here we need to allow Mal to search for any particular date in the **DateOut** field, so this will be a parameter query. The list could be sorted in order of **RegNo** or perhaps by **Make**, then **Model**. Again, this is a matter of opinion – in your own portfolio you will need to make decisions like these, and **Merit** and **Distinction** candidates will need to explain your reasons.

▶ Create a suitable query for this task. Figure 11.1 shows one possible design:

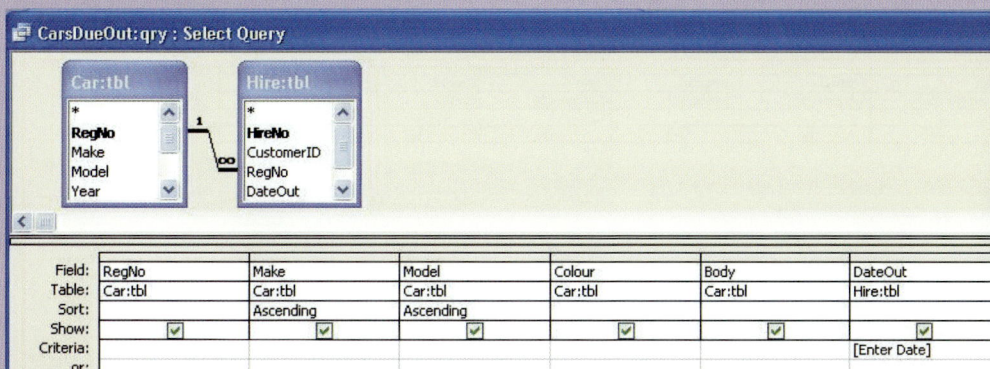

Figure 11.1: *A query to produce a list of cars due out on a particular day.*

▶ Run the query to make sure it works, then save it as **CarsDueOut:qry**.

An alternative would be to assume that Mal would always run this query at the beginning of the day, so the date could be entered automatically using the function **Date()** as shown in Figure 11.2.

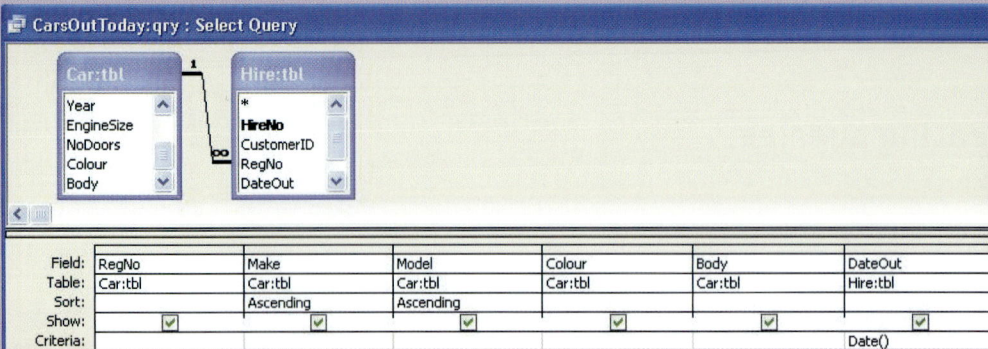

Field:	RegNo	Make	Model	Colour	Body	DateOut
Table:	Car:tbl	Car:tbl	Car:tbl	Car:tbl	Car:tbl	Hire:tbl
Sort:		Ascending	Ascending			
Show:	✔	✔	✔	✔	✔	✔
Criteria:						Date()

Figure 11.2: *A query to produce a list of cars due out today.*

▶ Create this query and save it as **CarsOutToday:qry**. You will need to add some new hire records with cars due out today in order to test this query properly.

You might decide that Mal would benefit from both of these – the **CarsOutToday:qry** for easy regular use and the **CarsDueOut:qry** as a more flexible option if ever he needs to create lists for other days.

Query 2

Mal's next requirement is for a list of cars that are due back in the day, with the name and telephone number of the customers who have these cars.

▶ Create a suitable query for this, choosing appropriate search and sort criteria. Make sure your query works, then save it using a suitable name. One option is shown in Figure 11.3.

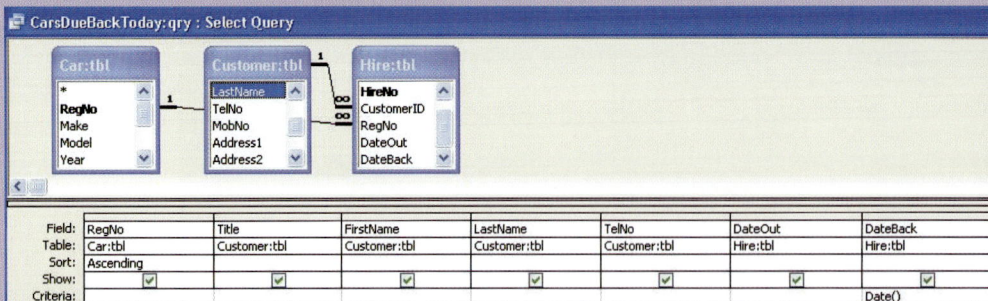

Field:	RegNo	Title	FirstName	LastName	TelNo	DateOut	DateBack
Table:	Car:tbl	Customer:tbl	Customer:tbl	Customer:tbl	Customer:tbl	Hire:tbl	Hire:tbl
Sort:	Ascending						
Show:	✔	✔	✔	✔	✔	✔	✔
Criteria:							Date()

Figure 11.3: *A design for a query to produce a list of cars due back today.*

The reason for sorting this list on **RegNo** is that when cars are brought back you can see the registration number and so find the car easily on the list. If you choose a different sort for your query you are not necessarily wrong, as you may have had a different reason. What is important is that you do have a reason, which you can explain.

Query 3

The next requirement – to quickly search for a list of cars that meet a customer's requirements – is not so straightforward. It is suggested that customers often request a particular make, model, engine size and/or body type (hatchback, saloon, estate, 4 x 4, etc.), so we need to consider a number of options. This sort of search is actually best done using a **Filter by form**, rather than a query.

If there are sufficient other queries to meet the assessment requirements, then it would be quite acceptable to leave this one, as long as you include an explanation that a query is not the best solution here. However, you could create a query where the user may or may not want to specify all the criteria, in which case you could use something like the query shown in Figure 11.4.

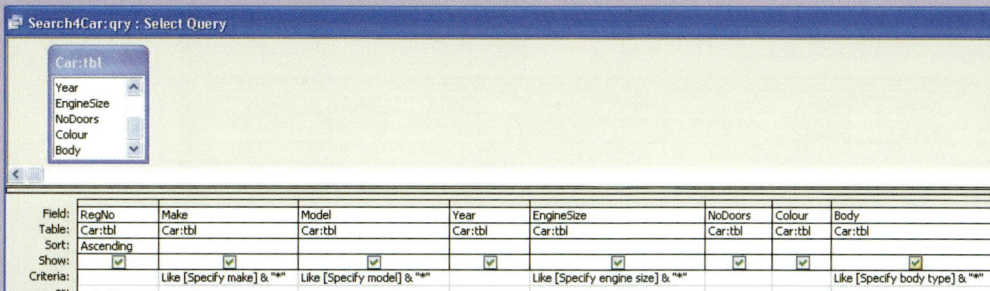

Figure 11.4: *A flexible query to allow searches for different features.*

▶ Create the query shown in Figure 11.4 and try it out a few times. You should see that you can specify any of the required fields – **Make**, **Model**, **EngineSize** and **Body**, but if you don't want to specify anything, simply pressing the **Enter** key at the prompt will not filter that field. For example, if you just wanted a list of all the **Ford**s with an engine size of **2** litres you would type **Ford** at the **Make** prompt, press **Enter** at the **Model** prompt, type **2** at the **EngineSize** prompt and **Enter** at the **Body** prompt.

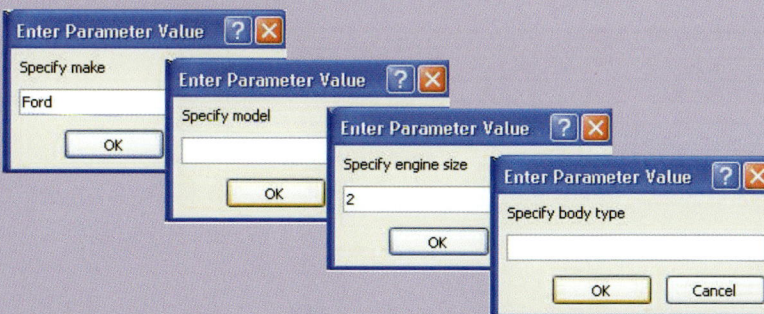

Figure 11.5: *Using the query to find all the Fords with an engine size of 2 litres.*

> ⓘNOTE
>
> If you think customers will want to specify 'at least' a particular engine size you
> need to put this into the query: >=[Specify minimum engine size]. With this you
> would then need to enter 0 if you didn't want to specify an engine size.

Query 4

The last requirement is to find lists of selected customers, e.g. those who have hired a 4 x 4 in the past year. Mal needs the customers' names and addresses. This could be quite complicated, as the selection might need to be on different fields. In situations like this it is best to create a query for a single example first, then see how it can be made more flexible.

▶ Create a query to produce a list of those who have hired a 4 x 4 in the past year. One possible design is shown in Figure 11.6.

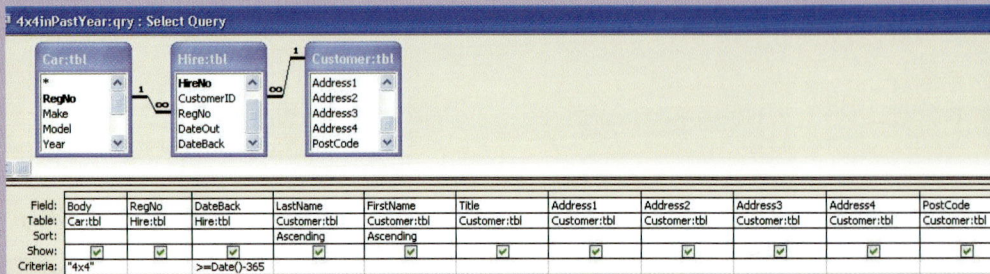

Figure 11.6: *Query to find customers who have hired a 4 x 4 in the past year.*

When you have created your initial query you can then think about what extra flexibility you might need. Here Mal might want to search on **Make** and/or **Model** rather than **Body**. He might also want more flexibility over the time limit. More flexible search criteria for this are shown in Figure 11.7.

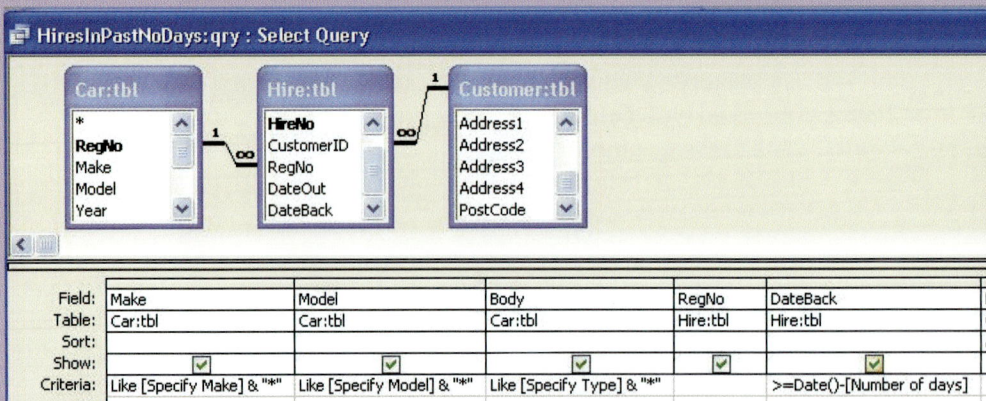

Figure 11.7: *A more flexible query.*

Creating portfolio evidence

When you have created your queries you should produce a word-processed page (or more than one page if necessary) for each one. First put an appropriate title and an explanation of what the query does. For **Merit** and **Distinction** you must also add an explanation of *why* you chose to create this query and *why* you designed it as you did. For a **Distinction** you should try to show that you have considered at least one alternative. You should then add a screenshot showing the design screen of your query and one showing the results. If you have used a parameter query it is a good idea to show at least two sets of results, with different inputs.

Do make sure that your screenshots are large enough to read easily. You may find it best to set your pages to landscape format.

Query write up.doc (provided in the downloadable Chapter 11 resources) shows a write-up for the query in Figure 11.7. It gives a full explanation of the query which would satisfy the **Distinction** requirements.

> **⊘TIP**
>
> If you have too many fields to show them all at once, you can create two screenshots – one of the fields on the left, and one of the fields on the right. You can also adjust the width of the columns by dragging or double clicking the lines on the bar at the top (see Figure 11.8).

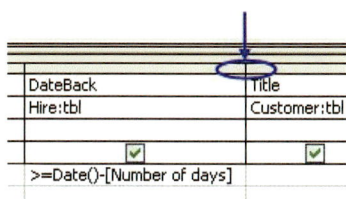

Figure 11.8: *Adjusting column widths in query design view.*

Checking the assessment requirements

Although you need to create queries to meet your user's needs, you must also make sure that you meet the assessment requirements. For example, for a **Distinction** you must have evidence of:

> **D1** a sort on one table using more than one field
>
> **D2** a range of queries, including one that searches on more than one criterion
>
> **D3** two queries that search using complex criteria – using AND, NOT, OR, BETWEEN or parameters – using more than one table.

You should see that D1 has been met in query 1 (and in others too): Figure 11.1 shows a table that is sorted on Make, then on Model.

D2 has been met in query 3, to find a car. Figure 11.4 shows searching on more than one criterion. We have also created queries for four purposes, which is sufficient for 'a range of queries'.

D3 has been met by queries 3 and 4, since both of these use parameters and both use more than one table. However, there is no evidence of any of the other types of criteria listed – AND, NOT, OR, BETWEEN. To safely deserve the **Distinction** you really should try to use at least one of these, so it would be advisable to go back and see if you can think of a way of either adjusting one of your existing queries, or of another query that might be useful to your user, which does use one of these. For your own portfolio you might ask your teacher for ideas at this point.

BETWEEN is often used with dates. We might adjust our last query to search for hires between particular dates rather than just over the last number of days. Figure 11.9 shows how the criteria for **DateBack** can be adjusted to ask for *two* dates and search for all the dates in between these.

| DateBack |
| Hire:tbl |
| |
| ☑ |
| Between [First date?] And [second date] |

Figure 11.9: *Searching between two dates entered by the user.*

In Chapter 9 it was emphasised that you should not set yourself too complex a problem. Here too you need to limit the number of queries you produce, as each query will require more work in future objectives. While it is important to cover all the assessment requirements you should also ensure you do not have too many queries – around four is a sensible number. If you find you have more than this, it would be wise to delete some of the simpler ones and remove evidence for these from your portfolio.

For this example, we might now look at the range of queries we have and make sure that we keep just the most appropriate one for each of Mal's requirements, while also demonstrating the best range of skills. We might, for example, choose to keep **CarsDueOut:qry** but delete **CarsOutToday:qry**, although in reality they might both be of use to Mal. We should also delete the query to find the people who have hired a 4 x 4 in the past year, since this has been replaced by a much more flexible query.

Portfolio builder

For your own portfolio you should create queries to meet the requirements you specified in your work for Assessment Objective 1.

You should save each query once you have tried it out to make sure it works. You should then create pages of evidence for each query, as outlined in the 'Creating portfolio evidence' section above.

Make sure you check what you have done against the requirements for the different levels shown in the 'How to achieve' section on page 180. Ideally you should be able to show the range of searches and sorts required in three or four different queries. If you find that there is a requirement you haven't met, then you will need to think of a query that would meet the requirement that could be of use.

➔ *Assessment Objective 4*
Create Reports

Overview:

This objective requires you to create reports for the queries you have created. You will use wizards to create standard reports and mailing labels. For a **Merit** or **Distinction** you will need to modify the reports to improve their appearance. In this chapter you will use the wizard to create reports for the four queries produced in Chapter 11, then you will learn how to modify these reports.

> In order to complete the activities in this chapter you will need access to a number of additional files. These files are contained in the Chapter 12 Resources zip file which can be downloaded from the OCR Nationals in ICT (Units 6 & 7) Student Resources page on the Payne-Gallway website: www.payne-gallway.co.uk.

How this assessment objective will be assessed...

- Printouts of the reports you produce using the wizard
- For **Merit** and **Distinction**, printouts to show your final, modified reports

Skills to use...

- Create reports using the wizard
- Create mailing labels
- Modify reports by:
  - adding a logo
  - changing the title
  - changing column widths
  - changing/removing column headings
  - changing font, colour and size
  - repositioning elements

How to achieve...

Pass requirements

P1 You will create a report for each query created for AO3.

P2 You will use a range of standard report styles.

Merit requirements

M1 You will create a report for each query created for AO3.

M2 You will customise at least one report.

Distinction requirements

D1 You will create a report for each query created for AO3.

D2 You will customise each report.

Standard reports

In Chapter 8 you created standard reports using the report wizard and investigated the different layouts and styles available. Although in reality you might choose to create all reports using the same layout and style for consistency, for this objective you need to show that you have used a range of styles. For example, you might produce some reports using landscape format and some using portrait; some might be in tabular form and some in columnar form. You might also choose different styles.

> **⊘TIP**
>
> Remember that because reports are so quick and easy to create using the wizard, it does not matter if you are not sure of the options to choose each time — experiment! If the final result is not what you want, delete the report and try again.

Activity 1: Producing standard reports...

In this activity you will:

● use the wizard to produce a standard report for three of the queries you produced in Chapter 11

● use a range of report types.

▶ Open up the database you saved at the end of Chapter 11. Alternatively you can use one of the files provided with the downloadable resources for this chapter (***Mals Car Hire P with queries.mdb***, ***Mals Car Hire MD1 with queries.mdb*** or ***Mals Car Hire MD2 with queries.mdb***).

▶ Click on **Reports** in the **Objects** panel and choose to **Create report by using wizard**.

▶ Choose the query you created to provide a list of cars due out on a particular day – query 1 from Chapter 11, then select all of the fields.

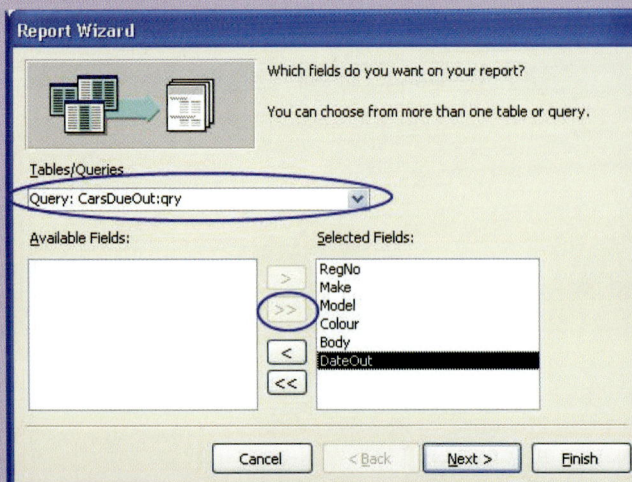

Figure 12.1: *Selecting the query and fields for the report.*

▶ The wizard suggests viewing this data by **Car:tbl**. This would give the details of each car, with the hire dates underneath. Since we are actually searching for one particular date, this is not appropriate, so choose to view by **Hire:tbl**:

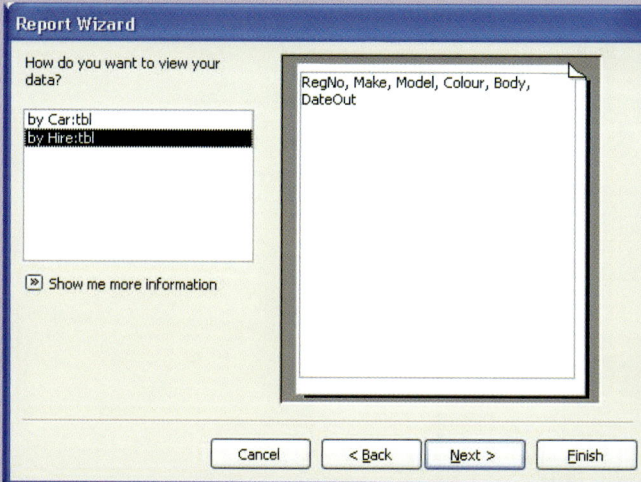

Report Wizard

How do you want to view your data?

by Car:tbl
by Hire:tbl

RegNo, Make, Model, Colour, Body, DateOut

» Show me more information

Cancel   < Back   Next >   Finish

Figure 12.2: *Viewing by Hire:tbl.*

▶ We don't want any grouping levels, but you might want to choose one or more fields to sort on. Remember, if you want to maintain the field order then you can sort in design view of the report.

▶ Choose an appropriate layout – **tabular** might be best for this sort of list.

▶ Choose a style, then save the report as **CarsDueOut:rpt**.

▶ You will then be able to test this report by entering a date. If you have used the data provided for your file, then try using 7/7/06 or 29/11/06 – you should find two cars for each date.

▶ Print out a copy of your report.

▶ Now create a similar report for your **CarsDueBackToday:qry**. Again you should choose to view the data by **Hire:tbl**. Because there are more fields to show here, landscape view might be best. Try a different style.

▶ Save the report as **CarsDueBackToday:rpt**.

▶ When you complete the report you may find it empty, as there may be no records in your file for cars due back today. If so, go back and enter a few more hires so that you will have some details to show on your report. Print out a copy.

▶ Now create a report for your query that searches for a car. You might think that a **columnar** layout is more appropriate here – if necessary try a few different ideas until you are happy with the one you want. Save your report as **Search4Car:rpt** and print a copy.

> **⊘TIP**
>
> Don't forget – you can easily delete or rename a report by right clicking on it in the main Reports window.

Using the Label Wizard

In addition to the standard report wizard you can also choose wizards that will help you create charts and mailing labels. To access these, click on **Reports** in the **Objects** panel, then choose **New**. You can then choose the **Chart Wizard** or the **Label Wizard**. By using one of these you can be sure of achieving the objective of using a 'range of report styles' as required.

Mal's requirements included the production of mailing labels, for which we will use the **Label Wizard**.

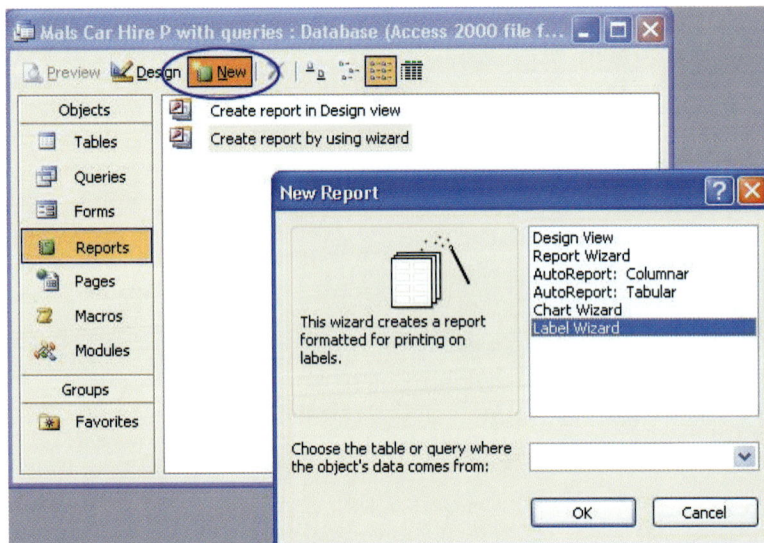

Figure 12.3: Selecting the Label Wizard.

When you have chosen the query to use you then need to specify the type of label required. If you are printing on real labels there should be a code on the packet. A commonly used type of label has 7 rows of 3 labels per sheet and has an Avery code J8160. To find these codes you need to ensure you choose the **Sheet feed** option under **Label Type**.

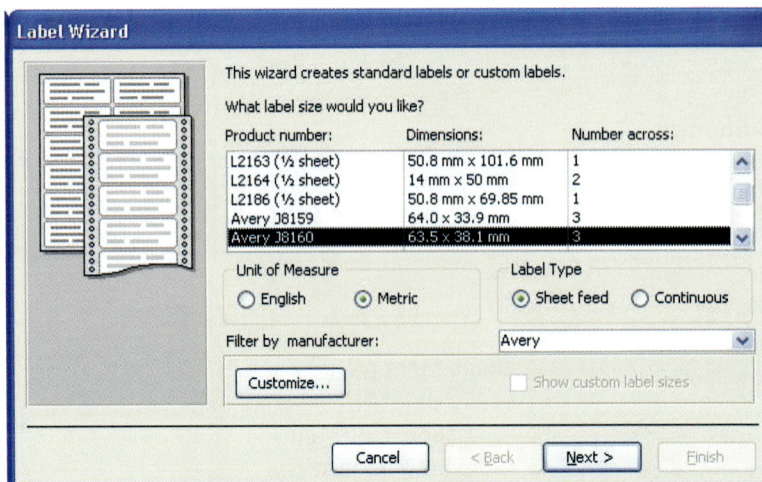

*Figure 12.4: Choosing the **Sheet feed** option and the appropriate code.*

You can then choose the font and size for the text on your label, although the defaults are likely to be fine.

The next stage is to choose the fields to include on each label. Choose the fields by double clicking on them, then insert spaces and new lines as required using the space bar and **Enter** key. A typical address label design would look like the one shown in Figure 12.5.

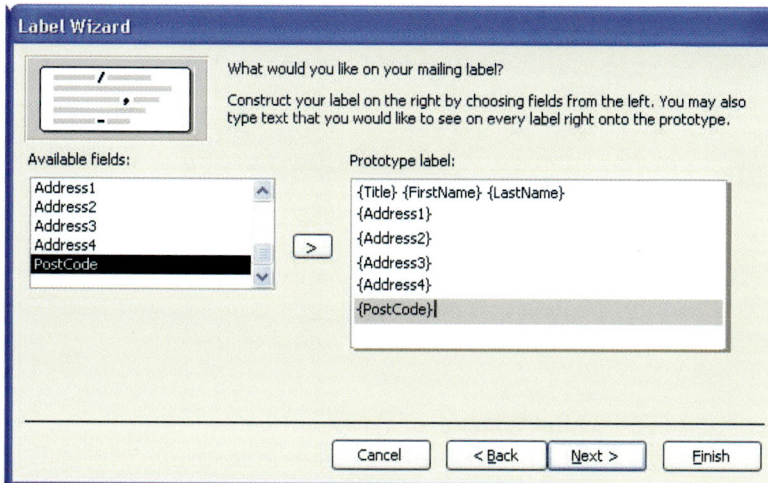

Figure 12.5: *The layout of an address label.*

When the report is run, you simply use a sheet of address labels instead of plain paper to print. For the purpose of your portfolio it will be perfectly acceptable (and a lot cheaper!) to print your labels on plain paper.

Activity 2: Creating mailing labels...

In this activity you will:

● create mailing labels for the fourth query that you produced in Chapter 11.

▶ Open the database file you used in Activity 1.

▶ Click on **Reports** in the **Objects** panel and choose **New**. Then choose the **Label Wizard** as shown in Figure 12.3.

▶ Choose the last query you saved in Chapter 11: to find customers who have hired particular types of cars over a given period.

▶ If you are using real labels then you need now to choose the correct label type and code. If you will be printing on plain paper, choose **Sheet feed** and then **J8160**, as shown in Figure 12.4.

▶ Leave the font and colour unchanged, just click on **Next**.

▶ The first line of the label needs to include the **Title**, **FirstName** and **LastName** with a space between each one. Double click on **Title**, press the space bar, then double click on **FirstName** and press the space bar again, then double click on **LastName** and press the **Enter** key.

▶ Now enter each line of the address, pressing the **Enter** key after each one, until your label layout matches the one in Figure 12.5.

▶ You can choose whether to sort the records or not. There might be an advantage to Mal of sorting in order of **LastName**.

▶ When you click on **Finish** your query will start to run, so you will need to set some search criteria. You might try to find the customers who have hired a Ford car during 2006 (i.e. from 1/1/06 to 31/12/06). Remember to just press the **Enter** key for any fields you don't want to specify.

▶ Print out a copy of your report.

Using the Chart Wizard

You might have user requirements that include the creation of a chart to summarise the data in a table or a query. Although Access allows the creation of quite complex charts, a simple chart would be sufficient to show the use of the 'range of report styles' required for this assessment objective.

The **Chart Wizard** is accessed in the same way as the **Label Wizard**. In Mal's Car Hire system we might choose to create a chart to show the different types of car he has in stock. We would therefore choose to use **Car:tbl**.

The wizard then asks for the fields to use in the chart. The simplest charts use just a single field. For example, we might want to create a chart to show the different makes of car Mal stocks, so we might just choose **Make**.

You can then choose the type and style of chart you require. A simple bar or pie chart is usually sufficient.

The next screen contains options that are only required for much more complex charts, so you can just click on **Next**.

You are then able to enter a suitable title for your chart. In a simple chart using one field you do not need a legend.

A simple chart, like the one shown in Figure 12.6, is then produced.

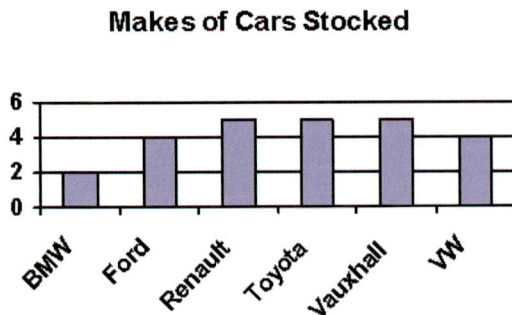

Figure 12.6: A simple chart produced by the **Chart Wizard**.

Customising report designs

For a **Pass** it is quite sufficient to produce a range of different types of report just by using the wizard. If you are aiming only for a **Pass** you can miss out this section and move straight onto the 'Portfolio builder' section at the end of this chapter.

For a **Merit** or a **Distinction** you must also be able to customise reports – change them to meet your particular requirements. There are a number of modifications that can easily be made by accessing the **Design View** of a report:

- adding a logo
- changing the title
- changing column widths
- changing/removing column headings
- changing font, colour and size
- repositioning elements.

The design view of a report is very similar to the design view of a form. You can add, delete, edit and move elements around in just the same way. You can also right click on elements and view and edit their **Properties**. You might like to look back at Activity 4 of Chapter 9 to remind yourself of some of the tools you can use.

Figure 12.7 shows the different parts of a report. The wizards do not create a report footer, but this can be added by dragging the bottom of the report down. The size of any element can be changed by dragging the edges. If you increase the size of the **Detail** section you will increase the space between each row of data.

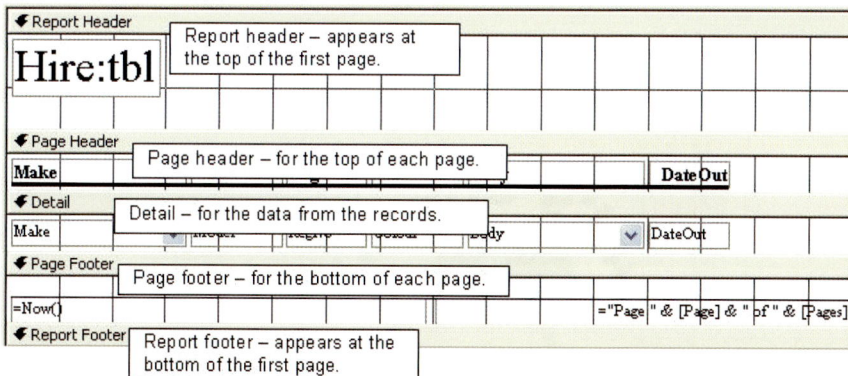

Figure 12.7: *The parts of a report.*

Activity 3: Customising reports...

In this activity you will:

- add a logo to a report
- change the title of a report
- move an element from the body of the report to the header
- change column widths on a report
- change column headings on a report
- remove a column heading from a report
- change font, colour and size on a report.

▶ Open the database file you used in Activity 2.

▶ Select **Reports** in the **Objects** panel and click
on the first report you created in Activity 1.
Open this up in **Design** view.

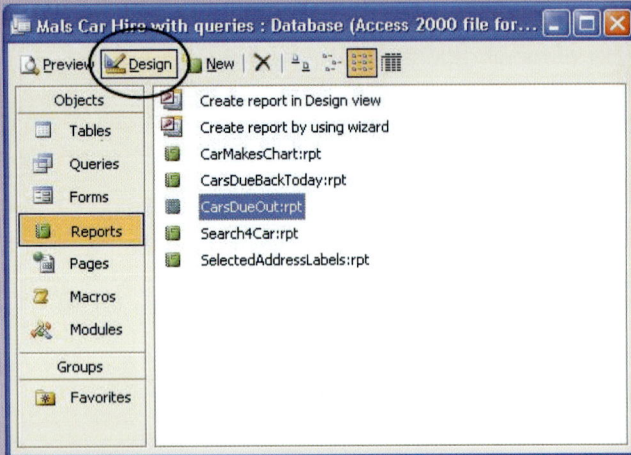

Figure 12.8: Opening up a report in Design view.

A picture can be inserted in this report by choosing **Insert** on the menu bar, then **Picture**.
Clipart can be inserted using **Insert/Object** and choosing **Microsoft Clip Gallery**.

▶ Insert the logo provided with the resources for this chapter: **Logo.bmp**. This will
automatically be placed in the report header, which is where we want it.

▶ Drag the logo to the right of the header and reduce its size, as shown in Figure 12.9.

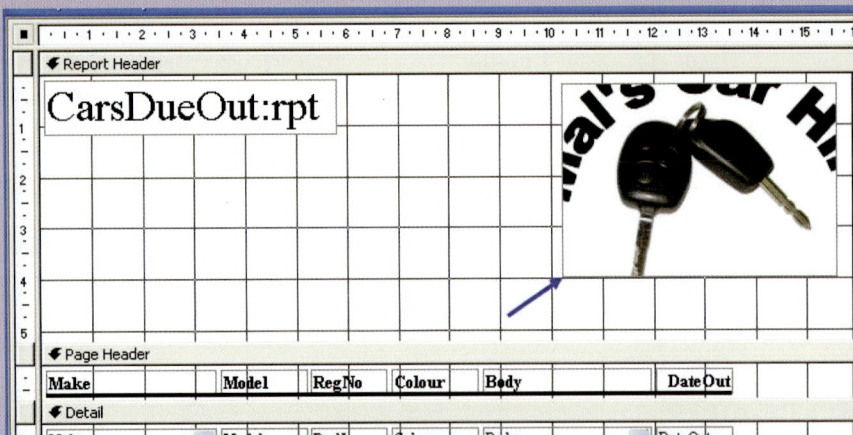

Figure 12.9: Moving and resizing the logo.

▶ To make the logo fit into the new size, right click on it, choose **Properties** and
change the **Size Mode** to **Zoom**.

▶ Now double click on the title, which at the moment is just the name of the report,
and change this to something more suitable, for example, **Cars Due Out**.

The **DateOut** field is actually set by the user of the report, and is the same for all cars, so this does not really need to be part of the table.

▶ Click on the heading **DateOut** in the page header section, and press the **Delete** key to delete it.

▶ Because **DateOut** will be the same for each record, this could be placed in the report header, as part of the title. You can move this by right clicking on it, choosing **Cut**, then right clicking under your title and choosing **Paste**.

▶ The **DateOut** field will first be placed in the top left corner of the header. You can drag this under the title – move the pointer to the edge of the item until the pointer becomes a hand, then drag.

▶ You can now spread out the remaining field headings and fields by dragging them in the same way. Be careful that you keep each field under its heading.

▶ The column headings are the field names. You can change any of these on your report by double clicking on them. If you need to, you can extend the size of the box by dragging the handle at the right-hand edge.

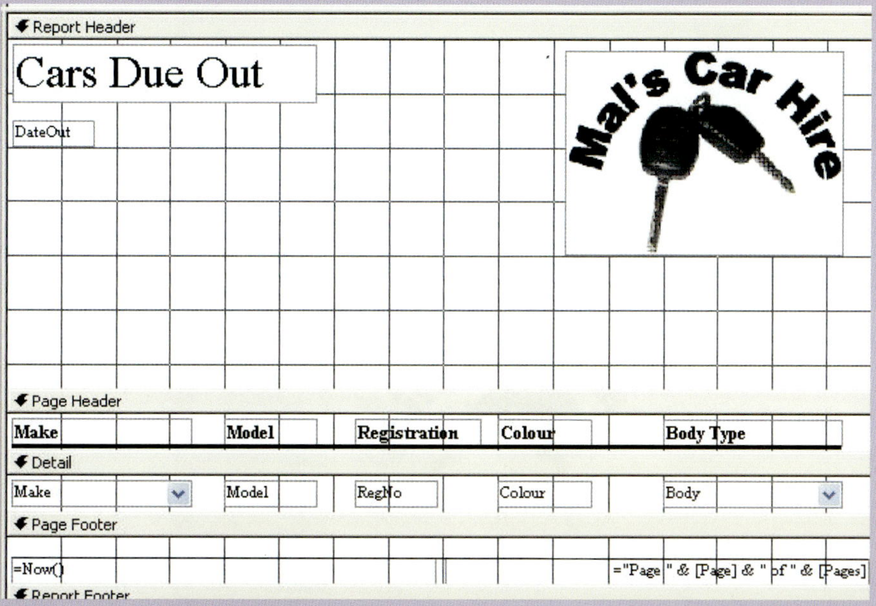

Figure 12.10: *The report with field names and fields moved, and some field names changed.*

You can change the font of any element by clicking on it (**not** double clicking). If there are a number of elements, such as the column headings, that you want to change in the same way, drag over these to select them all before choosing fonts, so that you can change them all at once.

▶ Experiment with a few changes to the text – you might change the font used, increase the size of the date in the report header, etc. You can change colours but this might depend on whether or not you will be printing in colour.

▶ Depending on the style of report you chose from the wizard, you may have lines and/or shaded boxes. These can be resized or deleted by clicking on them. You can also use the **Toolbox** to create additional labels, lines or boxes.

▶ Try out your report by changing to **Print Preview** view.

▶ Check that the whole report fits properly on the page by clicking the **Next Page** button at the bottom of the screen. If this is greyed out then your report does not go onto more than one page.

▶ If your report does not fit onto the page it is often sufficient to reduce the page margins a little. Click on **File** and choose **Page Setup** to do this.

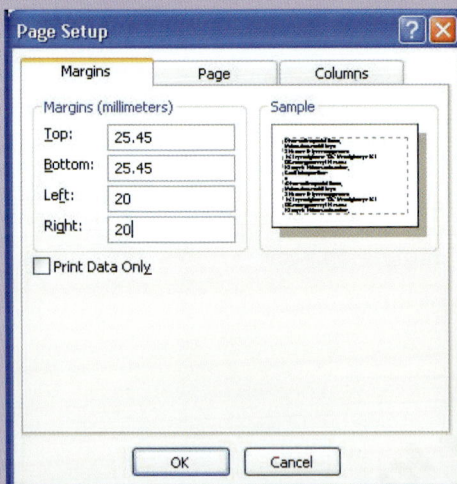

Figure 12.11: *Changing the left and right margins.*

▶ If it still doesn't fit on the page, you can try reducing the width of your report.

▶ When you are satisfied with your report, save it and print out a copy.

Cars Due Out:
07/07/2006

Make	Model	Registration	Colour	Body Type
Ford	Focus	BB56BNY	Silver	Estate
VW	Passat	YX55BPG	Tornado red	Hatch

Figure 12.12: *An example of a final customised report.*

▶ Customise your other two standard reports in the same way. If you want to change the auto style that a report is based on you can do this by clicking on the **AutoFormat** button on the toolbar.

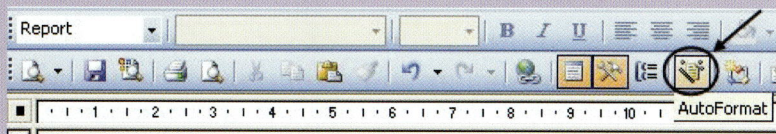

Figure 12.13: Changing the auto style of a report in design view.

There is very little that you either can or need to customise on a chart or label report. However, you can increase the size of the chart to help it fill the page better. You could also make the postcode on the address labels stand out by making it bold and/or using a slightly larger font.

You might like to compare your reports with those saved in the appropriate version of the database provided in the resources for this chapter – either *Mals Car Hire P with reports.mdb*, *Mals Car Hire MD1 with reports.mdb* or *Mals Car Hire MD2 with reports.mdb*.

Portfolio builder

For your own portfolio you must create a report for each of the queries you produced for Assessment Objective 3. This is one of the reasons why in the last chapter it was recommended that you limit your queries to no more than three.

For a **Pass** you simply need to use a range of standard templates – this might include tabular, columnar and/or justified layouts. You might use portrait orientation for some and landscape for others. You might also create a set of address labels and/or a chart. It is not necessary to do *all* of these things – you can choose the range for yourself.

You do not have to show *how* you created your reports – you can simply print each one out and put it in your portfolio.

For a **Merit** you need to customise at least *one* of your reports. This will probably be one that you have created using an ordinary wizard, where you might change the title, add a logo, change the font and size and rearrange some of the items on the page.

For a **Distinction** you need to customise *every* report you create. If you have created mailing labels and/or a chart there is very little you can do to these, but you should make at least one change to each – perhaps changing the size of the chart and making one element on the address label stand out by making it bold and/or changing its size.

Again, there is no requirement to show *how* you made changes, but you should print out each report twice – once when you have created it from the wizard and then after you have finished customising it. You should then put the two printouts next to each other in your portfolio, so that a reader can easily see how each report has changed.

→ *Assessment Objective 5*

Create a User Interface

Overview:

In this chapter you will learn how to create a menu system that will allow an Access database to be used much more easily. You will see how the database can be configured so that this menu appears automatically whenever the file is opened.

> In order to complete the activities in this chapter you will need access to a number of additional files. These files are contained in the Chapter 13 Resources zip file which can be downloaded from the OCR Nationals in ICT (Units 6 & 7) Student Resources page on the Payne-Gallway website: www.payne-gallway.co.uk.

How this assessment objective will be assessed...

- Screenshot(s) of menu screen(s)
- Your teacher may wish you to demonstrate that the menus work, and your final file may be saved as evidence

Skills to use...

- Creating a new switchboard (menu)
- Adding items to a switchboard
- Arranging items on a switchboard
- Setting a switchboard to open when the database is opened
- Customising the switchboard

How to achieve...

Pass requirements

P1 You will create a limited user interface, giving access to some of the forms and reports of the database.

Merit requirements

M1 You will create a clearly structured user interface, giving access to all the forms and reports of the database.

User Interfaces

A **user interface** is the term used to describe the way the user interacts with a system. The user interface of the current database system we have been developing consists of the main database window with the **Tables**, **Forms**, **Queries** and **Reports** buttons in the **Objects** panel. While this is not difficult to use, there could be some confusion for a new user because there are more options than s/he will need. For example, when you have set up the system there should be no need for the user to create new tables or forms. There may be very little need to create new queries or reports. The user doesn't really need to be able to see the tables, since data is entered via the forms and output is created by the reports. Queries are not needed either, as you should have created a report to format the output from each query.

Microsoft Access allows you to create a special type of form that can act as a menu to give easy access to the forms and reports you have created. An inexperienced user needs only use this form, so doesn't need to use the main database window. This form is called a **switchboard**.

To see an example of a switchboard, open the file **School Data Final.mdb** provided with the resources for this chapter. This is the database we used at the beginning of this unit, with a few more reports and a switchboard added.

Creating a switchboard

A switchboard is created by using the **Tools** menu and choosing **Database Utilities**. From here choose **Switchboard Manager**.

> ⊘**TIP**
>
> There is one other useful option found under Tools/Database Utilities. Use the Compact and Repair Database option if you have deleted a lot of records or if the file is getting very large. This can reduce the size of the file.

The first time you select the **Switchboard Manager** in a database you will see the message shown in Figure 13.1.

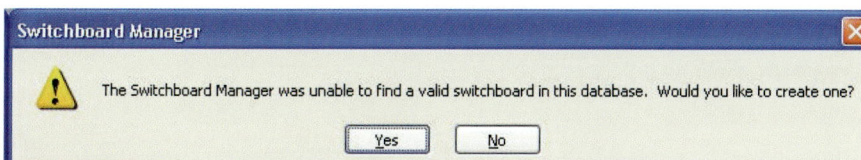

Figure 13.1: *Running the **Switchboard Manager** for the first time.*

You need to click on **Yes** and then you will be shown a list of all switchboards available. At first this will just be a blank **Main Switchboard** that has been created for you. Clicking on **Edit** will open this up so that you can add items.

Clicking on **New** on the next screen will allow you to create new menu items. For example, you could create a menu option that would allow the user to open up the **Customer** form as shown in Figure 13.2.

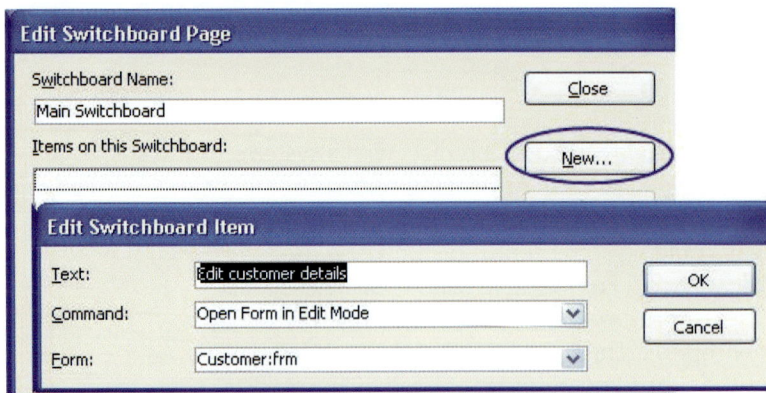

Figure 13.2: *Adding a new menu item.*

The main items you can add to a menu are:

- opening a form in edit mode – this is the same as opening the form from the database window. It shows the first record, from where you can move to any record you wish, or add a new one.
- opening a form in add mode – this is exactly the same as the previous option, except that it automatically chooses the **New Record** option. If you want to limit the number of switchboard items, then you might choose not to use this option, since new records can easily be added by opening the form in edit mode.
- opening a report – this runs the chosen report
- opening another switchboard
- exiting the application – this closes down Access.

There is a maximum of eight items that can be added to a switchboard. If you wish to add more than this, then you need to create more than one switchboard.

Activity 1: Creating a single switchboard...

In this activity you will:

- create a switchboard for Mal's Car Hire database
- set the switchboard to open when the database is opened.

▶ Open the database file you saved at the end of the last chapter. Alternatively you can use one of the files provided with the resources for this chapter. Use *Mals Car Hire P with reports.mdb*, *Mals Car Hire MD1 with reports.mdb* or *Mals Car Hire MD2 with reports.mdb*, according to the type of form you created in Chapter 10.

▶ Choose **Tools** and **Database Utilities** to open up the **Switchboard Manager**. Answer **Yes** to the question which asks if you would like to create a switchboard (see Figure 13.1).

▶ Click **Edit** to edit the main switchboard that has now been created for you.

▶ Choose **New** to add a new switchboard item. Create an item to edit customer details, as shown in Figure 13.2.

▶ Choose **New** again, and add an item to edit car details as shown in Figure 13.3.

Edit Switchboard Item

Text:	Edit Car details
Command:	Open Form in Edit Mode
Form:	Car:frm

Figure 13.3: Adding a menu item to edit car details.

▶ You will probably have a separate **Hire:frm**. If so, create another switchboard item to open this form in edit mode. If you have used subforms, as in *Mals Car Hire MD2 with reports.mdb*, you will not need to do this.

Edit Switchboard Item

Text:	Edit Hire Details
Command:	Open Form in Edit Mode
Form:	Hire:frm

Figure 13.4: Adding a menu item to edit hire details, if needed.

Now you have a menu item for each form you need to add links to all your reports.

▶ Add an item to **Open Report** for the report you created for the list of cars due back.

Edit Switchboard Item

Text:	Cars Due Out on a Particular Day
Command:	Open Report
Report:	CarsDueOut:rpt

Figure 13.5: Adding a menu item to open a report.

▶ Now add a menu item for the other reports you have created.

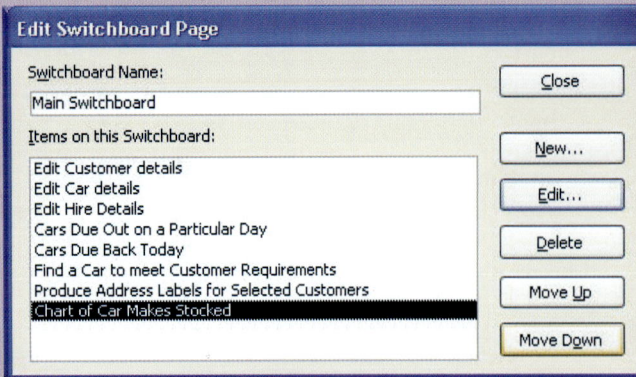

Figure 13.6: *Menu items to open up forms and reports.*

▶ Click on **Close** to close the main switchboard, then **Close** again to close down the **Switchboard Manager**.

▶ You will see your switchboard listed with your other **Forms**. Double click on this to open it. You should then be able to access all the forms and reports by clicking on the menu items.

The main reason for having a switchboard is to help users who are not familiar with the software, so that they don't have to use the main database window. This is not achieved if the switchboard has to be opened from the **Forms** button. You now need to set your database so that the switchboard is opened when the database is opened.

▶ Click on **Tools** from the menu bar and choose **Startup**.

▶ Change the **Display Form/Page** option to show your **Switchboard**.

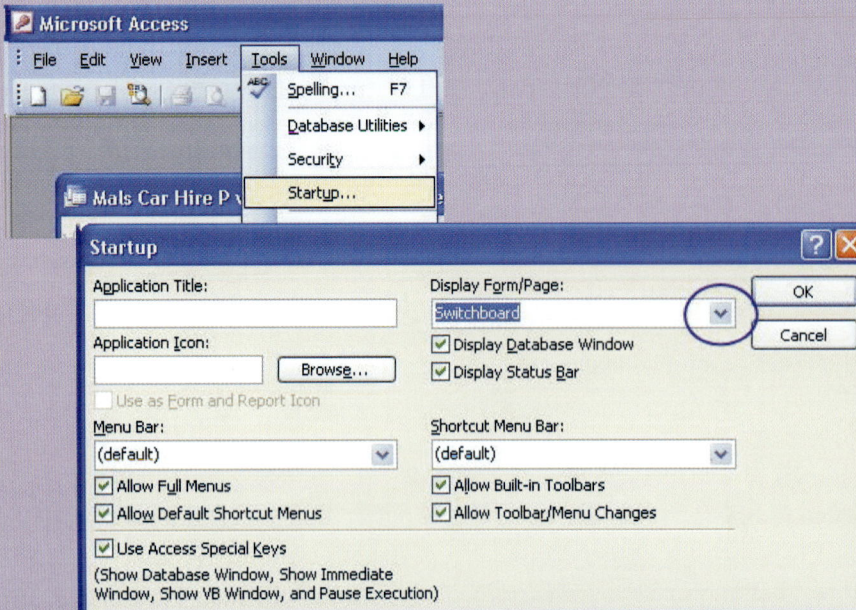

Figure 13.7: *Changing the **Startup** settings to show the switchboard automatically when the database is opened.*

▶ Close down your database and open it again, to see the switchboard open.

Pass candidates

If you are aiming for a **Pass** in this objective, there is no more that you need to know. You can move straight on to the 'Portfolio builder' section at the end of this chapter.

Merit and Distinction candidates

For a **Merit** or a **Distinction** you need to give access to all the main areas of your database. You should include menu items to open all your forms in both add and edit mode, as well as access to all your reports. You should also include a menu item to close down the database.

Because you cannot create more than eight menu items on a single switchboard, you will need to create more than one menu, as shown in Activity 2.

For a **Distinction** you need to customise your switchboard, perhaps by matching the design you used on your other forms. This is covered in Activity 3.

Activity 2: More than one switchboard...

In this activity you will:

- create separate switchboards for forms and reports
- rearrange switchboard items
- link all switchboards
- add an item to exit the database.

Forms switchboard

▶ Open up the file you saved in Activity 1.

▶ Use **Tools/Database Utilities** to access the **Switchboard Manager**.

▶ Click **New** to create a new switchboard. Call it **Forms**.

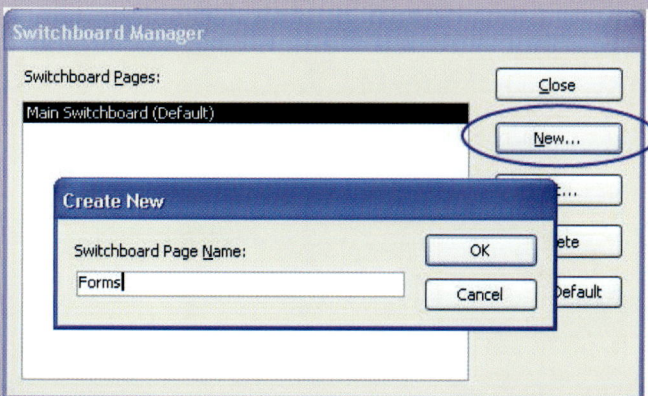

Figure 13.8: Creating a new switchboard for forms.

▶ Choose this new switchboard and click on **Edit**.

▶ You should now be able to add items to this new switchboard that will open up all of your forms in both add and edit mode. If you have one form for each main table your switchboard should contain the items shown in Figure 13.9. If you are using a subform then you will only have the items for customers and cars.

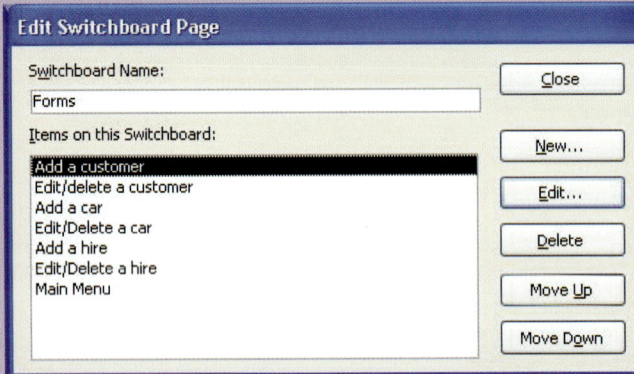

Edit Switchboard Page

Switchboard Name:

Forms

Close

Items on this Switchboard:

Add a customer
Edit/delete a customer
Add a car
Edit/Delete a car
Add a hire
Edit/Delete a hire
Main Menu

New...

Edit...

Delete

Move Up

Move Down

Figure 13.9: Switchboard items to open up all forms in both add and edit mode.

Use the **Edit** button to rename or change any item. Use the **Move Up** and **Move Down** buttons to change the position of items in the list.

▶ The last item you will need on this new menu is a link back to the main menu. Use the **New** button to add this, as shown in Figure 13.10.

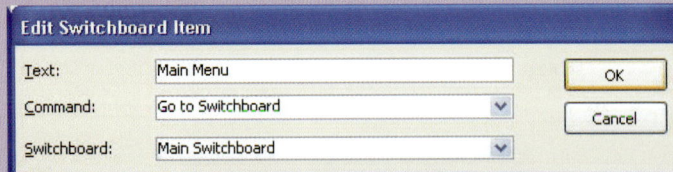

Edit Switchboard Item

Text: Main Menu

OK

Command: Go to Switchboard

Cancel

Switchboard: Main Switchboard

Figure 13.10: Adding an item to link back to the main menu.

▶ Close down this switchboard.

Reports switchboard

▶ Now choose **New** to add another new switchboard. Call this **Reports**.

▶ **Edit** this new switchboard and add new items to all your reports, and a link back to the main menu.

Edit Switchboard Page

Switchboard Name:

Reports

Items on this Switchboard:

Cars Due Out on a Particular Day
Cars Due Back Today
Find a Car to meet Customer Requirements
Produce Address Labels for Selected Customers
Chart of Car Makes Stocked
Main Menu

Close
New...
Edit...
Delete
Move Up
Move Down

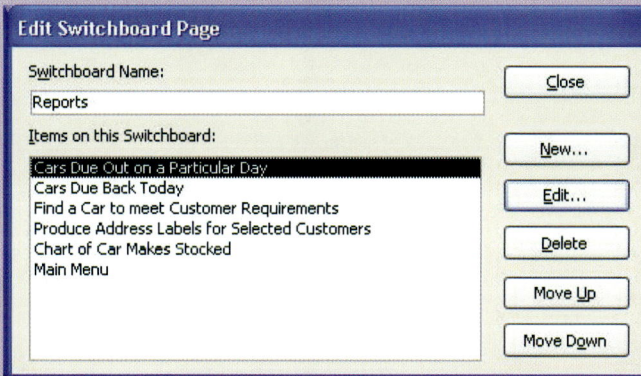

Figure 13.11: The items on the **Reports** switchboard.

▶ **Close** the **Reports** switchboard.

▶ Select the **Main Switchboard** and click **Edit**.

▶ Use the **Delete** button to delete the existing items, as these are now all on the new menus.

▶ Use the **New** button to add new items that will link to your two new switchboards.

▶ Add a third item, to exit the application.

Edit Switchboard Item

Text: Add, Edit or Delete Records
Command: Go to Switchboard
Switchboard: Forms

OK
Cancel

Edit Switchboard Item

Text: Search and Produce Lists
Command: Go to Switchboard
Switchboard: Reports

OK
Cancel

Edit Switchboard Item

Text: Close Database
Command: Exit Application

OK
Cancel

Figure 13.12: The three items to add to the revised main menu.

▶ Close down your switchboard and your database, then re-open it and test that your menu system works.

Activity 3: Customising a switchboard...

In this activity you will:

- change the size of a switchboard
- change the background colour
- add a logo
- increase the size of switchboard items
- add instructions.

In many ways a switchboard is treated like a form – you can edit its appearance using **Design View**. However, there is one major difference. It doesn't matter how many different switchboards you create, they are all related to the same design view. The actual items on the switchboards are stored in a table called **Switchboard Items**.

▶ Open the database you saved in Activity 2.

▶ With the switchboard showing, switch to **Design View**.

▶ Move the switchboard towards the top left of the screen, then drag out the bottom right-hand corner to increase the size of the window. Drag out the right-hand and bottom edge of the form to fill the window.

▶ Right click on a blank area of the form and choose a suitable **Fill/Back Color**. You might choose this to match the colour you used on your forms.

▶ The default switchboard uses three rectangles as decoration to the left and top of the form. There is also a small line underneath the last box. You can choose to delete these or alter them to suit your own design.

▶ The default switchboard uses two label boxes to create a shadow effect for the title. Again, you can either delete these to create your own title – perhaps using the same style as you used for your other forms – or you can edit the existing labels. Remember when choosing a title that this will be shown on *all* of your menu pages.

▶ Use the **Insert** menu to insert a picture/logo. Alternatively you can copy and paste from one of your other forms.

▶ Drag the boxes for the menu items to spread them out down the form. Leave a little space at the bottom for instructions. You should be able to use the gridlines to keep them even. Alternatively, right click and use the **Properties** box to adjust the measurement for the **Top** of each box.

▶ Now increase the size of the square buttons. Select them all by dragging over them, then right click and choose **Properties**. Increase the size by changing the **Width** and **Height**.

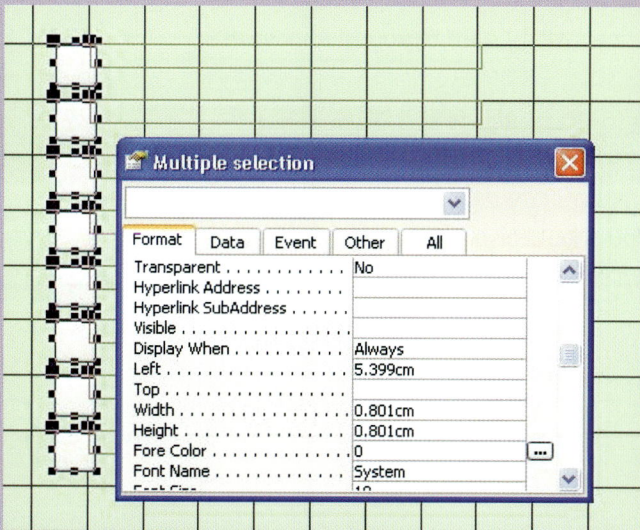

Figure 13.13: *Increasing the size of the buttons.*

▶ Change the size of the text boxes in the same way. You will also need to move these to the right a little, to make room for the larger buttons.

▶ Select the text boxes so that you can change the font and increase the size.

▶ Add a new label box at the bottom of the form to insert an instruction.

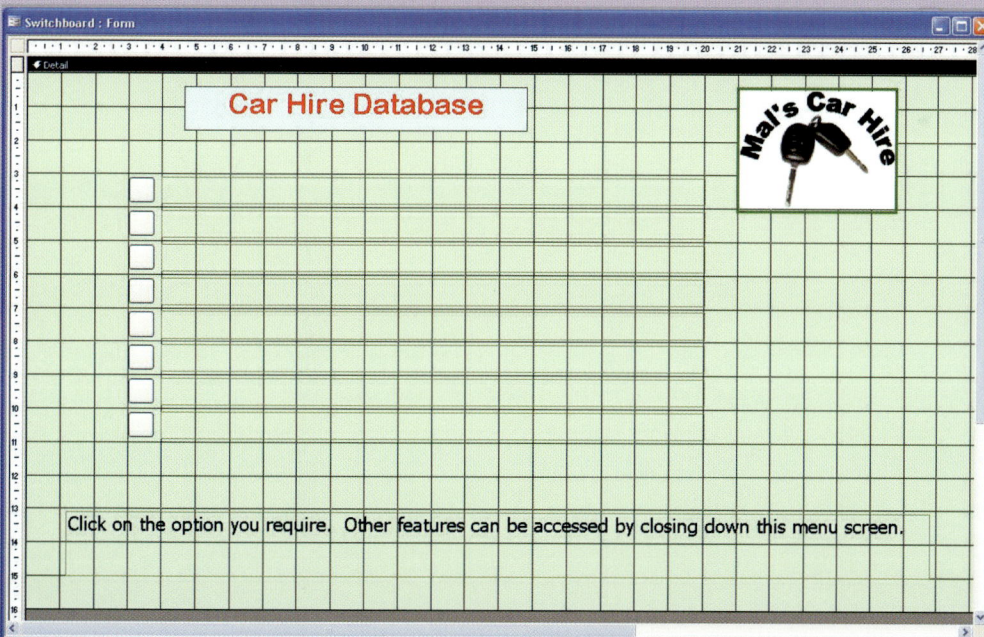

Figure 13.14: *A customised switchboard in* ***Design View***.

▶ Switch to **Form View** and test your switchboard. In particular you should make sure that there is enough space to view all of your menu items clearly. When you are happy that it is working, close down the switchboard.

Portfolio builder

For your own portfolio you will need to add at least one switchboard to your database as described in this chapter.

You should check carefully against the requirements for **Pass**, **Merit** and **Distinction** described in the 'How to achieve' section on page 198.

There is no need to create any evidence of *how* you created your switchboard, but you should provide a screenshot of each switchboard. You should also make sure that all the elements work as they should, as your teacher may ask to see this demonstrated.

CHAPTER (14)

→ *Assessment Objective 6*

Test the Database

. . . .

Overview:

As you have added elements to your database you have probably quickly checked that each does what you expected. This chapter will explain how to make sure that a database is more thoroughly tested. This will include planning the tests as well as carrying them out.

> In order to complete the activities in this chapter you will need access to a number of additional files. These files are contained in the Chapter 14 Resources zip file which can be downloaded from the OCR Nationals in ICT (Units 6 & 7) Student Resources page on the Payne-Gallway website: www.payne-gallway.co.uk.

How this assessment objective will be assessed...

- A completed test plan table, showing the tests to be carried out and the results obtained
- Evidence of any improvements that have been made as a result of the testing carried out
- Your teacher might also want to see your finished database to make sure that it really does work as you claim.

Skills to use...

- Organisation! You need to be very methodical and disciplined to make sure that every aspect of your database is tested.

How to achieve...

Pass requirements

P1 You will produce a test plan that contains evidence of some testing.

P2 You will make improvements *if* any problems are identified.

Merit requirements

M1 You will produce a test plan that contains evidence of testing most of the main areas of the database.

M2 You will make improvements *if* any problems are identified.

Although the wording of the requirements for the different levels may seem very similar, there is a lot of difference between the amount of testing required for a **Pass**, **Merit** and **Distinction**.

Why testing is necessary

When you create a system for someone else to use, it is important that all aspects work as intended. If there are any errors, an inexperienced user might not notice and then rely on incorrect data. Alternatively the user might find that there is an error but not know how to put it right.

There are six main areas you should test:

- testing validation checks and input masks
- testing that data can be input correctly using the forms created
- testing that the queries created produce the output required
- testing that the reports created produce output in an appropriate format
- testing the user interface
- testing that the database meets the original requirements.

The best way to ensure that you test all of the main elements of your database system is to create a **test plan**, sometimes called a **test table**. This is a table that shows all the elements that need to be tested and how they will be tested. There should also be space to show what you expect to happen, what actually did happen and any action that needs to be taken as a result of the testing.

A test plan template is provided with the resources for this chapter: ***Test plan template.doc***.

Key terms

Test plan

A table showing all the tests that need to be carried out, with space for adding the results.

Creating a test plan

You should try to create your test plan first, then carry out the tests afterwards. You can always add extra tests if you then think that they are necessary, but you are more likely to produce a thorough test plan if you think it out methodically first.

You will need all of your design work for Assessment Objective 1. That will show you most of the key items that will need to be tested.

Work through the six main areas shown in the bulleted list above. For each one you should plan testing of every example of that feature that you have used. For example, when testing validation checks and input masks you should test *each* validation check and *each* input mask.

The ***Test plan template.doc*** is split into the six areas. This gives you a more organised approach, which should help you think of all the necessary tests.

Some items require only one test. However, many items need more than one test to make sure that they will work in every possible situation.

- Validation checks should be tested by trying to input some valid data, some invalid data and some data that is just on the borderline. For example, the **Year** field in **Car:tbl** has a validation check **<=Year(Now())** to make sure that it will not accept years that are in the future. Suitable data to test this would be a year in the past, e.g. 2005, the current year, and a year in the future, e.g. 2050. If the validation check is working it should accept the first two but reject the last.

  If you have created combo boxes by looking up from another table, you should try adding another item to that table and testing that this will add another item to the combo box.

- Input masks should be tested by trying to input some data that is in the correct format and at least one example of data that is in an incorrect format. For a complex input mask you might test more than one of each. For example, you might test a postcode input mask with two different types of correct postcode, e.g. WS1 5TM and NE14 4BK, also two different types of incorrect format, e.g. 1WS TM5 and AAAAAAA. If you have used **>** or **<** to turn letters into upper or lower case, you should test this by entering a mixture of upper and lower case letters.

- Forms should be tested by entering a new record and then checking that all of this data has been added correctly to the relevant table(s). This is more important if you have used subforms. You should also check that there is space in each field for the maximum number of characters you planned.

- Ordinary queries can be tested by running them just once, then checking that the correct records have been found and that they have been sorted in the order you required. You will need to look back at the data in the table(s) to see if this has been done correctly. However, a parameter query should be tested with more than one input. You might test with data that should produce a number of records and data that should produce no records. If you have parameters that are designed so that the input can be left blank, as in our **Search4Car** query, you should test these with and without data entered.

- Since reports are based on the queries you have produced, it may be necessary only to run each report once. This report should be printed to test that it will all fit on the paper as you expected. You should look out especially to make sure that there is sufficient space in each column even for the longest possible item. You might enter a test record especially to test this.

- Your user interface should be tested by clicking once on every option and making sure it takes you to the correct item. You should also make sure that you can access every menu item and get back to the main menu.

- Once you have tested all the elements of your database you should go through your original user requirements, one by one, and make sure that you have met each of these in your database. If you have created your system for a real user, then you should show the user the output you have created and ask if this is what s/he wanted. If you have a judgemental requirement, for example Mal's requirement that the system should be 'easy to use', then you might ask someone else to look at your system as part of your testing.

  It may be that to keep the project of a reasonable size, you have limited the number of queries and reports you created. If this is so, then you should make sure there is a reason (other than your limited time) why you have not implemented a particular feature. An easier, if slightly less honest, method would be to delete the requirement from your planning section. This is another good reason for making sure that you don't set yourself too much in your original requirements.

Testing for different types of data

Figure 14.1 shows the start of a test plan table for the database we have constructed for Mal's car hire.

What is to be tested	Test to be done	Expected results	Actual results	Action necessary
Validation checks and input masks:				
Car:tbl – RegNo. Input mask = >AAaaaaa	Try entering a1, abc123, 123abc, a123abc, abc123a and ab12abc	All should be accepted but the letters should be made into capitals.		
Car:tbl – Make. Combo box – Lookup from another table – BMW, Ford, Renault, Toyota, Vauxhall, VW. Limit entries to this list.	Try entering BMW, Ford, Renault, Toyota, Vauxhall, VW and Kia	BMW, Ford, Renault, Toyota, Vauxhall, VW will be accepted but Kia will be rejected.		
Makes:tbl	Add Kia to the table, then try entering Kia into Car:tbl	Kia should now be accepted		
Car:tbl – EngineSize >=0.8 And <=4	Enter 0.7, 0.8, 2, 4, 5	0.8, 2 and 4 should be accepted. 0.7 and 5 should not.		

Figure 14.1: *Tests for validation checks and input masks.*

You should see that the **What is to be tested** column is virtually copied from the validation checks and input masks planned in the original database table planning sheets created for Assessment Objective 1.

The **Test to be done** column is to show what test(s) you plan to carry out to make sure your checks work. You will see here that a number of tests are planned for each one:

- to show that valid data will be accepted (called **normal** data), e.g. **BMW** for **Make** and **2** for **EngineSize**
- to show that impossible data will not be accepted (called **abnormal** data), e.g. **Kia** for **Make** and **5** for **EngineSize**
- there are also some tests planned on the edge of what is possible (called **extreme data**), e.g. **0.8** and **4** for **EngineSize**, both of which should be accepted.

A thorough test plan will make sure that **normal**, **abnormal** and **extreme** data and situations are all tested.

The third column, **Expected Results**, is where you write down what you expect will happen when you carry out the test.

These three columns should be completed *before* you carry out your tests. To gain a **Pass** you should have at least one test in every section. For a **Merit** you will need to make sure that most elements are tested at least once. For a **Distinction** you will need to include sufficient tests to thoroughly test every element in your database system.

Key terms

Normal data

Data that would be expected to be input in normal use, which should be **accepted**.

Abnormal data

Data that should **not** be accepted, because it is impossible.

Extreme data

Data that is on the boundary of what could be expected, which should be **accepted**.

Activity 1: Creating a test plan...

In this activity you will:

- identify tests that need to be carried out on Mal's Car Hire database.
- complete the first three columns of a test plan table.

(▶) Open the file ***Test Plan 1.doc***. This is a partly completed test plan table for Mal's Car Hire database.

(▶) Look at the first section, **Validation checks and input masks**, as shown in Figure 14.1 above.

(▶) Refer to your database table planning sheets. Add at least one test for every other field where there is a validation check or an input mask.

(▶) If there are any other tables used as lookup tables, where the plan suggests that Mal might want to add additional items at a later date, like **Makes:tbl**, add a test for these.

(▶) Add extra rows to the table if you need them. If there are too many rows you can leave them blank or delete them.

(▶) Now move to the next section, **Forms**. Two tests for **Car:frm** have been entered for you.

What is to be tested	Test to be done	Expected results	Actual results	Action necessary
Forms:				
Car:frm – data is input into Car:tbl	Enter a new record: AB12ABC Ford Focus 2007 2 5 Blue Saloon	The details should be entered as a new record in Car:tbl.		
Car:frm – Make, Model and colour should accept 15 characters.	Enter 15 characters into Make, model and colour	Although the entry won't be accepted for make, because of the lookup list, it should be possible to fit 15 characters into each box		

Figure 14.2: *Tests for forms.*

(▶) Enter some more tests, to test the other form(s) you have created.

(▶) Now look at the next section: **Queries**.

What is to be tested	Test to be done	Expected results	Actual results	Action necessary
Queries:				
CarsDueOut:qry	Test with 7/7/06	Two hires should be found		
CarsDueBackToday:qry	Input three hires due back today, then run the query.	The three hires input should be found.		
HiresBetweenDates:qry	Test with no input for make, model or type, 1/1/06 for first date and 31/12/10 for second date	All hire records should be found		
HiresBetweenDates:qry	Ford Focus Estate between 1/1/06 and 31/12/06	Three records should be found		

Figure 14.3: *Tests for queries.*

▶ You should be able to add more tests, to make sure you have tested all your queries.

▶ Move onto the **Reports** section.

What is to be tested	Test to be done	Expected results	Actual results	Action necessary
Reports:				
CarsDueOut:rpt	Create hires for JN05LDY (longest make), KB05AYJ (longest colour) and VP55VBJ (longest model) due out today and due back today. Run report with today's date. Print the report.	The three new records will be found. The data will all be shown and will fit on the paper.		

Figure 14.4: Tests for reports.

▶ Add tests for the other reports in your system.

▶ The **User Interface** section will usually only have one or two tests, so there is no need for you to add any more to the ones already entered. If you have only one switchboard menu, then you should delete the second test from the file. If you don't have a **close database** option, then delete this reference too.

What is to be tested	Test to be done	Expected results	Actual results	Action necessary
User Interface:				
Switchboard	Click on every option	The correct form or report should open. The 'Close database' option should close Access.		
Multiple switchboards	Move from the main menu to each submenu and back again	I should be able to move between the menus		

Figure 14.5: Tests for the user interface.

▶ You will see that for the final section, **User requirements**, some of the columns have been merged because any necessary tests have already been specified. However, you need to find some way of showing that every requirement from your original specification has been considered.

What is to be tested	Test to be done	Expected results	Actual results	Action necessary
User Requirements:				
Print out a list every morning of those cars that need to be ready to go out that day.	CarsDueOut:rpt meets this requirement			
The information Mal wants to store about his cars is: registration number, make, model, year of manufacture, engine size, number of doors, colour, body type.	This is stored in Car:tbl			
The system should be easy to use.	Ask another person to use my system	They will find it easy to use		

Figure 14.6: Testing user requirements.

▶ Think of a suitable person to test your system. If you have access to a computer and the right software at home, you might choose a relative who has less experience of using Access. Otherwise you might choose a fellow student. Change the reference to 'another person' to specify the person you have chosen.

▶ Add more references to make sure you have covered all the user requirements we specified in Chapter 9.

▶ You might like to compare your final test plan with the file *Test Plan 2.doc*. This is sufficiently detailed for a Distinction. You are unlikely to have chosen exactly the same tests as are planned here, but you should be able to use this to see how detailed your plan really is.

Carrying out the tests

When you have completed your test plan, the hard work is done! Now all you need to do is to carry out each of the tests you have listed.

Again, you will be most successful if you are organised and methodical. You should go through the tests one by one, filling in the results after each one.

There is no need to repeat yourself. If you have described fully in the **Expected results** section exactly what happens, then all you need to enter into the **Actual results** column is something like 'As expected'. However, if anything different happens, or if you can add more detail, then you should write about this here.

If the test is successful, showing that the feature works as you expected it to, then you need only enter 'None' in the **Action necessary** column. If you have made sure each element worked as you created it, then you should find that this is what you enter in most, if not all, of this column. However, you might occasionally find something that needs some adjustment – perhaps a box on a form or a column of a report that is not quite wide enough. If so, then you enter into this column a brief comment about what needs to be done.

Correcting errors

If you do find anything that needs adjusting you *must* put it right. To pass this unit you *either* need to find no errors when you test *or* you need to provide evidence that you have put any errors right.

Activity 2: testing the system...

In this activity you will:

- carry out the tests in your test plan
- enter **Actual results** and **Action necessary** for each test
- make any improvements to your system that are necessary because of your testing.

Open the test plan table you created in Activity 1. Now open the final database you saved at the end of the last chapter. Alternatively you can load one of the files provided with the resources for this chapter (***Mals Car Hire P with switchboard.mdb***, ***Mals Car Hire MD1 with switchboard.mdb*** or ***Mals Car Hire MD2 with customised switchboard.mdb***).

Go through the plan and carry out each test indicated. When you have finished each test, write up your results in the **Actual results** and **Action necessary** columns.

If you find anything that needs adjustment or improvement, then make the improvement(s) necessary and create a screenshot/printout to show what you have done.

You might like to compare your final test plan with the file ***Test plan complete.doc***. This shows the results of testing on a similar file to your own. The results may not be the same, as all databases will be slightly different, but it shows how you might enter the results of both successful and unsuccessful tests.

Portfolio builder

For your own portfolio you will need to create a test plan to test every part of your database. You can use the ***Test plan template.doc*** provided in the resources for this chapter to create this plan. This template is already split to show the six main areas you should consider. You will probably have to insert or delete rows to fit your own requirements.

You will need the work you produced for Assessment Objective 1 (the user requirements and the table designs) in order to complete this plan.

You should first complete the first three columns, as you did in Activity 1. You should then carry out the tests and complete the last two columns and make any necessary improvements, as you did in Activity 2.

There is no need to produce any screenshots or other evidence to prove what you have done. It is sufficient to enter the results into your table. However, your teacher will probably want to see you carrying out the tests.

If part of the testing involves printing (for example, the reports) you may as well include these in your portfolio, but this is not required.

However, it is most important that you **do** provide evidence, in the form of annotated screenshots, to show any improvements you make as a result of problems found during testing. You cannot pass this objective unless you show that your final database works as it should. If you have been very careful as you have created your database and there are no problems identified during testing, then there is no need for anything other than the completed plan itself to go into your portfolio. However, do not be tempted to 'cheat' and pretend that parts of your database work when in fact they don't. Your teacher is likely to find these and will then not be able to pass you for this objective.

Index

Abbreviations: SS, spreadsheets; DB, databases.

Absolute cell referencing 26–9
Analysing data (SS) 66–76
Arithmetic functions 3–6

Bar charts 67–71, 75
Buttons (SS) 83–90
    on toolbars 87–90

Chart wizard (SS) 192
Checking entry data 128–30, 144–7
Comments (SS) 22–6
Conditional formatting 30–1

Data redundancy 114
Data types (DB) 137–44
Databases
    about databases 96–7
    construction 162–78
    criteria with queries 104–7
    data entry 176–7
    data storage 127, 135
    interrogating 179–86
    planning 148
    see also Queries (DB); Relational databases
Date functions (SS) 11–13
Decision making (SS)
    with 'IF' 14–16
    modelling example 62–4
Default values (DB) 147
Design example (SS) 35–48
    initial ideas 38–41, 44–5
    planning sheets 42
    user requirements 41, 46

Error prevention 21–6, 32–4
Excel program 56–7

Fields (DB) 97, 135
Files (DB) 97
Filtering data (SS) 57–60
Form design (DB) 148–60, 174–5
    subforms 158–60
Formatting (SS) 6–11, 52–4

conditional formatting 30–1
    for error prevention 21–6
Graphs (SS)
    comparative graphs 71–3
    line graphs 73–5, 76

IF for decision making 14–16
Input forms (DB) 148–50
Input masks (DB) 146–7

Label wizard 190–2
Links (DB) 118–23
Logical functions
    databases 106–7
    spreadsheets 14–16
Lookup tables/functions 16–21

Macros (SS) 77–94
    about macros 77–8
    macro codes 81–3, 92–3
    multiprocess 85–7
    recording macros 78–81
    see also Buttons (SS)
Mailing labels 191–2
Modelling (SS) 61–5

Number formatting 10–11

Pie charts (SS) 67–71, 75
Planning (DB) 148
Prediction making 62–4

Queries (DB) 97–109
    complex queries 105–9
    parameter queries 102–4
    planning/creating 180–4

Records (DB) 97
Relational databases 114–18
    design example 131–61
    problem defining 133–4
Relationships (DB) 173
Relative cell referencing 26–9
Reports (DB) 109–13, 187–97
    with chart wizard 192
    customising 193–7
    with label wizard 190–2
    mailing labels 191–2

standard reports 188–9

Sorting data (SS) 55–7
Spreadsheets
    cell referencing 26–9
    creating/formatting 49–54
    data analysis 66–76
    decisions 14–16, 62–4
    tables/functions 16–21
    user-friendliness 21, 32–4
    validation 22–6
    worksheet protection 32–4
    see also Design example (SS); formatting (SS); Macros (SS)
Statistical functions 3–6
Switchboards (DB)
    creating 199–200
    customising 206–7
    multiple 203–5
    single 200–2

Tables (DB) 124–30
    data storage 127, 135
    fields for 125–6, 135
    links for 118–23, 126–7, 136, 171–3
    structures 135–9, 163–71
Testing (DB)
    about testing 209–10
    different data types 212
    error correction 215
    test plans 210–14
    test procedures 215
Time functions (SS) 11–13
Toolbars (SS) 87–92
    new with buttons 89–90
    showing/hiding 91–2

User interfaces (DB) 198–208
    see also Switchboards

Validation
    databases 128–30, 145–7
    spreadsheets 22–6
Visual Basic (VBA) 81

Worksheet protection 32–4